A Child's Histc

V. M. Hillyer

Alpha Editions

This edition published in 2024

ISBN : 9789367245194

Design and Setting By
Alpha Editions
www.alphaedis.com
Email - info@alphaedis.com

As per information held with us this book is in Public Domain.
This book is a reproduction of an important historical work. Alpha Editions uses the best technology to reproduce historical work in the same manner it was first published to preserve its original nature. Any marks or number seen are left intentionally to preserve its true form.

Contents

PREFACE .... - 1 -
INTRODUCTION .... - 2 -
1. .... - 7 -
2. .... - 12 -
3. .... - 15 -
4. .... - 18 -
5. .... - 21 -
6. .... - 25 -
7. .... - 29 -
8. .... - 33 -
9. .... - 37 -
10. .... - 41 -
11. .... - 45 -
12. .... - 48 -
13. .... - 50 -
14. .... - 54 -
15. .... - 57 -
16. .... - 60 -
17. .... - 63 -
18. .... - 66 -
19. .... - 68 -
20. .... - 72 -
21. .... - 75 -
22. .... - 79 -
23. .... - 83 -
24. .... - 88 -

25	- 91 -
26	- 94 -
27	- 99 -
28	- 102 -
29	- 105 -
30	- 109 -
31	- 112 -
32	- 115 -
33	- 119 -
34	- 123 -
35	- 127 -
36	- 130 -
37	- 134 -
38	- 137 -
39	- 139 -
40	- 143 -
41	- 146 -
42	- 149 -
43	- 153 -
44	- 158 -
45	- 163 -
46	- 167 -
47	- 170 -
48	- 172 -
49	- 176 -
50	- 180 -
51	- 185 -
52	- 188 -

53..- 192 -
54..- 197 -
55..- 200 -
56..- 203 -
57..- 206 -
58..- 210 -
59..- 213 -
60..- 218 -
61..- 223 -
62..- 226 -
63..- 229 -
64..- 233 -
65..- 236 -
66..- 239 -
67..- 242 -
68..- 245 -
69..- 250 -
70..- 253 -
71..- 256 -
72..- 261 -
73..- 265 -
74..- 269 -
75..- 274 -
76..- 278 -
77..- 281 -
78..- 285 -
79..- 288 -

PREFACE

To give the child some idea of what has gone on in the world before he arrived;

To take him out of his little self-centered, shut-in life, which looms so large because it is so close to his eyes;

To extend his horizon, broaden his view, and open up the vista down the ages past;

To acquaint him with some of the big events and great names and fix these in time and space as a basis for detailed study in the future;

To give him a chronological file with main guides, into which he can fit in its proper place all his further historical study—

Is the purpose of this first SURVEY OF THE WORLD'S HISTORY.

This part is not for you, either. It is for
your father, mother, or teacher, and is
what they would call the

INTRODUCTION

IN common with all children of my age, I was brought up on American History and given no other history but American, year in and year out, year after year for eight or more years.

So far as I knew 1492 was the beginning of the world. Any events or characters before that time, reference to which I encountered by any chance, were put down in my mind in the same category with fairy-tales. Christ and His times, of which I heard only in Sunday-school, were to me mere fiction without reality. They were not mentioned in any history that I knew and therefore, so I thought, must belong *not* to a realm in time and space, but to a spiritual realm.

To give an American child only American History is as provincial as to teach a Texas child only Texas History. Patriotism is usually given as the reason for such history teaching. It only promotes a narrow-mindedness and an absurd conceit, based on utter ignorance of any other peoples and any other times—an intolerant egotism without foundation in fact. Since the World War it has become increasingly more and more important that American children should have a knowledge of other countries and other peoples in order that their attitude may be intelligent and unprejudiced.

As young as nine years of age, a child is eagerly inquisitive as to what has taken place in the ages past and readily grasps a concept of World History. Therefore, for many years Calvert School nine-year-old pupils have been taught World History in spite of academic and parental skepticism and antagonism. But I have watched the gradual drift toward adoption of this plan of history teaching, and with it an ever-increasing demand for a text-book of general history for young children. I have found, however, that all existing text-books have to be largely abridged and also supplemented by a running explanation and comment, to make them intelligible to the young child.

The recent momentous studies into the native intelligence of children show us what the average child at different ages can understand and what he cannot understand—what dates, figures of speech, vocabulary, generalities, and abstractions he can comprehend and what he cannot comprehend—and in the future all text-books will have to be written with constant regard for these intelligence norms. Otherwise, such texts are very likely to be "over the child's head." They will be trying to teach him some things at least that, in the nature of the case, are beyond him.

In spite of the fact that the writer has been in constant contact with the child mind for a great many years, he has found that whatever was written in his study had to be revised and rewritten each time after the lesson had been tried out in the class-room. Even though the first writing was in what he considered the simplest language, he has found that each and every word and expression has had to be subjected again and again to this class-room test to determine what meaning is conveyed. The slightest inverted phraseology or possibility of double meaning has oftentimes been misconstrued or found confusing. For instance, the statement that "Rome was *on* the Tiber River" has quite commonly been taken to mean that the city was literally built *on top* of the river, and the child has had some sort of fantastic vision of houses built on piles in the river. A child of nine is still very young—he may still believe in Santa Claus—younger in ideas, in vocabulary and in understanding than most adults appreciate—even though they be parents or teachers—and new information can hardly be put too simply.

So the topics selected have not always been the most important—but the most important that can be understood and appreciated by a child. Most political, sociological, economic, or religious generalities are beyond a child's comprehension, no matter how simply told. After all, this History is only a preliminary story.

Excellent biographies and stories from general history have been written. But biographies from history do not give an historic outline. They do not give any outline at all for future filling in; and, indeed, unless they themselves are fitted into such a general historical scheme, they are nothing more than so many disconnected tales floating about in the child's mind with no associations of time or space.

The treatment of the subject in this book is, therefore, chronological—telling the story of what has happened century by century and epoch by epoch, not by nations. The story of one nation is interrupted to take up that of another as different plots in a novel are brought forward simultaneously. This is in line with the purpose, which is to give the pupil a continuous view or panorama of the ages, rather than Greek History from start to finish, then, retracing the steps of time, Roman History, and so on. The object is to sketch the whole picture in outline, leaving the details to be gradually filled in by later study, as the artist sketches the general scheme of his picture before filling in the details. Such a scheme is as necessary to orderly classification of historical knowledge as is a filing system in any office that can function properly or even at all.

The Staircase of Time is to give a visual idea of the extent of time and the progressive steps in the History of the World. Each "flight" represents a thousand years, and each "step" a hundred—a century. If you have a spare wall, either in the play-room, attic, or barn such a Staircase of Time on a large scale may be drawn upon it from floor to reaching height and made a feature if elaborated with pictures or drawings of people and events. If the wall faces the child's bed so much the better, for when lying awake in the morning or at any other time, instead of imagining fantastic designs on the wall-paper, he may picture the crowded events on the Staircase of Time. At any rate, the child should constantly refer either to such a Staircase of Time or to the Time Table as each event is studied, until he has a mental image of the Ages past.

At first a child does not appreciate time values represented by numbers or the relative position of dates on a time line and will wildly say twenty-five hundred B. C. or twenty-five thousand B. C. or twenty-five million B. C. indiscriminately. Only by constantly referring dates to position on the Staircase of Time or the Time Table can a child come to visualize dates. You may be *amused*, but do not be *amazed*, if a child gives 776 thousand years A.D. as the date for the First Olympiad, or says that Italy is located in Athens, or that Abraham was a hero of the Trojan War.

If you have ever been introduced to a roomful of strangers at one time, you know how futile it is to attempt even to remember their names to say nothing of connecting names and faces. It is necessary to hear something interesting about each one before you can begin to recall names and faces. Likewise an introduction to World History, the characters and places in which are utterly unknown strangers to the child, must be something more than a mere name introduction, and there must be very few introductions given at a time or both names and faces will be instantly forgotten. It is also necessary to repeat new names constantly in order that the pupil may gradually become familiarized with them, for so many strange people and places are bewildering.

In order to serve the purpose of a basal outline, which in the future is to be filled in, it is necessary that the Time Table be made a permanent possession of the pupil. This Time Table, therefore, should be studied like the multiplication tables until it is known one hundred per cent and for "keeps," and until the topic connected with each date can be elaborated as much as desired. The aim should be to have the pupil able to start with Primitive Man and give a summary of World History to the present time, with dates and chief events without prompting, questioning, hesitation, or mistake. Does this seem too much to expect? It is not as difficult as it may sound, if suggestions given in the text for connecting the various events into a sequence and for passing names and events in a condensed review are followed. Hundreds of Calvert children each year are successfully required to do this very thing.

The attitude, however, usually assumed by teachers, that "even if the pupil forgets it all, there will be left a valuable impression," is too often an apology for superficial teaching and superficial learning. History may be made just as much a "mental discipline" as some other studies, but only if difficulties of dates and other abstractions are squarely met and overcome by hard study and learned to be remembered, not merely to be forgotten after the recitation. The story part the child will easily remember, but it is the "who and when and where and why" that are important, and this part is the serious study. Instead of, "A man, once upon a time," he should say, "King John in 1215 at Runnymede because—"

This book, therefore, is not a supplementary reader but a basal history study. Just enough narrative is told to give the skeleton flesh and blood and make it living. The idea is not how much but how little can be told; to cut down one thousand pages to less than half of that number without leaving only dry bones.

No matter how the subject is presented it is necessary that the child do his part and put his own brain to work; and for this purpose he *should be required to retell each story after he has read it* and should be repeatedly questioned on names and dates as well as stories, to make sure he is retaining and assimilating what he hears.

I recall how once upon a time a young chap, just out of college, taught his first class in history. With all the enthusiasm of a full-back who has just kicked a goal from field, he talked, he sang; he drew maps on the blackboard, on the floor, on the field; he drew pictures, he vaulted desks, and even stood on his head to illustrate points. His pupils attended spellbound, with their eyes wide open, their ears wide open, and their mouths wide open. They missed nothing. They drank in his flow of words with thirst unquenched; but, like Baron Munchausen, he had failed to look at the other end of the drinking horse that had been cut in half. At the end of a month his kindly principal suggested a test, and he gave it with perfect confidence.

There were only three questions:

(1) Tell all you can about Columbus.
(2) "   "   "   "   " Jamestown.
(3) "   "   "   "   " Plymouth.

And here are the three answers of one of the most interested pupils:

(1) He was a *grate* man.
(2) "   "   "   "   "
(3) "   "   "   "   " *to.*

- 5 -

Here is the

STAIRCASE OF TIME

It starts far, far, below the bottom of the pages and rises up, UP, UP to where we are NOW—each step a hundred years, each flight of steps a thousand. It will keep on up until it reaches high heaven. From where we are NOW let us look down the flights below us and listen to the Story of what has happened in the long years gone by.

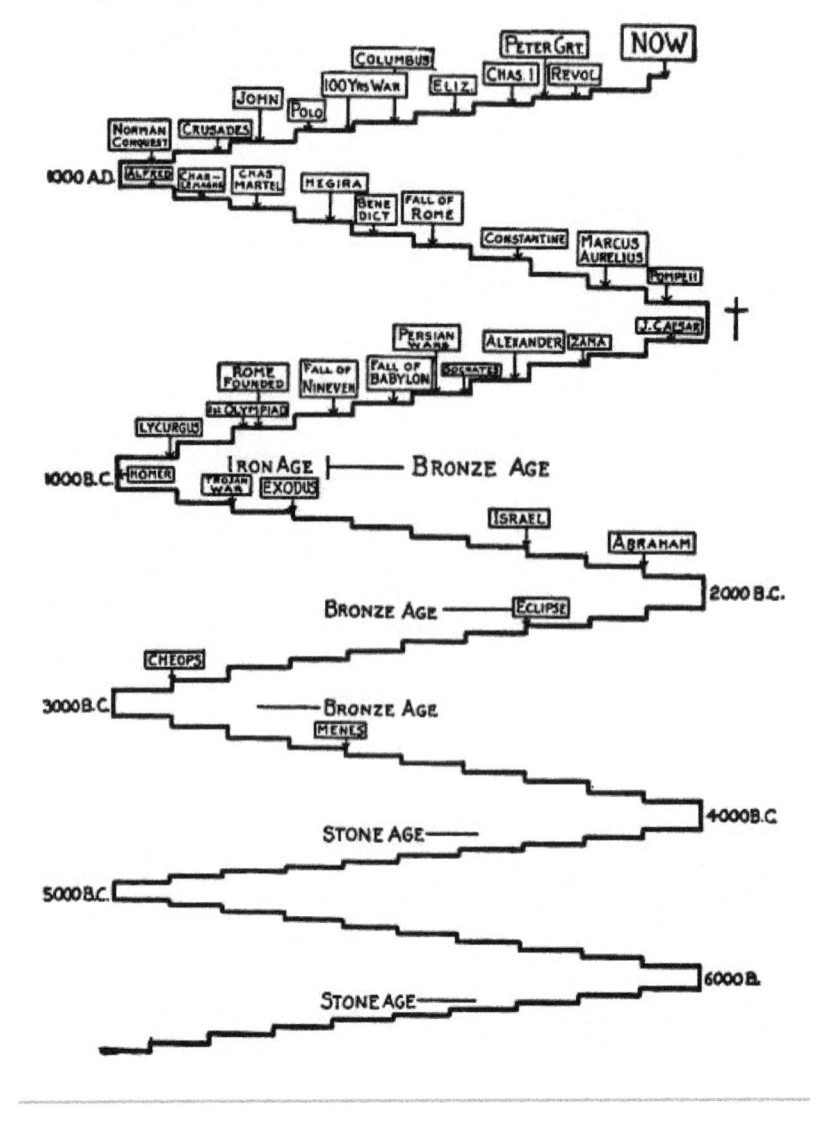

# 1

How Things Started

ONCE upon a time there was a boy—

Just like me.

He had to stay in bed in the morning until seven o'clock until his father and mother were ready to get up;

So did I.

As he was always awake long before this time, he used to lie there and think about all sorts of curious things;

So did I.

One thing he used to wonder was this:

What would the world be like if there were—

No fathers and mothers,

No uncles and aunts,

No cousins or other children to play with,

No people at all, except himself in the whole world!

Perhaps you have wondered the same thing;

So did I.

At last he used to get so lonely, just from thinking how dreadful such a world would be, that he could stand it no longer and would run to his mother's room and jump into bed by her side just to get this terrible thought out of his mind;

So did I—for *I was the boy*.

Well, there *was* a time long, long, long ago when there were no men or women or children, NO PEOPLE of any kind in the whole world. Of course there were no houses, for there was no one to build them or to live in them, no towns or cities—nothing that people make. There were just wild animals—bears and wolves, birds and butterflies, frogs and snakes, turtles and fish. Can you think of such a world as that?

Then,

long, long, long

before that, there was a time when there were *NO PEOPLE* and *NO ANIMALS* of any sort in the whole world; there were just growing plants, trees and bushes, grass and flowers. Can you think of such a world as that?

Then,

long, long, long,
long, long, long

before that, there was a time when there were *NO PEOPLE, NO ANIMALS, NO PLANTS*, in the whole world; there was just bare rock and water everywhere. Can you think of such a world as that?

Then,

long, long, long
long, long, long—you might
keep on saying—
"long, long, long," all day, and
to-morrow, and all
next week, and next
month, and next
year, and it would
not be long enough—

before this, there was a time when there was *NO WORLD AT ALL!*

There were only the Stars

Nothing else!

Now, real Stars are not things with points like those in the corner of a flag or the gold ones you put on a Christmas tree. The real stars in the sky have no points. They are huge burning coals of fire—coals of fire. Each star, however, is so huge that there is nothing in the world now anywhere nearly as big. One little bit, one little scrap of a star is bigger than our whole world—than our whole world.

One of these stars is our Sun—yes, our Sun. The other stars would look the same as the Sun if we could get as close to them. But at that time, so long, long ago, our Sun was not just a big, round, white, hot ball as we see it in the sky to-day. It was then more like the fireworks you may have seen on the Fourth of July. It was whirling and sputtering and throwing off sparks.

The sun sputtering and throwing off sparks.

One of these sparks which the Sun threw far off got cool just as a spark from the crackling log in the fireplace gets cool, and this cooled-off spark was—

What do you suppose?
See if you can guess—
It was our World!—yes, the World
on which we now live.

At first, however, our World or Earth was nothing but a ball of rock. This ball of rock was wrapped around with steam, like a heavy fog.

Then the steam turned to rain and it rained on the World,

        a a a
        n n n
        d d d

        i i i
        t t t

        r r r
        a a a
        i i i
        n n n
        e e e
        d d d

until it had filled up the hollows and made enormously big puddles. These puddles were the oceans. The dry places were bare *rock*.

Then, after this, came the first living things—*tiny plants* that you could only have seen under a microscope. At first they grew only in the water, then along the water's edge, then out on the rock.

Then dirt or soil, as people call it, formed all over the rock and made the rock into land, and the plants grew larger and spread farther over the land.

Then, after this, came the first *tiny animals* in the water. They were wee *Mites* like drops of jelly.

Then, after this, came things like *Insects*, some that live *in* the water, some *on* the water, some *on* the land, and some *in* the air.

Then, after this, came *Fish*, that live only in the water.

Then, after this, came *Frogs*, that live in the water and on the land, too.

Then, after this, came *Snakes* and huge *lizards* bigger than alligators, more like dragons; and they grew so big that at last they could not move and died because they could not get enough food to eat.

Then, after this, came *Birds* that lay eggs and those *Animals* like foxes and elephants and cows that nurse their babies when they are born.

Then, after this, came *Monkeys*.

Then, last of all, came—what do you suppose? Yes—*People*—men, women, and children.

Here are the steps; see if you can take them:

STAR, SUN;

SUN, SPARK;

SPARK, WORLD;

WORLD, STEAM;

STEAM, RAIN;

RAIN, OCEANS.

OCEANS, PLANTS;

    PLANTS, MITES;

        MITES, INSECTS;

            INSECTS, FISH;

                FISH, FROGS;

                    FROGS, SNAKES.

SNAKES, BIRDS;

    BIRDS, ANIMALS;

        ANIMALS, MONKEYS;

            MONKEYS, PEOPLE;

                AND HERE WE ARE!

What do you suppose will be next?

2

Umfa-Umfa and Itchy-Scratchy

How do you suppose I know about all these things that took place so long ago?

I don't.

I'm only guessing about them.

But there are different kinds of guesses. If I hold out my two closed hands and ask you to guess which one has the penny in it, that is one kind of a guess. Your guess might be right or it might be wrong. It would be just luck.

But there is another kind of a guess. When there is snow on the ground and I see tracks of a boot in the snow, I guess that a man must have passed by, for boots don't usually walk without some one in them. That kind of a guess is not just luck but common sense.

And so we can guess about a great many things that have taken place long ago, even though there was no one there at the time to see them or tell about them.

Men have dug down deep under the ground in different parts of the world and have found there—what do you suppose?

I don't believe you would ever guess.

They have found the heads of arrows and spears and hatchets.

The peculiar thing about these arrows and spears and hatchets is that they are not made of iron or steel, as you might expect, but of stone.

Now, we are sure that only men could have made and used such things, for birds and fish or other animals do not use hatchets or spears. We are also sure that these men must have lived long, long years ago before iron and steel were known, because it must have taken long, long years for these things to have become covered up so deep by dust and dirt. We have also found the bones of the people themselves, who must have died thousands upon thousands of years ago, long before any one began to write down history. So we know that the people who were living on the earth then were working and playing, eating and fighting—doing many of the same things we are to-day—especially the fighting.

This time in the pre-history of the world, when people used such things made of stone, is therefore called THE STONE AGE.

These First Stone Age People we call *Primitive*, which simply means First as a Primer means First Reader. Primitive People were wild animals. Unlike other wild animals, however, they walked on their hind legs.

These First People had hair growing, not just on their heads, but all over their bodies, like some shaggy dogs. They had no houses of any sort in which to live. They simply lay down on the ground when night came. Later, when the earth became cold, they found caves in the rocks or in the hillsides where they could get away from the cold and storms and other wild animals. So men, women, and children of this time were called *Cave People*.

They spent their days hunting some animals and running and hiding from others. They caught animals by trapping them in a pit covered over with bushes, or they killed them with a club or a rock if they had a chance, or with stone-headed arrows or hatchets. They even drew pictures of these animals on the walls of their caves, scratching the picture with a pointed stone, and some of these pictures we can still see to-day.

They lived on berries and nuts and grass-seeds. They robbed the nests of birds for the eggs, which they ate raw, for they had no fire to cook with. They were blood-thirsty; they liked to drink the warm blood of animals they killed, as you would a glass of milk.

They talked to each other by some sort of grunts—

"Umfa, umfa, glug, glug."

They made clothes of skins of animals they killed, for there was no such thing as cloth. And yet, although they were real men, they lived so much like wild animals that we call such people *savages*.

Primitive Men were not pleasant people. They were fearful and cruel creatures, who beat and killed and robbed whenever they had a chance.

A cave man got his wife by stealing a girl away from her own cave home, knocking her senseless, and dragging her off by her hair, if necessary. The men were fighters but not brave. They would kill other animals and other men if the others were weaker or if they could sneak upon them and catch them off their guard, but if others were stronger they would run and hide.

Their only rule of life was hurt and kill what you can, and run from what you can't. This is what we call the first law of nature—every man for himself. They knew if they didn't kill they would be killed, for there were no laws nor police to protect them.

These primitive cave people are our ancestors, and we get from them many of their wild ways. In spite of our religion and manners and education, there are many men still living who act in the same way when they get a chance.

Jails are made for such men.

Suppose you had been a boy or a girl in the Stone Age, with a name like Itchy-Scratchy. I wonder how you would have liked the life.

When you woke up in the morning, you would not have bathed or even washed your hands and face or brushed your teeth or combed your hair.

You ate with your fingers, for there were no knives or forks or spoons or cups or saucers, only one bowl—which your mother had made out of mud and dried in the sun to hold water to drink—no dishes to wash and put away, no chairs, no tables, no table manners.

There were no books, no paper, no pencils.

There was no Saturday or Sunday, January or July. Except that one day was warm and sunny or another cold and rainy, they were all alike. There was no school to go to. Every day was a holiday.

There was nothing to do all day long but make mud pies or pick berries or play tag with your brothers and sisters.

I wonder how you would like that kind of life!

"Fine!" do you think?—"a great life—just like camping out?"

But I have only told you part of the story.

The cave would have been cold and damp and dark, with only the bare ground or a pile of leaves for a bed. There would probably have been bats and big spiders sharing the cave with you.

You might have had on the skin of some animal your father had killed but as this only covered part of your body and as there was no fire, you would have felt cold in winter, and when it got very cold you might have frozen to death.

For breakfast you might have had some dried berries or grass-seed or a piece of raw meat, for dinner the same thing, for supper still the same thing.

You would never have had any bread or milk or griddle-cakes with syrup, or oatmeal with sugar on it, or apple pie or ice-cream.

There was nothing to do all day long but watch out for wild animals—bears and tigers; for there was no door with lock and key, and a tiger, if he found you out, could go wherever you went and "get you" even in your cave.

And then some day your father, who had left the cave in the morning to go hunting, would not return, and you would know he had been torn to pieces by some wild beast, and you would wonder how long before your turn would come next.

Do you think you would like to have lived then?

3

Fire! Fire!! Fire!!!

THE first things are usually the most interesting—the first baby, the first tooth, the first step, the first word, the first spanking. This book will be chiefly the story of first things; those that came second or third or fourth or fifth you can read about and study later.

Primitive People did not at first know what fire was. They had no matches nor any way of making a light or a fire. They had no light at night. They had no fire to warm themselves by. They had no fire with which to cook their food. Somewhere and sometime, we do not know exactly when or how, they found out how to make and use fire.

If you rub your hands together rapidly, they become warm. Try it. If you rub them together still more rapidly, they become hot. If you rub two sticks together rapidly, they become warm. If you rub two sticks together very, very, very rapidly, they become hot and at last, if you keep it up long enough and fast enough, are set on fire. The Indians and boy scouts do this and make a fire by twisting one stick against another.

This was one of the first inventions, and this invention was as remarkable for them at that time as the invention of electric light in our own times.

People of the Stone Age had hair and beards that were never cut, because they had nothing to cut them with, even had they wanted them short, which they probably didn't.

Their finger-nails grew like claws until they broke off.

They had no clothes made of cloth, for they had no cloth and nothing with which to cut and sew cloth if they had.

They had no saws to cut boards, no hammer or nails to fasten them together to make houses or furniture.

They had no forks nor spoons; no pots nor pans; no buckets nor shovels; no needles nor pins.

The People of the Stone Age had never seen or heard of such a thing as iron or steel or tin or brass or anything made of these metals. For thousands and thousands of years Primitive People got along without any of the things that are made of metal.

Then one day a Stone Age Man found out something by accident; a "discovery" we call it.

He was making a fire; and a fire, which is to us such a common, every-day thing, was still to him very wonderful. Round his fire he placed some rock to make a sort of camp-fire stove. Now, it happened that this particular rock was not ordinary rock but what we now call "ore," for it had copper in it. The heat of the fire melted some of the copper out of the rock, and it ran out on the ground.

A cave man discovering copper.

What were those bright, shining drops?

He examined them.

How pretty they were!

He heated some more of the same rock and got some more copper.

Thus was the first metal discovered.

At first people used the copper for beads and ornaments, it was so bright and shiny. But they soon found out that copper could be pounded into sharp blades and points, which were much better than the stone knives and arrow-heads they had used before.

But notice that it was not iron they discovered first, it was copper.

We think people next discovered tin in somewhat the same way. Then, after that, they found out that tin when mixed with copper made a still harder and better metal than either alone. This metal, made of tin and copper together, we now call bronze; and for two or three thousand years people made their tools and weapons out of bronze. And so we call the time when men used bronze tools, and bronze weapons for hunting and fighting, the Bronze Age.

At last some man discovered iron, and he soon saw that iron was better for most useful things than either copper or bronze. The Iron Age started with the discovery of iron, and we are still in the Iron Age.

As people who lived in the Bronze and Iron Ages were able, after the discovery of metal, to do many things they could not possibly have done before with only stone, and as they lived much more as we do now, we call people of the Bronze and Iron Ages "civilized."

You may have heard in your mythology or fairy tales of a Golden Age also, but by this is meant something quite different. The Golden Age means a time when everything was beautiful and lovely and everybody wise and good. There have been times in the World's History which have been called the Golden Age for this reason.

But I am afraid there never has been really a golden age—only in fairy-tales.

4

From an Airplane

PEOPLE of the Bronze and Iron Ages thought the world was flat, and they knew only a little bit of the world, the small part where they lived; and they thought that if you went too far the world came to an end where you would

T
U
M
B
L
E

O
F
F

The far-away land which nobody knew they called the Ultima Thule. This is a nice name to say—Ultima Thule, Ultima Thule—far-away Ultima Thule.

If we should go up in an airplane and look down on the world at the place where the first civilized people once lived, we should see two rivers, a sea and a gulf, and from so high up in the air they would look something like this:

Map of Mesopotamia and Mediterranean.

Now, you probably have never even heard of these rivers and seas, and yet they have been known longer than any other places in the world. One of these lines is the Tigris River, and the other is the Euphrates. They run along getting closer and closer together until at last they join each other and flow into what is called the Persian Gulf.

You might make these two rivers in the ground of your yard or garden or draw them on the floor if your mother will let you. Just for fun you might name your drinking-cup "Tigris" and your glass "Euphrates." Then you might call your mouth, into which they both empty, the "Persian Gulf," for you will hear a great many new names by and by, and as grown-up people give names to their houses and boats, to their horses and dogs, why shouldn't you give names to things that belong to you? For instance, you might call your chair, your bed, your table, your comb and brush, even your hat and shoes, after these strange names.

Then, if we flew in our airplane to the west, we should see a country called Egypt, another river, the Nile, and a sea now named the Mediterranean. Mediterranean simply means "between the land," for this sea is surrounded by land. It is, indeed, almost like a big lake. It is supposed that long, long ago in the Stone Age, there was no water at all where this sea now is, only a dry valley, and that people once lived there.

Along the Nile in Egypt and the Tigris and Euphrates were the only civilized nations living in the Bronze Age. The rest of the World people knew nothing about. There may have been Cave Men living in other parts of the World, but it is only of the people in these two places that we have any written history until after the Iron Age began.

All of the people who lived in the country of the Tigris and Euphrates were white. We don't know how nor when nor where colored people first lived, though it is interesting to guess. There were, we think, just three different white families and from these three families all the white people in the world are descended. Yes, your family came from here, 'way, 'way, 'way, 'way, back. So you will want to know the names of these three families and which one was your own. They were:

<blockquote>
The Indo-Europeans, often called Aryans,
The Semites, and
The Hamites.
</blockquote>

Most of us belong to the Aryan family, some are Semites, but very few in this part of the World are Hamites.

If your name is Henry or Charles or William, you are probably an Aryan.

If it is Moses or Solomon, you are probably a Semite.

If it is Shufu or Rameses, you are probably a Hamite.

The Aryans came from higher up on the map than the other two families, we think. They were the first people to tame wild horses and to use them for riding and drawing carts. They also had tamed cows which they used for milk, and sheep for their wool.

5

Real History Begins or 'Way 'Way Back to the Time of the Gipsies

YOU can remember the big things that have happened in your own lifetime.

And you have of course heard your father tell about things that happened in his own life—how he fought the Germans in the Great War, perhaps.

And if your grandfather is still living, he can tell you still other stories of things that took place when he was a boy before even your father was born.

Perhaps your
great,
great,
grandfather

may have been living when Washington was President, and *his*

great,
great,
great,
great,
grandfather

may have been living when there were only wild Indians in this country.

Although these ancestors, as they are called, are dead long since, the story of what did happen in all their lifetimes 'way, 'way back has been written down in books and this story is history—"his story" one boy named it.

Christ was living in the Year 1—no, not the first year of the world, of course.

Do you know how many years ago that was?

You can tell if you know what year this is now.

If Christ were living to-day, how old would He be?

Nineteen hundred and more years may seem a long time. But perhaps you have seen or heard of a man or a woman who was a hundred years old. Have you?

Well, in nineteen hundred years only nineteen men each a hundred years old might have lived one after the other—nineteen men one after the other since the time of Christ—and that doesn't seem so long after all!

Everything that happened *before* Christ was born is called B.C., which you can guess are the initials of Before Christ, so B.C. stands for Before Christ. So much is easy.

Everything that has happened in the world *since* the time of Christ is called A.D. This is not so easy for though A. might stand for After, we know D. is not the initial of Christ. As a matter of fact, A. D. are the initials of two Latin words, "Anno Domini." Anno means "in the year," Domini "of the Lord"; so that Anno Domini is "in the year, of the Lord," which in ordinary, every-day language means of course "since the time of Christ."

The things I have told you that I have had to guess at we call Before-History, or *Pre-History*—which means the same thing. But the things that have happened in the lifetime of people, who have written them down—the stories I don't have to guess at—we call *History*.

The first history that we feel fairly sure is really true begins with the Hamite family. The Hamites, you remember, were one of the three families of the white race I have already told you about who lived by the Tigris and Euphrates. We think that they moved away from the Tigris and Euphrates Rivers and went down to Egypt long before history began.

Of course they didn't pack all their furniture on a big wagon and move to Egypt, as you might move from the house where you now live to another. They lived in tents then and not in houses at all, and they only moved along a day's journey at a time as campers or Gipsies might do. In fact, Gipsy is short for Egyptian. When they got tired of one place or had eaten up everything there was near-by, they rolled up their tents, packed them on camels, and moved a little farther along to a new place. And so camping here for a while, then gradually moving farther along to the next good place and camping there, they at last got as far off as the land we now call Egypt. When they finally reached Egypt they found it such a fine country in which to live that there they stayed for good and were called Egyptians.

Why do you suppose they found Egypt such a fine country in which to live? It was chiefly on account of a habit of the river Nile—a bad habit you might at first think it—a habit of flooding the country once every year.

It rains so hard in the spring that the water fills up the river Nile, overflows its banks, and spreads far out over the land, but not very deep. It is as if you had left a water-spigot turned on and the water running, or had begun to water your garden with a hose, and then you had gone off and forgotten it.

But the people know when the overflow is coming and they are glad for it to come, so they put banks around some of it so that it is stored up for watering the land during the rest of the year when there is no rain. After most of the water has dried up, it has left a layer of rich, dark, moist earth over the whole country. In this earth it is easy to grow dates, wheat, and other things which are good for food.

Menes, 3400 B. C.

If it were not for this yearly overflow of the Nile, the country of Egypt would be a sandy desert in which no plant or living thing would grow—for all plants as well as animals must have water and will die without it. Egypt, without water, would be like the great Sahara Desert, which is not far away. It is the Nile, therefore, that makes the land so rich and Egypt such an easy and cheap country to live in, for food grows with little or no labor and costs almost nothing. Besides this, the climate is so warm that people need little clothing and do not have to buy coal or make fires to heat their houses. So it was to this country that the Hamites at last came, finally settled down, and were thereafter called Egyptians.

The first Egyptian king whose name we know was Menes, but we do not know much about him. We believe he built some kind of waterworks so that the people might better use the water of the Nile, and he probably lived about 3400 B. C. He may have lived either earlier or later, but as this is an easy date to remember, we shall take it for a starting-point. You might remember it by supposing it is a telephone number of a person you wanted to call up:

Menes, First Egyptian king . . 3400 B.C.

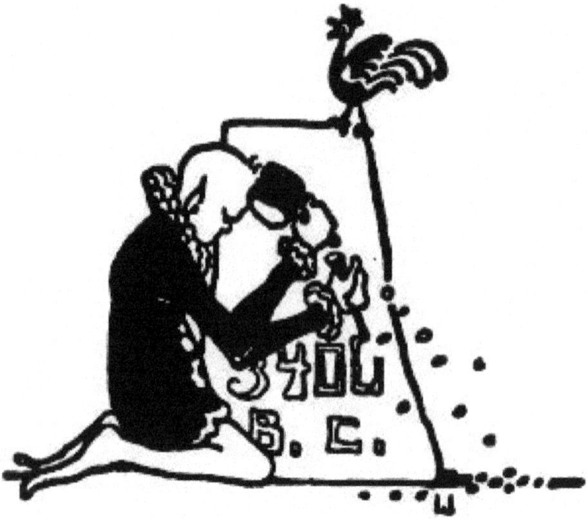
3400
B. C.

6

The Puzzle-Writers

PEOPLE of the Stone Age had learned how to talk to each other, but they could not write, for there was no such thing as an alphabet or written words, and so they could not send notes or messages to one another or write stories. The Egyptians were the first people to think of a way to write what they wanted to say.

The Egyptians did not write with letters like ours, however, but with signs that looked like little pictures, a lion, a spear, a bird, a whip. This picture-writing was called hieroglyphics—see if you can say "Hi-e-ro-glyph-ics." Perhaps you have seen, in the puzzle sections of a newspaper, stories written in pictures for you to guess the meaning. Well, hieroglyphics were something like that.

Here is the name of an Egyptian queen, whom you will hear about later—written in hieroglyphics; her name you would never guess from this funny writing. It is "Cleopatra."

Cleopatra in hieroglyphic writing.

A king's or queen's name always had a line drawn around it, like the one you see around the above name in order to mark it more prominently and give it more importance. It was something like the square or circle your mother may put around her initials or monogram on her letter-paper.

But there was no paper in those days and so the Egyptians wrote on the leaves of a plant called papyrus that grew in the water. It is from this name "papyrus" that we get the name "paper." Can you see that "paper" and "papyrus" look and sound something alike? The Egyptians' books were written by hand, of course, but they had no pencils nor pens nor ink to write with. For a pen they used a reed, split at the end, and for ink a mixture of water and soot.

Their books were not made of separate pages like our books, but from a long sheet of papyrus-leaves pasted together. This was rolled up to form what was called a scroll, something like a roll of wall-paper, and was read as it was unrolled.

Stories of their kings and battles and great events in their history they used to write on the walls of their buildings and monuments. This writing they carved into the stone, so that it would last much longer than that on the papyrus-leaves.

All the old Egyptians, who wrote in hieroglyphics and knew how to read this writing, had died long since, and for a great many years no one knew what such writing meant. But a little over a hundred years ago a man found out by accident how to read and understand hieroglyphics once again. This is the way he happened to do so.

The Nile separates into different streams before it flows into the Mediterranean Sea. These separate streams are called mouths and one of these mouths has been given the name "Rosetta."

One day a man was digging nearby this Rosetta Mouth when he dug up a stone something like a tombstone with several kinds of writing on it. The top writing was in pictures which we now call hieroglyphics, and no one understood what it meant. Below this was written what was supposed to be the same story in the Greek language, and a great many people do understand Greek. All one had to do, therefore, to find out the meaning of the hieroglyphics, was to compare the two writings. It was like reading secret writing when we know what the letters stand for. You may have tried to solve a puzzle in the back of your magazine, and this was just such an interesting puzzle, only there was no one to tell the answer in the next number.

The puzzle was not so easy as it sounds, however, for it took a man almost twenty years to solve it. That is a long time for any one to spend in trying to solve a puzzle, isn't it? But after this "key" to the puzzle was found, men were able to read all of the hieroglyphics in Egypt and so to find out what happened in that country long before Christ was born.

This stone is called the Rosetta Stone, from the Rosetta Mouth of the Nile where it was found. It is now in the great British Museum in London and is very famous, because from it we were able to learn so much history which we otherwise would not have known.

Egypt was ruled over by a king who was called a Pharaoh. When he died his son became the Pharaoh and so on. All the other people were divided into classes, and the children in each class usually became just what their fathers had been. It was very unusual for an Egyptian to start at the bottom and work up to the top, as a poor boy in this country may do, though once in a great while this happened even in Egypt, as we shall see by and by.

The highest class of people were called priests. They were not like priests or ministers of the church nowadays, however, for there was no church at that time. The priests made the religion and rules, which every one had to obey as everybody does the laws of our land.

But the priests were not only priests; they were doctors and lawyers and engineers, as well. They were the best-educated class, and they were the only people who knew how to read and write, for it was very difficult, as you might suppose, to learn how to read and write hieroglyphics.

The next highest class to the priests were the soldiers, and below these were the lower classes—farmers, shepherds, shopkeepers, merchants, mechanics, and last of all the swineherds.

The Egyptians did not worship one God as we do. They believed in hundreds of gods and goddesses, and they had a special god for every sort of thing, who ruled over and had charge of that thing—a god of the farm, a god of the home, and so on. Some of their gods were good and some were bad, but the Egyptians prayed to them all.

Osiris was the chief god, and Isis was his wife. Osiris was the god of farming and judge of the dead. Their son Horus had the head of a hawk.

Many of their gods had bodies of men with heads of animals. Animals they thought sacred. The dog and the cat were sacred animals. The ibis, which was a bird like a stork, was another. Then there was the beetle, which was called a scarab. If any one killed a sacred animal he was put to death, for the Egyptians thought it much worse to kill a sacred and holy creature than to kill even a human being.

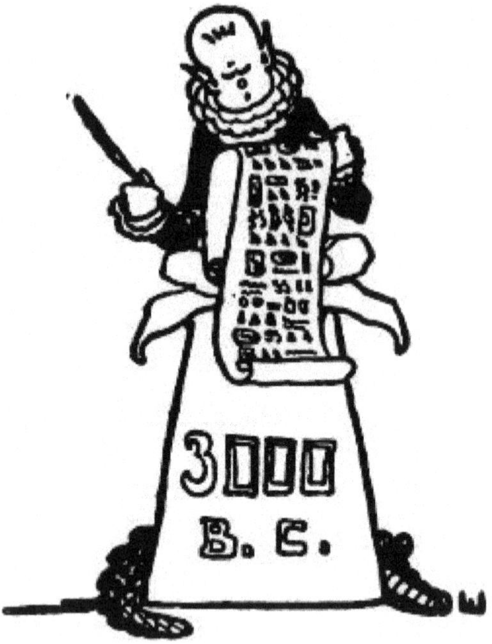
3000
B. C.

7

The Tomb-Builders

Tu-tank-amen's tomb showing foods preserved.

THE Egyptians believed that when they died, their souls stayed near by their bodies. So when a person died they put in the tomb with him all sorts of things that he had used in daily life—things to eat and drink, furniture and dishes, toys and games. They thought the soul would return to its own body at the day of judgment. They wanted their bodies to be kept from decaying until judgment day, in order that the soul might then have a body to return to. So they pickled the bodies of the dead by soaking them in a kind of melted tar and wrapping them round and round and round with a cloth like a bandage. A dead body pickled in this way is called a mummy, and after thousands of years the mummies of the Egyptian kings may still be seen. Most of them are not, however, in the tombs where they were at first placed. They have been moved away and put in museums, and we may see them there now. Although they are yellow and dried up, they still look like

"Little old men

All skin and bones."

At first only kings or important people of the highest classes were made mummies, but after a while all the classes, except perhaps the lowest, were treated in the same way. Sacred animals from beetles to cows were also made into mummies.

When an Egyptian died his friends heaped up a few stones over his body just to cover it up decently and keep it from being stolen or destroyed by those wild animals that fed on dead bodies. But a king or a rich man wanted a bigger pile of stones over his body than just ordinary people had. So to make sure that his pile would be big enough, a king built it for himself before he died. Each king tried to make his pile larger than any one else's until at last the pile of stones became so big it was a hill of rocks and called a pyramid. The pyramids therefore were tombs of the kings who built them while they were alive to be monuments to themselves when they were dead. In fact a king was much more interested in building a home for his dead body than he was in a home for his live body. So, instead of palaces, kings built pyramids. There are many of these pyramids built along the bank of the Nile, and most of them were built, we think, just after 3000 B.C.

When a building is being put up nowadays, men use derricks and cranes and engines to haul and raise heavy stones and beams. But the Egyptians had no such machinery, and though they used huge stones to build the pyramids, they had to drag these stones for many miles and raise them into place simply by pushing and pulling them. The three biggest of all the pyramids are near the city of Cairo. The largest one of them, which is called the Great Pyramid, was built by a king named Cheops. To remember when he lived, simply think of this as another telephone number:

>Cheops ....2900 B.C.

It is said that one hundred thousand men worked twenty years to build his pyramid. It is one of the largest buildings in the world, and some of the blocks of stone themselves are as big as a small house. I have been to the top of it, and it is like climbing a steep mountain with rocky sides. I have also been far inside to the cave-like room in the center where Cheop's mummy was placed. There is nothing in there now, however, except bats that fly about in the darkness, for the mummy has disappeared—been stolen, perhaps.

Cheops building his pyramid.

Near the Pyramid of Cheops is the Sphinx. It is a huge statue of a lion with a man's head. It is as big as a church, and though it is so big, it has been carved out of one single rock. The rock, however, was already there and so did not have to be carried. The Sphinx is a statue of the god of the morning, and the head is that of one of the Egyptian Pharaohs who built a pyramid near that of Cheops. The desert sand has covered the paws and most of the body. Though the sand has been dug away from time to time, the wind quickly covers the body with sand again.

The Egyptians carved other large statues of men and women out of rock. These figures are usually many times bigger than life-size, and sit or stand stiffly erect with both feet flat on the ground and hands close to the body in the position some children take when they "sit" for their photograph.

They built huge houses for their gods. These were called temples and took the place of our churches. These temples had gigantic—that's the way it is spelled, though it means "giant-ic"—columns and pillars. Ordinary people standing beside them look like dwarfs. Here is one of these temples, and you can see how different it is from our churches:

Egyptian temple.

They decorated their temples and pyramids, and the cases in which the mummies were put, with drawings and paintings. The pictures they made, however, looked something like those a young child might draw. For example, when they wanted to make a picture of water, they simply made a zigzag line to represent waves; when they tried to draw a row of men back of a row in front, they put those in the back *on top* of those in front. To show that a man was a king, they made him several times larger than the other men in the picture. When they painted a picture they used any color they thought was pretty, usually blue or yellow or brown. Whether the person or thing was really that color or not made no difference.

8

A Rich Land Where There Was No Money

YOU have read in fairy-tales of a land where cakes and candy and sugar-plums grow on trees, where everything you want to eat or to play with can be had just by picking it. Well, long, long ago people used to think there had been really such a country, and where do you suppose they said it was? Somewhere near the Tigris and Euphrates Rivers—those rivers with the strange names I asked you to learn—and they called this spot the Garden of Eden. We do not know exactly where it was, for there is no such place now quite as wonderful as the Garden of Eden was supposed to be.

Egypt was a land of one river, the Nile. The land of the Two Rivers had several names.

Let us suppose we are flying over the country in an airplane and looking down at the land between these two rivers. It is called Mesopotamia, which is two Greek words simply meaning "Between the Rivers."

See the land over there by the upper Tigris. It is called *Assyria*.

See the land near where the rivers join each other. That is called *Babylonia*.

See the land near where they empty. That is called *Chaldea*.

And see over there is *Mount Ararat*, where it is supposed Noah's Ark rested after the flood.

Here are a lot of new names. A young friend of mine had a train of toy cars. He had noticed that the Pullman cars on which he had ridden had names, and so he gave his toy cars names also. He called them:

ASSYRIA   MESOPOTAMIA
BABYLONIA   ARARAT
CHALDEA   EUPHRATES

Babylonia was a very rich country, for the two rivers brought down and dropped great quantities of earth just as the Nile did in Egypt, and this made very rich soil. Wheat, from which we make bread, is called the staff of life. It is the most valuable of all foods which grow. It is supposed that wheat first grew in Babylonia. Dates in that part of the world are almost as important a food as wheat. Dates, too, grow there very plentifully. Now, you may think dates are something to be eaten almost like candy but in Babylonia dates took the place of oatmeal. In the rivers there were quantities of good fish, and as fishing was just fun, you see that the people who lived in Babylonia—the Babylonians, as they were called—had plenty of good food without having to do much work for it. No one had any money in those days; people had cows and sheep and goats, and a man was rich who had much of these "goods." But if a man wanted to buy or sell, he had to buy or sell by trading something he had for something he wanted.

Somewhere in Babylonia the people built a great tower called the *Tower of Babel*, which you have probably heard about. It was more like a mountain than a tower. They built other towers, too. Some say the Tower of Babel and towers like it were built so that the people might have a high place to which they could climb in case of another flood. But others give a different reason. They say that the people who built these towers came to Babylonia from farther north where there were mountains. In this northern land they had always placed their altars on the top of a mountain, to be close to heaven. So when they moved to a flat country like Mesopotamia and Babylonia, where there were no mountains, they *built* mountains in order to have a high place for the altar on top. To reach the top of these mountains or towers, they made, instead of a staircase on the inside, a slanting roadway that wound around the outside in somewhat the way a road winds around a mountain.

There was hardly any stone either in or near Babylonia as there was in Egypt, and so the Babylonians built their buildings of bricks, which were made of mud formed into blocks and dried in the sun. In the course of time, bricks of this sort crumble and turn back into dust again just as mud pies that you might make would do. This is the reason why all that is left of the Tower of Babel and the other buildings that were put up so long ago are now simply hills of clay into which the brick has turned.

The Egyptians wrote on papyrus or carved their history in stone, but the Babylonians had neither papyrus nor stone. All they had were bricks. So they wrote on bricks before they were dried, while they were still soft clay. This writing was made by punching marks into the clay with the end of a stick. It was called *cuneiform*, which means wedge-shaped, for it looked like little groups of wedge-shaped marks, like chicken-tracks, made in the mud. I have seen boys' writing that looked more like cuneiform than it did like English.

The Babylonians as they watched their flocks by night and by day watched also the sun and the moon and the stars moving across the sky. So they came to know a great deal about these heavenly bodies.

Did you ever see the moon in the daytime?

Oh, yes, you can.

Babylonians watching eclipse.

Well, every once in a great while the moon as it moves across the sky gets in front of the sun and shuts out its light—just as, if you should put a white plate in front of an electric light, the electric light would be darkened. It may be ten o'clock in the morning and broad daylight when suddenly the sun is covered up by the moon as by a white plate and it becomes night and the stars shine out and chickens, thinking it is night, go to roost. But in a few moments the moon passes by and the sun shines out once again. This is called an *eclipse* of the sun.

Now you probably have never seen an eclipse of the sun, but some day you may. At that time, and even to-day when ignorant people see an eclipse of the sun, they think that something dreadful is going to happen—the end of the world, perhaps, just because they have never seen such a strange sight before and do not know that it is a thing that happens regularly and that no harm comes from it.

Well, nearly twenty-three hundred years before Christ, 2300 B. C., the Babylonians told beforehand just when there was going to be an eclipse of the sun. They had watched the moon moving across the sky and they had figured out how long it would be before it would catch up with the sun and cross directly over it. So you see how much the old Babylonians knew about such things. Men who study the stars and other heavenly bodies are called astronomers, and the Babylonians, therefore, were famous astronomers.

The Egyptians worshiped animals; but it was quite natural that the Babylonians should worship these wonderful heavenly bodies, the sun, moon, and stars, and they did.

The first king of Babylonia whom we know much about—and that much is very little—was Sargon I, who may have lived about the same time that the pyramids were built in Egypt.

About 2100 B. C. Babylonia had a king known far and wide for the laws he made. His name was Hammurabi, and we still have the laws he made though we no longer obey them; for they were carved into a stone in cuneiform, and we have the stone. Sargon and Hammurabi are strange names like no one's name you ever heard before, yet they are real names of real kings who ruled over real people.

9

The Wandering Jews

"YOU are" spells "Ur." It is one of the shortest names I know. It is the name of a little place in that part of Babylonia called Chaldea. In this place—about nineteen hundred years B.C.—there lived a man named Abraham. Abraham had a very large family and though he had no money he was rich. He had large herds of sheep and goats, and these were the chief riches in those days. Now, Abraham believed in one God, as we do, while his neighbors, the Babylonians, worshiped idols and the heavenly bodies, such as the sun, moon, and stars, as I have just said. Abraham did not like his neighbors for this reason; and his neighbors didn't like him, either, for they thought his ideas were peculiar or even crazy. So, about nineteen hundred years before Christ, Abraham took his large family, his flocks, and his herds and moved to a land called Canaan, far away on the edge of the Mediterranean Sea.

Abraham lived to be a very old man, and he had a large family. One of his grandsons named Jacob, who was also known by the name of Israel, had a son Joseph. You probably remember the Bible story of Jacob's favorite son Joseph with the coat of many colors. Joseph's brothers were jealous of him, as boys and even dogs are apt to be jealous of any one who is liked better than they are. So they put Joseph into a well and then sold him as a slave to some Egyptians who were passing by. Then they told their father Jacob that Joseph had been killed by wild animals. The Egyptians took Joseph to far-off Egypt—far away from Canaan.

Abraham leaving Ur. 1900 B.C.

But although Joseph was a slave in Egypt, and although, as I told you, it was very difficult for any one to work his way up out of his class to a higher class, he was so bright that at last he became one of the rulers in Egypt.

Now, at that time when he was ruler there came a famine in Canaan and there was no food. In Egypt, however, there was plenty of food stored up. So Joseph's wicked brothers went down to Egypt to beg the rulers for bread. They probably thought by that time their brother was dead. They did not know that he had become such a great man and that he was now the ruler of whom they were begging food. You can imagine how surprised they were and how ashamed they must have felt when they found out that the great ruler was their own brother, whom they had planned to kill and then had sold as a slave.

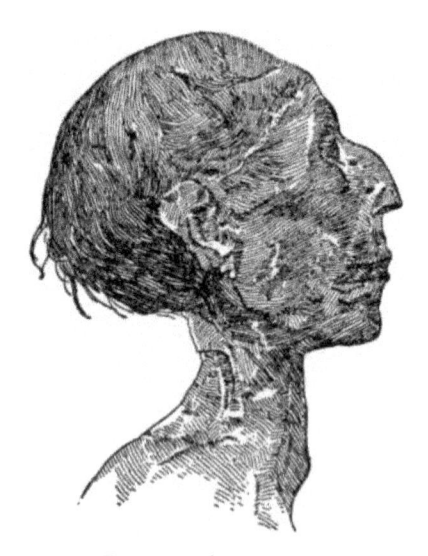

Rameses' mummy.

Joseph might have let his brothers starve to death or put them in prison, or sent them back to Canaan without anything, if he had wanted to revenge himself on them. But instead of doing any of these things, he gave them not only all the food they wanted and more to take back home, but made them rich presents besides. Then he told them to go back and get the rest of his family and return with them to Egypt, and he promised to give them a piece of land called Goshen where there would be no famines and they might live happily. So they did as they were told, and Israel and his sons and all their families came down and settled in Goshen about 1700 B.C. They were called Israelites, which means of course the children of Israel, and they believed they were God's chosen people. These are the people we now call the Jews.

After Joseph, who was of course an Israelite himself, died, the kings or Pharaohs of Egypt did not like these foreign people who belonged to the Semite family, and treated them very badly, as other peoples have always treated the Jews badly ever since. Though the Jews and their sons and sons' sons lived in Egypt for about four hundred years, they were always hated by the Egyptians.

Now about four hundred years from the time the Jews first came into Egypt—400 from 1700 is 1300 B.C.—there was a ruler of Egypt called Rameses the Great.

Rameses the Great.

Rameses so hated the Jews that finally he gave orders to have every Jewish boy baby killed. In this way he thought to get rid of these people. One little Jewish boy named Moses, however, was saved, and when he grew up he became the greatest leader of his people. Moses wanted to get the Jews out of this unfriendly country where the people worshiped false gods. And so at last he led all his people out of Egypt across the Red Sea. This was called the Exodus, and it took place about 1300 B.C.

After the Jews had left Egypt they first stopped at the foot of a mountain called Mount Sinai, while Moses went up to the top where he could be by himself and learn what God wanted him and the Jews to do. Moses spent forty days praying on top of the mountain. When he came down from the mountain-top, he brought with him the Ten Commandments, the same Ten Commandments you may have learned in Sunday-school. But Moses had been gone so long that when he came back again to his people he found them worshiping a golden calf as the Egyptians had done. They had lived in Egypt until they had come to think it was all right to worship idols.

Moses was very angry. It was high time, he thought, that they should get rid of the bad influence of their old Egyptian neighbors. And at last he succeeded in making them worship God again and gave them the Ten Commandments for their rule of life. So Moses is called a lawgiver and the founder of the Jewish religion. Then Moses died, and the Jews wandered from place to place for a great many years before they finally settled in Canaan.

The Jews had no kings. They were ruled by men called judges, but the judges lived very simply, just like every one else and not like kings in palaces with servants and fine robes and rich jewels. But the Jews wanted a real king as their enemies had and other nations who were their neighbors. Strange they wanted a king which so many countries have tried to get rid of—we should think they would have preferred a President as we have.

So at last a judge who was named Samuel said they should have a king, and Saul was chosen. Then Samuel poured olive-oil over Saul's head. This may seem a queer thing to do, but it took the place of putting a crown on his head and was a sign that he was to be king. Samuel, therefore, was the last one of their judges, and Saul was their first king.

All other nations at that time believed as the Egyptians and Chaldeans did, in fairy-tale gods or idols. But the Jews alone believed in one God. They had a Holy Book which had been written by their prophets. This book is the Old Testament part of the Christian Bible.

So this is the story of the Wandering Jews who gave us the Old Testament and the Ten Commandments, and here is the way they wandered:

From Ur to Canaan—1900 B.C.

From Canaan to Egypt—1700 B.C.

From Egypt back to Canaan—1300 B.C.

10

Fairy-Tale Gods

THERE was once a man named Hellen—strange-sounding name for a man, isn't it? He was not a Semite and not a Hamite. He was an Aryan. He had a great many children and children's children, and they called themselves Hellenes. They lived in a little scrap of a country that juts out into the Mediterranean Sea, and they called their land Hellas. I once upset a bottle of ink on my desk, and the ink ran out into a wriggly spot that looked exactly as Hellas does on the map. Though Hellas is hardly any bigger than one of our States, its history is more famous than that of any other country of its size in the world. We call Hellas "Greece" and the people who lived there "Greeks."

About the same time the Jews were leaving Egypt, about the time when people were beginning to use iron instead of bronze, that is, about 1300 B.C., we first begin to hear of Hellas and the Hellenes, of Greece and the Greeks.

The Greeks believed in many gods, not in one God as we do and as the Jews did, and their gods were more like people in fairy-tales than like divine beings. Many beautiful statues have been made of their different gods, and poems and stories have been written about them.

There were twelve—just a dozen—chief gods. They were supposed to live on Mount Olympus, which was the highest mountain in Greece. These gods were not always good, but often quarreled and cheated and did even worse things. The gods lived on a kind of food that was much more delicious than what we eat. It was called nectar and ambrosia, and the Greeks thought it made those who ate it immortal; that is, so that they would never die.

Let me introduce you to the family of the gods. I know you will be pleased to meet them. Most of them have two names.

Jupiter or Zeus is the father of the gods and the the king who rules over all human beings. He sits on a throne and holds a zigzag flash of lightning called a thunderbolt in his hand. An eagle, the king of birds, is usually by his side.

Juno or Hera is his wife and therefore queen. She carries a scepter, and her pet bird, the peacock, is often with her.

Neptune or Poseidon is one of the brothers of Jupiter. He rules over the sea. He rides in a chariot drawn by sea-horses and carries in his hand a trident, which looks like a pitchfork with three points. He can make a storm at sea or quiet the waves simply by striking them with his trident.

Vulcan or Hephæstus is the god of fire. He is a lame blacksmith and works at a forge. His forge is said to be in the cave of a mountain, and as smoke and fire come forth from some mountains they are called volcanoes after the god Vulcan inside.

Apollo is the most beautiful of all the gods. He is the god of the sun and of song and music. Every morning—so the Greeks said—he drives his sun-chariot across the sky from the east to the west, and this makes the sun-lighted day.

Diana or Artemis is the twin sister of Apollo. She is the goddess of the moon and of hunting.

Mars or Ares is the terrible god of war, who is only happy when a war is going on—so that he is happy most of the time.

Mercury or Hermes is the messenger of the gods. He has wings on his cap and on his sandals, and he carries in his hand a wonderful winged stick or wand, which, if placed between two people who are quarreling, will immediately make them friends. One day Mercury saw two snakes fighting and he put his wand between them, whereupon they twined around it as if in a loving hug, and ever since the snakes have remained entwined around it. This wand is called a *caduceus*.

Birth of Minerva or Athene.

Minerva or Athene is the goddess of wisdom. She was born in a very strange way. One day Jupiter had a terrible headache—what we call a "splitting" headache. It got worse and worse, until at last he could stand it no longer, but he took a very strange way to cure it. He called Vulcan, the lame blacksmith, and told him to hit him on the head with his hammer. Though

Vulcan must have thought this a funny request, of course he had to obey the father god. So he struck Jupiter a terrible blow on the head, whereupon there sprang forth Minerva in all her armor, and the headache, of which she had been the cause, had gone. So she was born from his brain, that is why she is the goddess of wisdom. Minerva's Greek name is Athene, and she founded a great city in Greece and named it after herself, Athens. She is supposed to look out for this city as a mother does for her child.

Venus or Aphrodite is the goddess of love and beauty. She is the most beautiful of the goddesses as Apollo is the most beautiful of the gods. She is said to have been born from the sea-foam. Cupid, her son, is a little chubby boy with a quiver of arrows on his back. He goes about shooting his invisible arrows into the hearts of human beings, but instead of dying when they are hit they at once fall in love with some one. That is why we put hearts with arrows through them on valentines.

Vesta is the goddess of the home and fireside, who looks out for the family.

Ceres or Demeter is the goddess of the farmer. These are the twelve gods of the Olympian family.

Pluto is a brother of Jupiter. He rules the world underground and lives down there.

There are many other less important gods and goddesses as well as some gods that are half human, such as the three Fates and three Graces and the nine Muses.

Some of the planets in the sky which look like stars are still called by the names of these Greek gods. Jupiter is the name of the largest planet. Mars is the name of one that is reddish—the color of blood. Venus is the name of one that is very beautiful. There is also a Mercury and a Neptune.

It is hard for us to understand how the Greeks could have prayed to such gods as these, but they did. Their prayers, however, were not like ours. Instead of kneeling and closing their eyes as we do, they stood up and stretched their arms straight out before them. They did not pray to be forgiven for their sins and to be made better. They prayed for victory over their enemies or to be protected from harm.

When they prayed they often made the god an offering of animals, fruit, honey, or wine in order to please him so that he would grant their prayer. The wine they poured out on the ground, thinking the god would like to have them do this. The animals they killed and then burned by building a fire under them on an altar. This was called a sacrifice. Their idea seemed to be that even though the gods could not eat the meat of the animals nor drink the wine themselves, they liked to have something *given up* for them. And so even to-day we say a person makes a sacrifice when he *gives up* something for another.

When the Greeks were sacrificing they usually looked for some sign from the god to see whether he was pleased or not with the sacrifice and whether he would answer their prayer and do what they asked him or not. A flock of birds flying overhead, a flash of lightning, or any unusual happening they thought was a sign which meant something. Such signs were called "omens." Some omens were good and showed that the god would do what he was asked, and some omens were bad and showed he would not. Omens were very much like some of the signs that people believe in even to-day when they say it is a good sign or good luck if you see the new moon over the right shoulder or a bad sign or bad luck if you spill the salt.

Not so very far from Athens is a mountain called Mount Parnassus. On the side of Mount Parnassus was a town called Delphi. In the town of Delphi there was a crack in the ground, from which gas came forth, somewhat as it does from cracks in a volcano. This gas was supposed to be the breath of the god Apollo, and there was a woman priest called a priestess who sat on a three-legged stool or tripod over the crack so as to breathe the gas. She would become delirious, as some people do when they are sick with fever and we say they are "out of their heads," and when people asked her questions she would mutter strange things and a priest would tell what she meant. This place was called the Delphic Oracle, and people would go long distances to ask the oracle questions, for they thought Apollo was answering them.

The Greeks went to the oracle whenever they wanted to know what to do or what was going to happen, and they firmly believed in what the oracle told them. Usually, however, the answers of the oracle were like a riddle, so that they could be understood in more than one way. For instance, a king who was about to go to war with another king asked the oracle who would win. The oracle replied, "A great kingdom will fall." What do you suppose the oracle meant? Such an answer, which you can understand in two or three ways, is still called "oracular."

11

A Fairy-Tale War

THE history of countries usually begins—and also ends—with war. The first great happening in the history of Greece was a war. It was called the Trojan War and was supposed to have taken place about twelve hundred years before Christ, or not long after the beginning of the Iron Age. But we are not only not sure of the date; we are not even sure that there ever was such a war, for a great deal of it, we know, is simply fairy-tale. This is the way the tale goes.

Once there was a wedding feast of the gods and goddesses on Mount Olympus, when suddenly a goddess who had not been invited threw a golden apple on the table. On the apple was written these words:

To the Fairest.

The goddess who had thrown the apple was the goddess of quarreling; and true to her name she *did* start a quarrel, for each of the goddesses, like vain human beings, thought she was the fairest and should have the apple. At last they called in a shepherd boy named Paris to decide which was the fairest.

Each goddess offered Paris a present if he would choose her. Juno, the queen of the gods, offered to make him a king; Minerva, the goddess of wisdom, offered to make him wise; but Venus, the goddess of beauty, offered to give him the most beautiful girl in the world for his wife.

Now, Paris was not really a shepherd boy but the son of Priam, the king of Troy, which was a city on the sea-shore opposite Greece. Paris when a baby had been left on a mountain to die, but had been found by a shepherd and brought up by him as his own child.

Paris didn't care about being wise; he didn't care about being king; what he did want was to have the most beautiful girl in the world for his wife, and so he gave the apple to Venus.

Now the most beautiful girl in the world was named Helen, and she was already married to Menelaus, the king of Sparta. But in spite of that fact Venus told Paris to go to Sparta in Greece, where he would find Helen, and then run away with her. So Paris went to Sparta to visit King Menelaus and was royally entertained by him. And then Paris, although he had been treated so kindly and been trusted, one night stole Helen away and carried her off across the sea to Troy. Though this was in the Iron Age, it was the way a Cave Man of the Stone Age might have acted.

Menelaus and the Greeks were naturally very angry and immediately prepared for war and sailed off for Troy to get Helen back. Now, in ancient times all cities had walls built around them to protect them from the enemy. As there were no cannons nor guns nor deadly weapons such as are used in war nowadays, it was very hard to get into a walled city or capture it. Troy was protected in this way with walls; and though the Greeks tried for ten years to capture it, at the end of the ten years Troy was still unconquered.

So at last the Greeks decided to try a trick to get into the city. They built a huge horse of wood, and inside this wooden horse they put soldiers. They placed the horse in front of the city walls and then sailed away as if at last they were giving up the war. The Trojans were told by a spy that the horse was a gift of the gods and that they ought to take it into the city. A Trojan priest named La-oc-o-on, however, told his people not to have anything to do with the horse, for he suspected a trick. But people seldom take advice when told *not* to do what they want to do.

Just then some huge snakes came out of the sea and attacked Laocoon and his two sons and, twining round them, strangled them to death. The Trojans thought this was a sign from the gods, or an omen as they would have said, that they should not believe Laocoon; so they determined to take the horse into the city against his advice. The horse was so big, however, that it would not go through the gates, and in order to get it inside of the walls they had to tear down part of the wall itself. When night fell, the Greek soldiers came out of the horse and opened the gates of the city. The other Greeks, who had been waiting just out of sight, returned and entered through the gates and the hole the Trojans had made in the wall. Troy was easily conquered then, and the city was burned to the ground, and Helen's husband carried her back to Greece. For reason of this horse trick, we still have a saying, "Beware of the Greeks bearing gifts," which is as much as to say, "Look out for an enemy who makes you a present."

The story of the Trojan War was told in two long poems. Some people think they are the finest poems that were ever written. One of these poems is called the "Iliad," from the name of the city of Troy, which was also known as Ilium. The "Iliad" describes the Trojan War itself. The other poem is called the "Odyssey" and describes the adventures of one of the Greek heroes on his way home after the war was over. This Greek hero's name was Odysseus, which gives the name Odyssey to the book, but he was also called Ulysses. These poems, the "Iliad" and the "Odyssey," were composed by a blind Greek poet named Homer, who is supposed to have lived about two hundred years after the war; that is about 1000 B.C.

Homer was a bard; that is, a singing poet who went about from place to place and sang his poems to the people. Usually a bard played on the lyre as he sang, and the people gave him something to eat or a place to sleep to pay him for his songs. Nowadays, instead of a Homer singing the "Iliad" and

"Odyssey," we have the organ-grinder and street piano playing their tunes in front of our houses.

Homer never wrote down his poems, for he was blind; but the people were very fond of hearing his songs, and they learned them by heart, and mothers taught them to their children after Homer had died. At last, many years later, another man wrote the poems down in Greek, and you may some day read them in Greek, if you study that language, or at least in an English translation.

Although the Greeks thought so much of Homer, he could hardly make a living, and he almost had to beg his daily bread. After his death however, the people of nine different cities each proudly said that Homer was born in their city. And so some one has made this rime:

Nine cities claimed blind Homer dead,

Through which, alive, he'd begged his bread.

Some people now doubt that there ever was a poet named Homer. Others think that instead of only one man there must have been several men, perhaps nine, who composed these poems, and this might explain how he could be born in nine different cities.

12

The Kings of the Jews

WHILE the blind beggar Homer was singing his wonderful songs through the streets of Greece, a great king of the Jews was singing other wonderful songs in Canaan. This king was named David, and he wasn't born a king. He was only a shepherd boy in King Saul's army. This is the way he happened to become king.

At first, as you remember, the Jews had no kings; but they had asked for kings, and at last they were given one by the name of Saul.

David had killed the giant Goliath. We all love this Bible story because we are always glad when the skilful little chap beats the great, big, bragging bully.

Well, King Saul had a daughter, and she fell in love with this brave and athletic young David the Giant-Killer, and at last they were married.

So after Saul died David became king, and he was the greatest king the Jews ever had. Although Saul had been king he had lived in a tent, not in a palace, and he didn't even have a capital city.

So David conquered a city in Canaan called Jerusalem and made this city the capital of the Jews.

But David was not only a brave warrior and a great king; he wrote beautiful songs as well.

The blind beggar Homer sang of his fairy-tale gods. The great King David sang of his one God.

These songs are the Psalms, which you hear read and sung in church.

Nowadays even a popular song is popular for only a few months, but the songs which David wrote almost three thousand years ago are still popular to-day! The Twenty-third Psalm, which starts, "The Lord is my shepherd," is one of the most beautiful and a good one to learn by heart. David likens himself to a sheep and his Lord to a good shepherd who tenderly looks out for the comfort and safety of his sheep.

David's son was named Solomon, and when David died Solomon became king.

If a good fairy had asked you what you would rather have than anything in the world, I wonder what you would have chosen. When Solomon became king, God is said to have appeared to him in a dream and asked him what he would rather have than anything else in the world. Instead of saying he wanted to be made rich or powerful, Solomon asked to be made wise, and

God said He would make him the wisest man that ever lived. Here is a story that shows how wise he was.

Once upon a time two women came to Solomon with a baby, and each woman said the baby was her own child. Solomon called for a sword and said, "Cut the baby in two, and give each a half." One of the women cried out to give the baby to the other rather than do this, and Solomon then knew who was the real mother and ordered the baby to be given to her.

Solomon built a magnificent temple made of cedar-wood from the famous forest of Lebanon, and of marble and gold and studded with jewels. Then he built himself a wonderful palace, which was so gorgeous and splendid that people came from all over the world to see it. The Bible tells us just how large this temple and palace were, not in feet but in cubits. A cubit was the distance from a man's elbow to the end of his middle finger, which is about one foot and a half.

The queen of Sheba, among others, came a long distance across Arabia to hear the wise sayings of Solomon and see his palace and the temple he had built.

Although the palace and temple were considered extraordinarily magnificent at that time, you must remember that this was a thousand years before Christ. Solomon's temple and palace have disappeared long since, and there is left of them neither stick nor stone. But his wise sayings are preserved in every language and read by every people in every part of the world. There are thousands of buildings now in the world that would make his palace, if still standing, look like a child's toy-house. But no one has ever been able to say any better the things he said. Do you think you could? Suppose you try. Here are some of them. They are called proverbs.

A soft answer turneth away wrath; but grievous words stir up anger.

What's that mean?

A good name is rather to be chosen than great riches and loving favor rather than silver and gold.

What's that mean?

Let another man praise thee and not thine own mouth.

What's that mean?

Solomon was the last great king the Jews ever had. After he died the Jewish nation gradually broke up and went to pieces, and the great Jewish people are to-day without a king, without a capital, and without a country of their own, but are found in every other country of the world.

13

The People Who Made Our A B C's

LONG before people knew how to write, there lived a carpenter named Cadmus. One day he was at work on a house when he wanted a tool that he had left at home. Picking up a chip of wood, he wrote something on it and, handing it to his slave, told him to go to his home and give the chip to his wife, saying that it would tell her what he wanted. The slave, wondering, did as he was told. Cadmus's wife looked at the chip, and without a word handed the tool to the amazed slave, who thought the chip in some mysterious way had spoken the message. When he returned to Cadmus with the tool, he begged for the remarkable chip, and when it was given him, hung it around his neck for a charm.

Cadmus' slave and the chip.

This is the story the Greeks told of the man they say invented the alphabet. We believe, however, that Cadmus was a mythical person, for the Greeks liked to make up such stories, and we think no *one* man made the alphabet. But Cadmus was a Phenician and we do know that the Phenician people invented the alphabet. You probably call it your A B C's, but the Greeks had much harder names for the letters. They called *A* "alpha," *B* "beta," and so on. So the Greek boy spoke of learning his "alpha beta," and that is why we call it the "alphabet."

You may never have heard of Phenicia or the Phenician people. Yet, if there had been no such country as Phenicia, you might now be learning at school to read and write in hieroglyphics or in cuneiform.

Up to this time, you know, people had very clumsy ways of writing. The Egyptians had to draw pictures, and the Babylonians made writing like chicken-tracks. The alphabet that the Phenicians invented had twenty-two letters, and from it we get the alphabet we use to-day.

Of course, we do not use just the same alphabet now that the Phenicians did, but some of the letters are almost, if not quite, like those we now have after three thousand years. For instance the

Phenician A was written on its side —☐

    E "   "   backward   —Ǝ

    Z "   "   just the same   Z

    O "   "   "   "   "   O

The Phenicians lived next door to the Jews; in fact they belonged to the same family—the Semites. Their country was just north of the kingdom of the Jews; that is, above it on the map and lying along the shore of the Mediterranean Sea.

The Phenicians had a great king named Hiram who lived at the same time as Solomon. In fact, Hiram was a friend of Solomon and sent him some of his best workmen to help build a temple at Jerusalem. And yet Hiram himself and the Phenicians did not believe in the Jewish God.

The Phenicians worshiped idols, terrible monsters named Baal and Moloch, which they called gods of the sun. They also believed in a goddess of the moon named Astarte and made sacrifices of live children to her idol, Fe-Fi-Fo-Fum; this is a real story and not a fairy-tale. Just suppose you had been a child then!

The Jews, as we have learned, were very religious, but their neighbors, the Phenicians, though Semites and therefore relatives, were business people and thought of nothing but money, money, money—all the time. And they were not particular how they earned it, whether honestly or not. Nowadays, dealers know that they must be honest if they are to be very successful, but the Phenicians were usually tricky in their trading with people. They always drove a good bargain and sometimes even cheated when they had a chance.

The Phenicians made many things to sell, and then they went far and near to sell them.

They knew how to make beautiful cloth and glassware and objects in gold and silver and ivory.

They knew the secret of making a wonderful purple dye from the body of a little shell-fish that lived in the water near the city of Tyre. This dye was known as Tyrian purple from the name of that city, and it was so beautiful that kings' robes were colored with it.

Tyre and Sidon were the two chief cities of Phenicia, and once upon a time they were two of the busiest cities in the world.

In order to find people to sell to, the Phenicians traveled in boats all over the Mediterranean Sea and even went outside this sea into the Great Ocean. This opening is now called the Strait of Gibraltar but was then known as the Pillars of Hercules. They went as far as the British Isles. Other people in those days had not dared to go so far in boats; they thought they would come to the edge of the ocean and tumble off. But the Phenicians had no such fear, and so they were the greatest sailors as well as the greatest traders of their times. Their ships were built from the cedar-trees that grew on the slopes of their hills, which were called Lebanon.

Wherever the Phenicians found good harbors for their boats, they started little towns where they traded with the natives, who at that time were almost savage. With ignorant savages they found they could drive a good bargain. For a few glass beads or a piece of purple dyed cloth worth very little they could get in return gold and silver and other things worth a great deal. On the African coast, one of these towns they started was called Carthage. Of Carthage we shall hear more by and by, for it grew to be so wealthy and important that—but wait until I come to that story.

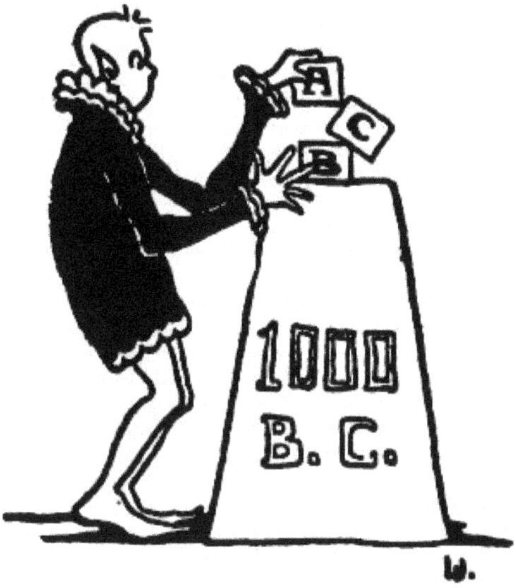
A
C
B
1000
B. C.
W.

14

Hard as Nails

OUR story goes back again to Greece, the land of Homer and the fairy-tale gods and to Sparta, where Helen once lived.

About nine hundred years before Christ was born, there lived in Sparta a man named Lycurgus. That is a hard name, and when you hear about this man you may think he was hard, too. Lycurgus wanted his city to be the greatest in the world.

But first he had to find out what it was that made a city and a people great.

So he started off and traveled for years and years visiting all the chief countries of the world to see if he could learn what it was that made them great. And this is what he learned.

Wherever the people thought chiefly of fun and pleasure, of amusing themselves and having a good time—he found they were not much good, not much account—*not* great.

Wherever the people thought chiefly of hard work and did what they ought, whether it was pleasant or not, he found they were usually good for something—some account—great.

So Lycurgus came back to his home Sparta and set to work to make a set of rules which he thought would make his people greater than all other people in the world. These rules were called a Code of Laws, and I think you'll agree they were very hard, and they made the Spartans hard, too—as "hard as nails." We shall see whether they made the Spartans really great, also.

To begin with, babies, as soon as they were born, were examined to see that they were strong and perfect. Whenever one was found that did not seem to be so, he was put out on the mountain-side and left to die. Lycurgus wanted no weaklings in Sparta.

When boys were seven years old, they were taken from their mothers and put in a school, which was more like a soldiers' camp than a school, and they never lived anywhere else until they were sixty years old.

In this school they were not taught the things you are, but only the things that trained them to be good soldiers.

There were no such things as school-books then.

There were no spelling-books.

There were no arithmetics.

There were no geographies. No one knew enough about the world to write a geography.

There were no histories. No one knew much about things that had happened in the world before that time, and of course none of the history since then that you now study had taken place.

At certain times, the Spartan boy was whipped, not because he had done anything wrong, but just to teach him to suffer pain without whimpering. He would have been disgraced forever if he had cried, no matter how badly he was hurt.

He was exercised and drilled and worked until he was ready to drop. But still he was obliged to keep on, no matter how tired or hungry or sleepy or aching he might be, and he must never show by any sign how he felt.

He was made to eat the worst kind of food, to go hungry and thirsty for long periods of time, to go out in the bitter cold with little or no clothing, just to get used to such hardships and able to bear all sorts of discomforts. This kind of training, this kind of hardening, is therefore called "Spartan discipline." How do you think you would have liked it?

The Spartans' food, clothing, and lodging were all furnished them, though it was very poor food and poor clothing and poor lodging. They were not allowed good things to eat, soft beds to lie on, or fine clothing to wear. Such things were called luxuries, and luxuries, Lycurgus thought, would make people soft and weak, and he wanted his people hard and strong.

The Spartans were even taught to speak in a short and blunt manner; they were taught not to waste words; they must say what they had to say in as few words as possible. This manner of speaking we call "Laconic" from the name Laconia, the state in which Sparta was located.

Once a king wrote to the Spartans a threatening letter, saying that they had better do what he told them to, for *if* he came and took their country, he would destroy their city and make them slaves.

The Spartans sent a messenger back with their answer, and when the letter was opened, it contained only one word:

"*IF!*"

Even to-day, we call such an answer, short but to the point, a Laconic answer.

Did all this hard training and hard work make the Spartans the greatest people in the world?

Lycurgus did make the Spartans the strongest and best fighters in the world—but—

The Spartans conquered all the peoples around about them, though there were ten times as many—but—

They made these people their slaves, who did all their farming and other work—but—

We shall see later whether Lycurgus's idea was right.

North of Sparta was another great city of Greece called Athens. There were, of course, many other towns in Greece, but Sparta and Athens were the most important. In Athens the people lived and thought quite differently from those in Sparta.

The Athenians were just as fond of everything beautiful as the Spartans were of discipline and of everything military.

The Athenians loved athletic games of all sorts just as the Spartans did, but they also loved music and poetry and beautiful statues, paintings, vases, buildings, and such things that are known as the "arts."

The Athenians believed in training the mind *as well* as the body. The Spartans believed the training of the body was the all-important thing. Which do you like better, the Athenians' idea or the Spartans' idea?

Once at a big game a very old man was looking for a seat on the Athenians' side. There was no seat empty, and no Athenian offered to give him one. Whereupon the Spartans called to the old man and gave him the best seat on their side. The Athenians cheered the Spartans to show how fine they thought this act. At this the Spartans said:

"The Athenians *know* what is right but they don't *do* it."

15

The Crown of Leaves

GREEK boys and young men and even girls loved all sorts of outdoor sports.

They didn't play football or baseball or basketball, but they ran and jumped and wrestled and boxed and threw the discus—a thing like a big, heavy dinner-plate of iron.

From time to time matches were held in different parts of Greece to see who was the best in these sports.

The Big Meet, however, took place only once every four years at a place called Olympia in southern Greece; and these Olympic games, as they were called, were the most important affairs held in Greece, for all the winners from different parts of the country were here matched against each other to see who should be the champion of all Greece.

The time when the games were held was a great national holiday, for the games were in honor of the head god Jupiter, or Zeus as the Greeks called him. People came from all over the known world to see the games much as they do now when a World's Fair is held or a big football game.

Only Greeks could enter this contest, and only those who had never committed a crime or broken any laws—as a boy nowadays must have a clean record in order to be allowed to play on his college or school team.

If there happened to be a war going on at the time, and there usually was, so important was this holiday that a truce was declared, and everybody went off to the games. Nothing could be allowed to interfere with the games, and even war was not as important. "Business before pleasure!" When the games were finished, they started fighting again!

The Greek boys and young men would train for four years getting ready for this big event, and then nine months before the great day they would go to Olympia to get in training at an open-air gymnasium near the field.

The games lasted five days and began and ended with a parade and prayers and sacrifices to the Greek gods, beautiful statues to whom were placed all about the field, for this was not only sport, but a religious service in honor of Jupiter and the other gods.

There were all sorts of matches—in running, jumping, wrestling, boxing, chariot-racing, and throwing the discus.

Any one who cheated would have been put out and never again allowed to take part. The Greek believed in what we call being a good sport. He didn't brag if he won. He didn't make excuses if he lost; he didn't cry out that the decision was unfair.

The athlete who won one or more of these games was the hero of all Greece, and in particular of the town from which he came. The winner received no money prize but was crowned with a wreath made of laurel leaves. This he valued much more than an athlete nowadays does the silver cup or gold medal he may win. Besides receiving the laurel wreath, the winner had songs written to him by poets, and often statues were made of him by sculptors.

There were not only athletic matches but contests between poets and musicians to see who could write the best poetry or compose and play the sweetest music on a kind of small harp called the lyre. The winners of these contests did not receive a laurel wreath, but they were carried in triumph on the shoulders of the throng, as you may have seen the captain of a winning team picked up and raised aloft by his fellow-players after he has won.

Greek runner.

Now, in Greek History the first event which we can be absolutely sure is true is the record of the winner of a foot-race in these Olympic Games 776 years before Christ was born. And from this event the Greeks began to count their history dates, as we do now from the birth of Christ. It was their Year 1.

The four years' time between the Olympic Games was called an Olympiad. Up to this time, they had no calendar that gave the year or date, so 776 is the date of the first Olympiad. Greek History before that time may have been partly true, but we know much of it was mythical. Beginning with 776, however, Greek history is pretty much all true.

After a long while they stopped having the games, but a few years ago it was thought it would be a good thing to start them again. So, for the first time since before Christ, new Olympic Games were again held in 1896 A.D., not in Olympia, however, but in Athens. The games used to be held only in Greece. Now they are held each time in a different country. Only Greeks used to be allowed to take part. Now, however, athletes from almost all the countries of the world are invited to compete. War used to be stopped when the time for the games arrived. Now the games are stopped when war is on.

From what we have learned of the Spartans' training, we might guess that they used to win most of the athletic prizes, and they did.

Do the Spartans still continue to win most of the prizes in the New Olympic Games?

No. Not even the Greeks now carry off the chief prizes.

16

A Bad Beginning

HAVE you ever heard of the Seven-League Boots, the boots in which one could take many miles at a single step?

Well, there is a still bigger boot; it is over five hundred miles long, and it is in the Mediterranean Sea.

No, it's not a real boot, but it would look like one if you were miles high in an airplane and looking down upon it.

It is called Italy.

Something very important happened in Italy, not long after the First Olympiad in Greece. It was so important that it was called the Year 1, and for a thousand years people counted from it as the Greeks did from the First Olympiad, and as we do now from the birth of Christ. This thing that happened was not the birth of a man, however. It was the birth of a city, and this city was called Rome.

The history of Rome starts with stories that we know are fairy-tales or myths in the same way that the history of Greece does. Homer told about the wanderings of the Greek, Odysseus. A great many years later a poet named Vergil told about the wanderings of a Trojan named Æneas.

Æneas fled from Troy when that city was burning down and started off to find a new home. Finally after several years he came to Italy and the mouth of a river called the Tiber. There Æneas met the daughter of the man who was ruling over that country, a girl by the name of Lavinia, and married her, and they lived happily ever after. So the children of Æneas and Lavinia ruled over the land, and they had children, and their children had children, and their children had children, until at last boy twins were born. These twins were named Romulus and Remus. Here endeth the first part of the story and the trouble begins, for they did not live happily ever after.

At the time the twins were born, a man had stolen the kingdom, and he feared that these two boys might grow up and take his stolen kingdom away from him. So he put the twins in a basket and set them afloat on the river Tiber, hoping that they might be carried out to sea or upset and be drowned. This, he thought, was nearly all right, so long as he didn't kill them with his own hands. But the basket drifted ashore instead of going out to sea or upsetting, and a mother wolf found the twins and nursed them as if they were her own babies. And a woodpecker also helped and fed them berries. At last a shepherd found them and brought them up as if they were his own sons until they grew up and became men. This sounds a good deal like the story of Paris who was left out to die and was found and brought up by a shepherd also.

Romulus and Remus with the wolf.

Each of the twins then wished to build a city. But they could not agree which one was to do it, and in quarreling over the matter, Romulus killed his own twin brother Remus. Romulus then built the city by the Tiber River, on the spot where he and his brother had been saved and nursed by the mother wolf. Here there were seven hills. This was in 753 B.C., and he named the city Roma after his own name, and the people who lived there were called Romans. So that is why, ever afterward, the Roman kings always said they were descended from the Trojan hero, Æneas, the great-great-great-grandfather of Romulus.

Don't you believe this story? Neither do I. But it is such an old, old story every one is supposed to have heard it even though it is only a legend.

In order to get people for the city which he had started, it is said that Romulus invited all the thieves and bad men who had escaped from jail to come and live in Rome, promising them that they would be safe there.

Then as none of the men had wives, and there were no women in his new city, Romulus thought up a scheme to get the men wives. He invited some people called Sabines, who lived near-by, both men and women, to come to Rome to a big party.

They accepted, and a great feast was spread. In the middle of the feast, when every one was eating and drinking, a signal was given, and each of the Romans seized a Sabine woman for his wife and ran off with her.

The Sabine husbands immediately prepared themselves for war against the Romans, who had stolen their wives. When the battle had begun between the two armies, the Sabine women ran out in the midst of the fighting between their new and old husbands and begged them both to stop. They said they had come to love their new husbands and would not return to their old homes.

What do you think of that?

It sounds like a pretty bad beginning for a new city, doesn't it? and you may well wonder how Rome turned out—a city that started with Romulus killing his brother and that was settled by escaped prisoners who stole the wives of their neighbors. We must remember, however, that then they were nearer the time when Primitive Men lived whose only rule of life was: kill or be killed, steal or be stolen; and whose usual way of getting wives was to knock them in the head and drag them off to their caves while they were senseless. Besides, they believed in the same gods as the Greeks, and we have heard how their gods did all sorts of wicked things themselves. This, too, was long before Christ was born, and at that time they did not know anything about the Christian religion or what we call right and wrong.

You see I have tried to think of some good excuses for the actions of these first Romans.

17

Kings with Corkscrew Curls

AFTER Rome's bad start she had one king after another, and some of these kings were pretty good and some were pretty bad.

But the most important city in the world at this time was far away from Rome on the Tigris River. This city was called Nineveh, and here lived the kings of the country called Assyria, which I told you about some time ago.

As usual, the chief thing we hear about Assyria and the Assyrians is that they were fighting with their neighbors. This, however, was not the fault of their neighbors.

The Assyrian kings who lived in Nineveh wanted more land and power, and so they fought their neighbors in order to take their land away from them. These kings had long corkscrew curls, and you may think that only girls wear long curls and that a man with curls would be "girl-like." But these kings were not at all that kind. They were such terrible fighters that they were feared far and near. They treated their prisoners terribly; they skinned them alive, cut off their ears, pulled out their tongues, bored sticks into their eyes, then bragged about it. They made the people whom they conquered pay them huge sums of money and promise to fight with them whenever they went to war.

And so Assyria became so strong and powerful that she at last owned everything of importance in the world, the land between the rivers called Mesopotamia, and the land to the east, north, and south, and Phenicia, and Egypt, and pretty nearly everything except Greece and Italy.

This big, big country of Assyria was ruled by the kings at Nineveh, who lived in great magnificence. They built wonderful palaces for themselves, and on each side of the way that led to the palace they placed rows of huge statues of bulls and lions with wings and men's heads as a rich man nowadays might plant a row of trees along the driveway that leads up to his home. These winged animals are what are called cherubs in the Bible.

Perhaps you have heard a particularly sweet and pretty little baby called a cherub. Isn't it strange that these hideous Assyrian monsters should be called cherubs also?

When the Assyrian kings were not fighting men they were fighting wild animals, for they were very fond of hunting with bow and arrow, and they had pictures and statues made of themselves on horseback or in chariots fighting lions. Often they would capture the animals they hunted alive and put them in cages so that the people could come and see them. This was something like a "zoo" such as we have nowadays.

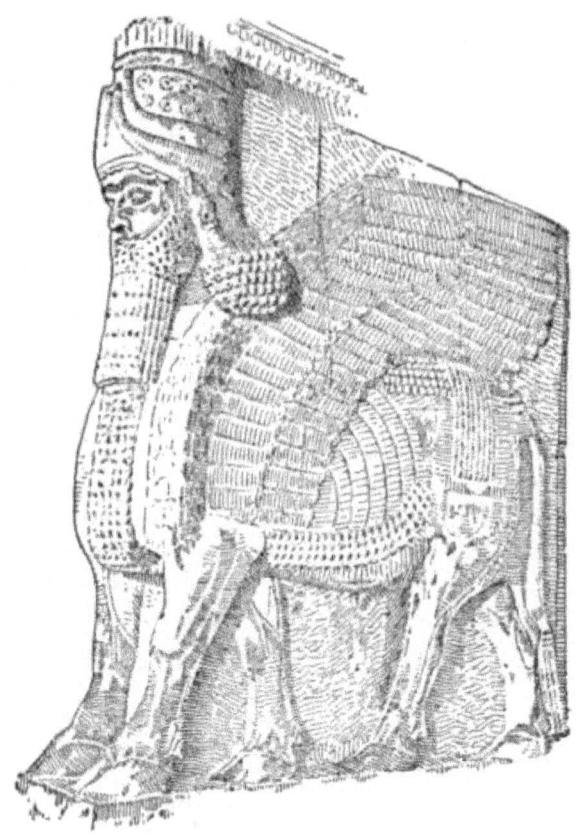

An Assyrian cherub.

The rulers of Assyria had very strange names. Sennacherib was one of the most famous. Sennacherib lived about 700 B.C. Once upon a time Sennacherib was fighting Jerusalem. His whole army was camped one night when as they lay asleep something happened, for when the morning came, none woke up; all were dead, both men and horses. An English poet named Byron has written a poem called "The Destruction of Sennacherib" describing this event. Perhaps they were poisoned; what do you think?

Assur-bani-pal was another king who ruled later—about 650 B.C. He was a great fighter too, but he was also very fond of books and reading; so Assur-bani-pal started the first public library. The books in that first public library were, however, very peculiar. Of course they were not printed books, and they were not even made of paper. They were made of mud with the words pressed into the clay before it dried. This writing was cuneiform, which I have already told you about. The books were not arranged in bookcases, either, but were placed in piles on the floor. They were, however, kept in careful order and numbered so that a person who wanted to see a book in the library could call for it by its number.

Assyria reached the height of her power during the reign of Sennacherib and Assur-bani-pal, and everything in Nineveh was so lovely for the Ninevites that the time when Assur-bani-pal reigned was called the Golden Age.

But although everything in Nineveh was so lovely for the Ninevites, everywhere else the Assyrians were hated and feared, for their armies brought death and destruction wherever they went.

So it came to pass that not long after Assur-bani-pal died, two of the neighbors of Nineveh could stand it no longer. These two neighbors were the king of Babylon, who lived south, and a people called the Medes, who lived to the east and belonged to the Aryan family. So the king of Babylon and the Medes got together and attacked Nineveh, and together they wiped that city off the face of the earth. This was in 612 B.C.—Six-One-Two—and the power of Nineveh and Assyria was killed dead. This, therefore is called the Fall of Nineveh, the end of Nineveh. We might put up a tombstone:

18

A City of Wonders and Wickedness

THE king of Babylon had beaten Nineveh. But he didn't stop with that. He wanted his Babylon to be as great as Nineveh had been. So he went on conquering other lands to the left and right until Babylon, in its turn, became the leader and ruler of other countries. Was Babylon, also, in its turn, to fall, as Nineveh had fallen?

When at last the king of Babylon died, he left his vast empire to his son. Now, the king's son was not called John or James or Charles or anything simple like that. It was—Nebuchadnezzar, and I wonder if his father called him by all that long name or shortened it to a nickname like "Neb," for instance, or "Chad," or perhaps "Nezzar." This is the way Nebuchadnezzar wrote his name, for he used cuneiform writing. How would you like to write your name in such a queer way?

Name of Nebuchadnezzar in cuneiform writing.

Nebuchadnezzar set to work and made the city of Babylon the largest, the most magnificent and the most wonderful city of that time and perhaps of any time. The city was in the shape of a square and covered more ground than the two largest cities in the world to-day—New York and London—put together. He surrounded it with a wall fifty times as high as a man—fifty times—whew!—and so broad that a chariot could be driven along on the top, and in this wall he made one hundred huge brass gates. The Euphrates River flowed under the wall, across the city, and out under the wall on the other side.

Nebuchadnezzar could not find any one in Babylon who was beautiful enough to be his queen. The Babylonian girls must have felt pretty bad—or mad—about that. So he went to Media, the country that had helped his father conquer Nineveh. There he found a lovely princess, and so he married her and brought her home to Babylon.

Now, Media was a land of hills and mountains, whilst Babylon was on level ground and without even a hill in sight. Nebuchadnezzar's queen found Babylonia so flat and uninteresting that she became homesick, and she longed for her own country with its wild mountain scenery. So, just to please her and keep her contented Nebuchadnezzar set to work and *built* a hill for her, but the queer thing was he built it on top of the roof of his palace! On the sides of this hill he made beautiful gardens, and these gardens he planted not only with flowers but also with trees, so that his queen might sit in the shade and enjoy herself. These were called Hanging Gardens. The Hanging Gardens and the tremendous walls were known far and wide as one of the Seven Wonders of the world.

Would you like to know what the other Wonders were?

Well, the pyramids in Egypt were one; the magnificent statue of Jupiter at Olympia, where the Olympic Games were held, was another—so those with the Hanging Gardens make three.

Nebuchadnezzar believed in idols like those terrible monsters the Phenicians worshiped. The Jews away off in Jerusalem believed in one God. Nebuchadnezzar wanted the Jews to worship his gods, but they would not. He also wanted them to pay him taxes, and they would not. So he sent his armies to Jerusalem, destroyed that city, burnt the beautiful Temple that Solomon had built, and brought the Jews and all their belongings to Babylon. There in Babylon Nebuchadnezzar kept the Jews prisoners, and there in Babylon the Jews remained prisoners for fifty years.

Babylon had become not only the most magnificent city in the world; it had become also the most wicked. The people of Babylon gave themselves up to the wildest pleasures. Their only thought seemed to be, "Let's eat, drink, and be merry"; they thought nothing of the morrow; the more wicked the pleasure the more they liked it.

But although Nebuchadnezzar seemed able to do and able to have everything in the world he wanted, he finally went crazy. He thought he was a bull, and he used to get down on his hands and knees and eat grass, imagining he was a beast of the field.

And Babylon, in spite of its tremendous walls and brass gates, was doomed. Babylon was to be conquered. It didn't seem possible. How could it be conquered, and who was to do the conquering? You would probably never guess.

19

A Surprise Party

WHEN I was a boy I was always told, and you have probably been told the same thing:

"You can have no dessert until you have eaten your dinner."

No matter whether I was hungry or not, "No dinner, no dessert." This was a rule which my father said was "like the laws of the Medes and Persians."

I didn't know then who the Medes and Persians were, but I know now that they were two Aryan families living next to Babylon—you remember Nebuchadnezzar had married a Median girl—and that they were governed by laws which were fixed so hard and fast and were so unchangeable that we still speak of any such thing that does not change as like "the laws of the Medes and Persians."

The Medes and the Persians had a religion which was neither like that of the Jews nor like the idol worship of the Babylonians. It had been started by a Persian named Zoroaster, who was a wise man like Solomon. He may even have lived about the same time as Solomon, but probably a good deal later.

Zoroaster went about among the people, teaching them wise sayings and hymns. These wise sayings have been gathered into a book, which is now the Persian Bible.

Zoroaster taught that there were two great spirits in the world, the Good Spirit and the Bad Spirit.

The Good Spirit, he said, was Light, and the Bad Spirit, Darkness. The Good or Light he called Mazda; where have you heard that word, I wonder. So the Persians kept a fire, in which they thought was the Good Spirit, constantly burning on their altars, and they had men watch over this flame to see that it never went out. These men who watched the flame were called Magi, and they were supposed to be able to do all sorts of wonderful things, so that we call such wonderful things "magic," and the people who are able to do them we call "magicians."

At the time of this story which I'm telling you, the ruler of the Medes and the Persians was a great king named Cyrus.

But before I go on with this story I must tell you about a little country not far from Troy. This little country was called Lydia. Perhaps you may know a girl named Lydia. I do. Lydia was ruled over by a king named Crœsus who was the richest man in the world. When we want to describe a man as very wealthy, we still say he is "as rich as Crœsus."

Crœsus owned nearly all the gold-mines, of which there were a great many in that country, and besides this he collected money in the form of taxes from all the cities near him.

Before the time of Crœsus people did not have money such as we have now. When they wished to buy anything, they simply traded something they had for something they wanted—so many eggs for a pound of meat or so much wine for a pair of sandals. To buy anything expensive, such as a horse, they paid with a lump of gold or silver, which was weighed in the scales to see just how heavy it was. It is hard for us to think how people could get along without cents and nickels, dimes, quarters and dollars—with no money at all—and yet they did.

Crœsus, in order to make things simpler, cut up his gold into small bits. Now, it was not easy for every one to weigh each piece each time it was traded, for he might not have any scales handy. So Crœsus had each piece weighed and stamped with its weight and with his name or initials to show that he guaranteed the weight. These pieces of gold and silver were only lumps with Crœsus' seal pressed into them, but they were the first real money even though they were not round and beautifully engraved like our coins.

Now, Cyrus, the great Persian king, thought he would like to own this rich country of Lydia with all its gold-mines, so he set out to conquer it.

When Cyrus was on the way Crœsus sent in a hurry to the oracle in Greece to ask what was going to happen and who was going to win. You will remember what I said about the oracle at Delphi and how people used to ask the oracle questions—to have their fortunes told, as nowadays some people ask the ouija board.

The oracle replied to Crœsus' question:

"A great kingdom shall fall."

Crœsus was delighted, for he thought the oracle meant that Cyrus' kingdom would fall. The oracle *was* right, but not in the way Crœsus had thought.

A great kingdom did fall, but it was his own kingdom of Lydia and not Cyrus' that fell.

But Cyrus was still not satisfied with the capture of Lydia, and so at last he attacked Babylon.

Now, the people in Babylon who thought of nothing but pleasure were busy feasting and drinking and having a good time. Why should they worry about Cyrus? Their city had walls that were so high and thick and was protected by such strong gates of brass that it seemed as if no one could possibly have captured it.

Delphic Oracle.

But you remember that the Euphrates River ran beneath the walls and crossed right through the city. Well, one night when the young prince of Babylon named Belshazzar was having a gay party and enjoying himself, feeling quite certain that no one could enter the city, Cyrus made a dam and turned the waters of the river to one side. Then Cyrus' army marched into the city through the dry river-bed and captured the surprised Babylonians without even a fight. It is supposed that some of the Babylonian priests helped him to do this and even opened the gates, for Babylon had become so wicked that they thought it time for it to be destroyed.

Old Lycurgus would have said: "I told you so. People who think of nothing but pleasure never come to a good end."

This surprise party was in 538—5 and 3 are 8.

Two years later Cyrus let the Jews, who had been carried away fifty years before from Jerusalem, return to the home of their fathers, thus ending the Babylonian Captivity.

To-day the only thing left of this great city of Babylon, which was once bigger than New York and London together—Babylon the Wicked, Babylon the Magnificent, Babylon with all its great walls and brass gates and Hanging Gardens—is only a mound of earth. A few miles away is a ruined tower. This tower, we think, may once have been the Tower of Babel.

20

The Other Side of the World

THERE used to be a "missionary box" in my Sunday-school, and into this box we dropped our pennies to send a missionary to the heathen.

The heathen, we were told, were people who lived on the other side of the world and worshiped idols.

There was the heathen "Chinee," the heathen "Japanee," and the heathen Indian.

These heathen Indians were not our American Indians. They lived in a country called India on the other side of the world. India looks on the map like the little thing that hangs down in the back of your mouth when the doctor says: "Stick out your tongue. Say 'Ah.'" Our Indians are red, but the Indians from India are white. The white Indians belong to the Aryan family, the same family that Cyrus belonged to.

Two thousand years before the time of Cyrus, an Aryan family had moved away from the other Aryan families in Persia until they had come to this country we now call India.

In the course of time there came to be four chief classes of people in India, four chief classes of society—high society, low society, and two classes of society in between. These classes were called castes, and no one in one caste would have anything to do with one in another caste. A boy or girl in one caste would never play with a boy or girl in another caste. A man from one caste would never marry a woman in another. No one from one caste would eat with one in another caste, even though he were starving. Men in different castes were even afraid of touching each other in passing on the street. It was almost as if they were afraid of catching some horrible disease.

The highest caste of all were the Fighters and Rulers. The Rulers were the Fighters, and the Fighters were the Rulers, for they had to be fighters in order to keep their rule.

In the next caste were the Priests; and, as in the case of the Egyptian priests, these men were not what we think of as priests nowadays. They were what we should call professional men—doctors, lawyers, engineers, etc.

Next came the farmers and tradespeople—the butcher, the baker, and candlestick maker.

Fourth and last were the common laborers. These were the men who knew nothing and could do nothing but dig or chop wood or carry water.

Below these four castes were still other people so low and mean that they were called outcastes or Pariahs. We now call any person who has done something so disgraceful that no one, not even the lowest, will have anything to do with him a "pariah."

The people in India believed in a god whom they called Brahma, and so we call their religion Brahmanism. The Brahmanists believed that when a person died his soul was born again in the body of another person or perhaps of an animal. If he had been good while alive they thought his soul went into the body of a higher caste man when he died—as if he were promoted from one grade to the next. If, however, he had led a bad life they thought his soul went into the body of a lower caste man or even of an animal.

When a man died, his body was not buried, it was burned. If he were a married man, his wife was obliged to throw herself alive upon the burning flames. She was not allowed to live after her husband was dead. If the wife died, that was another matter; the man simply got another wife. In the Brahman temples were hideous idols, which the people worshiped as gods. These idols had several heads apiece or many arms, or many legs, or they had tusks sticking out of their mouths—or they had horns coming out of their heads.

About the year 500 B.C. there was born a prince in India by the name of Gautama. Gautama saw so much suffering and trouble in the world that he felt it was not right that he himself, just because he by chance had been born rich, should be happy while others were miserable and unhappy. So he gave up the life to which he had been born and brought up, a life of ease and luxury with all its good things, and spent his entire time trying to make things better for his people.

Gautama taught the people to be good; he taught them to be honest; and he taught them to help the poor and unfortunate. After a while people began to call him Buddha, and he was so holy and pure that at last they thought he must be god himself, and so they worshiped him as god.

These people who believed in Buddha were called Buddhists, and many, many Brahmanists left their hideous idols and became Buddhists. You see there was no such thing as a Christian religion as yet, for this was still five hundred years before Christ was born, and Buddhism seemed so much better than Brahmanism that we do not wonder that great numbers of people became Buddhists.

Buddhists thought their religion was so good that they wanted everyone to become Buddhists; so they sent missionaries across country and sea to the island of Japan just as we send Christian missionaries now, and this new religion spread far and wide.

Perhaps you have never met nor seen nor even heard of a Buddhist, and yet to-day there are many more Buddhists on the other side of the world than there are Christians!

About the same time that Gautama was starting Buddhism in India, a man in China, a teacher by the name of Confucius, was teaching the people of China what they ought to do and what they ought not to do. His teachings filled several books and formed what came to be a religion for the Chinese.

Confucius taught his people to obey their parents and teachers and to honor their ancestors. This sounds something like one of the Ten Commandments: "Honor thy father and thy mother."

Confucius also taught the golden rule, the same golden rule you are taught to-day, only instead of saying, "*Do* unto others as you would be done by," he said, "Do *not* do to others what you would *not* want others to do to you."

In China there are still as many people who follow the teachings of Confucius as there are Christians in all the rest of the world. So here are two religions each as large or larger than the Christian religion.

China was highly civilized, even at this time, 500 B.C., and many inventions were known and used in that country long before the rest of the world ever heard of them. Yet we know little of China's history until a great deal later.

21

Rich Man, Poor Man

WHENEVER I pass a group of street boys playing ball, I almost always hear some one shout, "That's no fair!"

There always seem to be some players who think the others are not playing fair. Sides are always quarreling.

They need an umpire.

When Athens was young there were two sides among the people—the rich and the poor, the aristocrats and the common people—and they were always quarreling. Each side was trying to get more power, and each side said the other wasn't playing fair.

They needed an umpire.

Athens had had kings, but the kings took the side of the rich, and so at last the Athenians had kicked out the last king, and after that they would have no more kings.

About the year 600 B.C. things became so very bad that a man named Draco was chosen to make a set of rules for the Athenians to obey. These rules he made were called the Code of Draco.

Draco's Code made terrible punishments for any one who broke the rules. If a man stole anything, even as small a thing as a loaf of bread, he was not just fined or sent to jail; he was put to death! And no matter how small the wrong a man had done, he was put to death for it. Draco explained the reason for such a severe law by saying that a thief deserved to be put to death and should be. A man who killed another deserved *more* than to be put to death, but unfortunately there was no worse punishment to give him.

You can understand how much trouble the laws of Draco caused. They were so hard that a little later another man was called upon to make a new set of laws. This man was named Solon, and his laws were very just and good. We now call senators and other people who make our laws "Solons" after this man Solon who lived so long ago, even though their laws are not always just and good.

Still the people were not satisfied with Solon's laws. The upper classes thought the laws gave too much to the lower classes, and the lower classes thought they gave too much to the upper. Both classes, however, obeyed the laws for a while, although both classes complained against them.

But about 560 B.C. a man named Pisistratus stepped in and took charge of things himself. He was not elected nor chosen by the people. He simply made himself ruler, and he was so powerful that no one could stop him. It was as if a boy made himself captain or umpire without being chosen by those on the teams.

There were others from time to time in Greece who did the same thing, and they were called tyrants. So Pisistratus was a tyrant. Nowadays only a ruler who is cruel and unjust is called a tyrant. Pisistratus, however, settled the difficulties of both sides, and, though a tyrant in the Greek sense, he was neither cruel nor unjust. In fact, Pisistratus ruled according to the laws of Solon, and he did a great deal to improve Athens and the life of the people. Among other things he did, he had Homer's poems written down, so that people could read them, for before this time people knew them only from hearing them recited. So the people put up with Pisistratus and also with his son for a while. But finally the Athenians got tired of the son's rule and drove all the Pisistratus family out of Athens in 510 B.C.

The next man to try and settle the quarrels of the two sides was named Clisthenes. It is hard, sometimes, to learn the name of a stranger to whom we have just been introduced unless we hear his name repeated several times. So I will say over his name so that you can get used to hearing it:

CLISTHENES;
CLISTHENES;
CLISTHENES.

Your father may be poor or he may be rich.

If he is poor he has one vote when there is an election.

If he is rich he has one vote but only one vote and no more.

If he breaks the laws, whether he is rich or whether he is poor, he must go to jail.

It was not always so; it is not always so even now. But long ago it was much worse.

Ostracism.

Clisthenes gave every one a vote—rich and poor alike—and ruled wisely and well.

Clisthenes started something called ostracism. If for any reason the people wanted to get rid of a man, all they had to do was to scratch his name on any piece of a broken pot or jar they might find and drop it in a voting-box on a certain day. If there were enough such votes, the man would have to leave the city and stay away for ten years. This was called ostracism, and a man so treated was said to be ostracized, from the Greek name for such a broken piece of pottery, on which the name was written. Even to-day we use this same word to speak of a person whom no one will have anything to do with, whom no one wants around, saying he has been ostracized.

Have you ever been sent away from the table to the kitchen or to your room for being naughty?

Then you, too, have been ostracized.

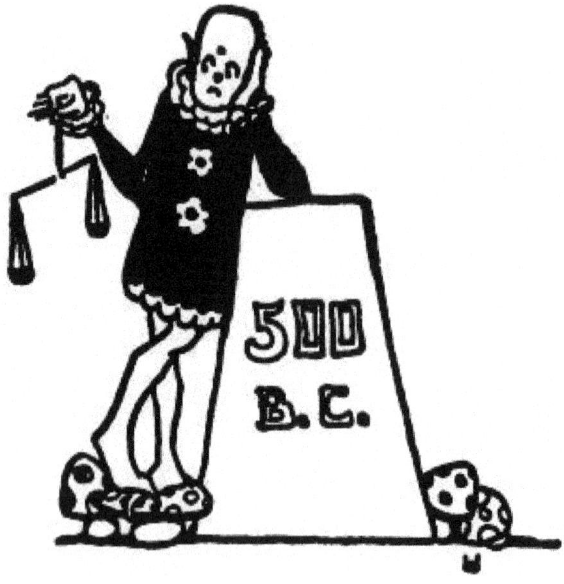
500
B. C.

22

Rome Kicks Out Her Kings

IN 509 B.C. something happened in Rome.

There were two classes of people in Rome, just as there were in Athens; the wealthy people who were called patricians and the poor people who were called plebeians. We use the same words now and call people who are rich and aristocratic "patricians," and the people who are poor and uneducated "plebeians." The patricians were allowed to vote, but the plebeians were not allowed to vote.

At last, however, the plebeians had been given the right to vote. But in 509 Rome had a king named Tarquin. He didn't think the plebeians should be allowed to vote, and so he said they should not. The plebeians would not stand this, and so they got together and drove Tarquin out of the city, as the Athenians had driven out their king. This was in 509, and Tarquin was the last king Rome ever had.

After King Tarquin had been driven out, the Romans started what is called a republic, something like our own country, but they were afraid to have only one man as president for fear he might make himself king, and they had had enough of kings.

Lictor carrying fasces.

So the Romans elected *two men* each year to be rulers over them, and these two men they called consuls. Each consul had a body-guard of twelve men—just a dozen. These men were given the name "lictors," and each lictor carried an ax tied up in a bundle of sticks. This bundle of sticks with the ax-head sticking out in the middle or at the end was known as "fasces" and signified that the consuls had power to punish by whipping with the sticks or by chopping off one's head with the ax.

Perhaps you have seen fasces used as ornaments or as a decoration around monuments or on buildings like a court-house, city hall, or capitol. Why do you suppose they are used in this way?

One of the first two consuls was named Brutus the Elder, and he had two sons. The king, Tarquin, who had been driven out of the city, plotted to get back to Rome and become king once more. He was able to persuade some Romans to help him. Among those whom he persuaded were, strange to say, the two sons of Brutus—the new consul of Rome.

Brutus found out this plot and learned that his own children had helped Tarquin. So Brutus had his sons tried. They were found guilty, and in spite of the fact that they were his own children, he had the lictors put both of them to death as well as the other traitors to Rome.

Tarquin did not succeed in getting back the rule of Rome in this way, and so the next year he tried again. This time he got together an army of his neighbors, the Etruscans, and with this army he attacked Rome.

Now, there was a wooden bridge across the Tiber River, which separated the Etruscans from the city of Rome. In order to keep the Etruscans from crossing into the city, a Roman named Horatius, who had already lost one eye in fighting for Rome, gave orders to have this bridge broken down.

While the bridge was being chopped down, Horatius with two of his friends stood on the far side of the bridge and fought back the whole Etruscan army. When the bridge was cracking under the blows of the Roman soldiers, Horatius ordered his two friends to run quickly to the other side before the bridge fell.

Then Horatius, all by himself, kept the enemy back until at last the bridge crashed into the river. Horatius then jumped into the water with all his armor on and swam toward the Roman shore. Though arrows the Etruscans shot were falling all around him, and though his armor weighed him down, he reached the other side safely. Even the Etruscans were thrilled at his bravery, and, enemies though they were, they cheered him loudly.

There is a very famous poem called "Horatius at the Bridge," which describes this brave deed, and most boys like to learn at least a part of it.

A few years after Horatius, there lived another Roman named Cincinnatus. He was only a simple farmer with a little farm on the bank of the Tiber, but he was very wise and good, and the people of Rome honored and trusted him.

One day when an enemy was about to attack the city—for in those days there always seemed to be enemies everywhere ready to attack Rome on any excuse—the people had to have a leader and a general. They thought of Cincinnatus and went and asked him to be dictator.

Now, a dictator was the name they gave to a man who in case of sudden danger was called upon to command the army and in fact all the people for the time being while there was danger. Cincinnatus left his plow, went with the people to the city, got together an army, went out and defeated the enemy, and returned to Rome, all in twenty-four hours!

The people were so much pleased with the quick and decided way in which Cincinnatus had saved Rome that they wanted him to keep right on being their general in time of peace. Even though they hated kings so much, they would have made him king if he would have accepted.

But Cincinnatus did not want any such thing. His duty done, he wanted to return to his wife and humble home and his little farm. So in spite of what many would have thought a wonderful chance, he did go back to his plow, choosing to be just a simple farmer instead of being king.

The city of Cincinnati in Ohio is named after a society which was founded in honor of this old Roman, who lived nearly five hundred years before Christ.

23

Greece *vs.* Persia

DO you know what those two little letters "vs." mean between Greece and Persia in the name of this story?

Perhaps you have seen them used on football tickets when there was to be a match between two teams, as, for example, Harvard vs. Yale.

They stand for "versus," which means "against."

Well, there was to be a great match between Greece and Persia, but it wasn't a game; it was a fight for life and death, a fight between little Greece and great big Persia.

Cyrus, the great Persian king, had conquered Babylon and other countries, as well, and he had kept on conquering until Persia ruled most of the world, all except Greece and Italy.

About the Year 500 B.C. the new ruler of this vast Persian Empire was a man named Darius. Darius looked at the map, as you might do, and saw that he owned and ruled over a large part of it. What a pity, thought he, that there should be a little country like Greece that did not belong to him!

So Darius said to himself, "I must have this piece of land called Greece to complete my empire." Besides, the Greeks had given him some trouble. They had helped some of his subjects to rebel against him. Darius said, "I must punish these Greeks for what they have done and then just add their country to mine."

So he called his son-in-law and told him to go over to Greece and conquer it.

His son-in-law did as he was told and started out with a fleet and an army to do the punishing. But before his fleet could reach Greece it was destroyed by a storm, and he had to go back home without having done anything.

Darius was very angry at this, mad with his son-in-law and mad with the gods who he thought had wrecked his ships, and he made up his mind that he himself would go and do the punishing and conquering the next time.

First, however, he sent his messengers to all the Greek cities and ordered each of them to send him some earth and some water as a sign that they would give him their land and become his subjects peaceably without a fight.

Many Greek cities were so frightened by the threat of Darius and by his mighty power that they gave in at once and sent earth and water as they were told to do.

But little Athens and little Sparta both hotly refused to do so, in spite of the fact that they were only two small cities against the vast empire of Darius.

Athens took Darius' messenger and threw him into a well, saying, "There is earth and water for you; help yourself"; and Sparta did likewise. Then these two cities joined their forces and called on all their neighbors to join with them to fight for their native land against Darius and Persia.

So Darius made ready to conquer Athens and then Sparta.

A Trireme.

In order to reach Athens his army had to be carried across the sea in boats. Of course, in those days there were no steamboats. Steamboats were invented thousands of years later. The only way to make a boat go was with sails or with oars. To make a large boat move with oars, it was necessary to have a great many rowers—three rows one above the other on each side of the boat.

Such a boat was called a trireme, which means three rows of oars. It took about 600 of these boats to carry Darius' army over to Greece. Each of these 600 boats carried, besides the rowers or crew, about 200 soldiers. So you can see for yourself how many soldiers Darius had in this army, if there were 600 ship-loads of them and 200 soldiers on each ship. Yes, that is an example in multiplication—120,000 soldiers—that's right.

So the Persians sailed across the sea; and this time there was no storm, and they reached the shore of Greece safely. They landed on a spot called the plain of Marathon, which was only about twenty-six miles away from Athens. You will see presently why I have told you just the number of miles—twenty-six.

When the Athenians heard that the Persians were coming, they wanted to get Sparta in a hurry to help, as she had promised to do.

Now, there were no telegraphs or telephones or railroads, of course, in those days. There was no way in which they could send a message to Sparta except to have it carried by hand.

So they called on a famous runner named Pheidippides to carry the message. Pheidippides started out and ran the whole way from Athens to Sparta, about one hundred and fifty miles, to carry the message. He ran night and day, hardly stopping at all to rest or to eat, and on the second day he was in Sparta.

The Spartans, however, sent back word that they couldn't start just then; the moon wasn't full, and it was bad luck to start when the moon wasn't full, as nowadays some superstitious people think it bad luck to start on a trip on Friday. They said they would come after a while, when the moon was full.

But the Athenians couldn't wait for the moon. They knew the Persians would be in Athens before then, and they didn't want them to get as far as that.

So all the fighting men in Athens left their city and went forth to meet the Persians on the plain of Marathon—twenty-six miles away.

The Athenians were led by a man named Miltiades, and there were only ten thousand soldiers of them. Besides these, there were one thousand more from a little near-by town, which was friendly with Athens and wished to stand by her—eleven thousand in all. If you figure it out, you will see that there were perhaps ten times as many Persians as there were Greeks, ten Persian soldiers to one Greek soldier.

The Greeks, however, were trained athletes, as we know, and their whole manner of life made them physically fit. The Persians were no match for them. And so, in spite of the small number of Greeks, the large number of Persians were beaten, and beaten badly. Of course the Greeks were far better soldiers than the Persians, for all their training made them so, but more than all this, they were fighting for themselves to save their homes and their families.

Perhaps you have heard the fable of the hound who was chasing a hare. The hare escaped. The hound was made fun of for not catching the little hare. To which the hound replied, "I was only running for my supper; the hare was running for his life."

The Persian soldiers were not fighting for their homes or families, which were away back across the sea; and it made little difference to them who won, anyway, for they were merely hirelings on slaves; they were fighting for a king because he ordered them to.

Naturally the Greeks were overjoyed at this victory.

Pheidippides, the famous runner, who was now at Marathon, started off at once to carry the joyful news back to Athens, twenty-six miles away. The whole distance he ran without stopping for breath. But he had not had time to rest up from his long run to Sparta, which he had taken only a few days before, and so fast did he run this long distance that as soon as he had reached Athens and gasped the news to the Athenians in the market-place he dropped down dead!

In honor of this famous run, they have nowadays, in the new Olympic Games, what is called a Marathon race, in which the athletes run this same distance.

"The First Marathon Race."

This battle of Marathon took place in 490 B. C. and is one of the most famous battles in all history, for the great Persian army was beaten by one little city and its neighbor, and the Persians had to go back to their homes in disgrace.

A little handful of people, who governed themselves, had defeated a great king with a large army of only hired soldiers or slaves.

But this was not the last the Greeks were to see of the Persians.

24

Fighting Mad

DARIUS was now angrier than ever, and still more determined to whip those stubborn Greeks, who dared to defy him and his enormous power; and he began to get ready for one more attempt. This time, however, he made up his mind that he would get together such an army and navy that there would be no chance in the world against it, and he made a solemn oath to destroy the Greeks. So for several years he gathered troops and supplies, but something happened, and in spite of his oath he did not carry out his plan. Why? You guessed it. He died.

But Darius had a son named Xerxes—pronounced as if it began with a Z.

When I was a boy, there was an alphabet rime that began, "A is for Apple," and went on down to, "X is for Xerxes, a great Persian king." I learned the rime, though I did not know at that time anything either about Xerxes or Persia.

Xerxes was just as determined as his father had been that the Greeks must be beaten, so he went on getting ready.

But the Greeks also were just as determined that they must *not* be beaten, so they, too, went on getting ready, for they knew the Persians would sooner or later come back and try again.

At this time there were two chief men in Athens, and each was trying to be leader. One was named Themistocles—pronounced The-mis-to-klees—and the other Aristides—pronounced Air-is-tie-dees. Notice how many Greek names seem to end in "es."

Themistocles urged the Athenians to get ready for what he knew was coming, the next war with Persia. Especially did he urge the Athenians to build a fleet of boats, for they had no boats and the Persians had a great many.

Aristides, on the other hand, didn't believe in Themistocles' scheme to build boats. He thought it a foolish expense and talked against it.

Aristides had always been so wise and fair that people called him Aristides the Just. Some of the people wanted to get rid of him, because they thought he was wrong and Themistocles was right. So they waited till the time came to vote to ostracize any one they wanted to get rid of. Do you remember who started this custom? Clisthenes—about 500 B.C.

When the day for voting came, a man who could not write and did not know Aristides by sight happened to ask his help in voting. Aristides inquired what name he should write, and the man replied, "Aristides."

Aristides did not tell who he was, but merely said:

"Why do you want to get rid of this man? Has he done anything wrong?"

"Oh, no," the voter replied. "He hasn't done anything wrong"; but with a long sigh he said, "I'm so tired of hearing him always called 'The Just.'"

Aristides must have been surprised by this unreasonable answer, but nevertheless he wrote his own name for the voter, and when the votes were counted there were so many that he was ostracized.

Though it did not seem quite fair that Aristides should be ostracized, it was fortunate, as it turned out, that Themistocles had his way, and it was fortunate the Athenians went on preparing for war.

They built a fleet of triremes. Then they got all the cities and towns in Greece to agree to join forces in case of war. Sparta, on account of its fame as a city of soldiers, was made the leader of all the others in case war should come.

And then, just ten years after the battle of Marathon, in 480 B. C., the great Persian army was again ready to attack Greece. It had been, brought together from all parts of the vast Persian Empire and was far bigger than the former army with its 120,000 men, although that was a large army for those days.

This time the army is supposed to have consisted of over two million soldiers—two million; just think of that! The question then was how to get so many soldiers over to Greece. Such a multitude could not be carried across to Greece in boats, for even the largest triremes only held a few hundred men, and it would have taken—well, can you tell how many boats, to carry over two million? Probably many more triremes than there were in the whole world at that time. So Xerxes decided to have his army march to Greece, the long way but the only way round. So they started.

Now, there is a strip of water called a strait, something like a wide river, right across the path the Persian army had to take. This strait was then called the Hellespont. It is, of course, still there, but if you look on the map now you will find it is now called the Dardanelles. But there was no bridge across the Hellespont, for it was almost a mile wide, and they didn't have bridges as long as that in those days. So Xerxes fastened boats together in a line that stretched from one shore to the other shore, and over these boats he built a floor to form a bridge so that his army could cross upon it.

Hardly had he finished building the bridge, however, when a storm arose and destroyed it. Xerxes, in anger at the waves, ordered that the water of the Hellespont be whipped as if it were a slave he were punishing. Then he built another bridge, and this time the water behaved itself, and his soldiers were able to cross over safely.

So vast was Xerxes' army that it is said to have taken it seven days and seven nights marching continuously all the time in two long unbroken lines to get over to the opposite shore. Xerxes' fleet followed the army as closely as they could along the shore, and at last they reached the top of Greece. Down through the north of Greece the army came, overrunning everything before it, and it seemed as though nothing on earth could stop such numbers of men.

25

One Against a Thousand

THERE is a little narrow passageway with the mountains on one side and the water on the other through which the Persians had to go to reach Athens. This pass is called Thermopylæ, and you might guess what Thermopylæ means if you notice that the first part is like Thermos bottle, which means "hot" bottle. As a matter of fact, Thermopylæ meant Hot Gateway, and was so named because this natural gateway to Greece had hot springs near-by.

The Greeks decided that it was best to stop the Persians at this gate—to go to meet them there first before they reached Athens. In such a place a few Greek soldiers could fight better against a much larger number.

It also seemed wise to send picked Greek troops to meet the Persians, the very best soldiers in Greece with the very bravest general to lead them.

So the Spartan king, who was named Leonidas—which in Greek means "like a lion"—was chosen to go to Thermopylæ, and with him seven thousand soldiers—seven thousand soldiers to block the way of two million Persians! Three hundred of these were Spartans, and a Spartan was taught that he must never surrender, never give up. A Spartan mother used to say to her son:

"Come back *with* your shield or *on* it."

When Xerxes found his way blocked by this ridiculously small band of soldiers, he sent his messengers ordering them to surrender, to give themselves up.

And what do you suppose Leonidas replied?

It was what we should expect a Spartan to answer, brief and to the point; that is, "Laconic." He said simply:

"Come and take us."

As there was nothing left for Xerxes to do but fight, he started his army forward.

For two days the Persians fought the Greeks, but Leonidas still held the pass, and the Persians were unable to get through.

Then a Greek traitor and coward, who thought he might save his own life and be given a rich prize by Xerxes, told that king of a secret path over the mountains by which he and his army might slip through and get around Leonidas and his soldiers who blocked the way.

The next morning Leonidas learned that the Persians had found out this path and were already on the way to pen him in from behind. There was still a chance, however, for his men to escape, and Leonidas told all those who wanted to do so to leave. Those that remained knew that the fight was absolutely hopeless and that it meant certain death for all them. In spite of this, however, one thousand men, including all the three hundred Spartans stood by their leader, for, said they:

"We have been ordered to hold the pass, and a Spartan obeys orders, and never surrenders, no matter what happens."

So there Leonidas and his thousand men fought to the bitter end until all except one of their number was killed.

The gateway to the city of Athens was now open, and things looked very black for the Greeks, for there was nothing to prevent the Persians from marching over the dead bodies of Leonidas and his men straight on to Athens.

The Athenians, wondering what was to happen to them, hurriedly went to the oracle at Delphi and asked what they should do.

The oracle replied that the city of Athens itself was doomed, that it would be destroyed, there was no hope for it, but that the Athenians themselves would be saved by wooden walls.

This answer, as was usually the case in whatever the oracle said, was a riddle, the meaning of which seemed hard to solve. Themistocles, however, said that he knew the answer. You remember that it was he who had been working so hard to have a fleet of ships built. Themistocles said that the oracle meant these ships when it spoke of the wooden walls.

So the Athenians, following the supposed advice of the oracle, left their city as Themistocles told them and went on board the ships, which were not far away, in a bay called Salamis.

The Persian army reached Athens and found it deserted. So they burned and destroyed the city as the oracle said. Then they marched on to the Bay of Salamis, where the Athenians were on board the ships. There, on a hill overlooking the bay, Xerxes had a throne built for himself so that he could sit, as if in a box at the theater looking at a play, and watch his own large fleet destroy the much smaller one of the Greeks with all the Athenians on board.

The Greek fleet was commanded, of course, by Themistocles. His ships were in this narrow bay or strait of water, somewhat in the same way that the soldiers of Leonidas had been in the narrow valley at Thermopylæ.

Xerxes on his throne watching battle of Salamis.

Themistocles, seeing that the Bay of Salamis looked somewhat like the Pass of Thermopylæ, had an idea. He made believe he was a traitor like the traitor at Thermopylæ and sent word to Xerxes that if the Persian fleet divided and one half stayed at one end of the strait and the other half closed off the other end of the strait, the Greeks would be penned in between and caught as in a trap.

Xerxes thought this a good idea, so he gave orders to have his ships do as Themistocles had suggested. But Xerxes, sitting smiling on his throne, had the surprise of his life. The result was just the opposite of what he had expected. With the Persian fleet separated in two parts, the Greeks in between could fight both halves of the divided fleet at the same time, and the space was so narrow that the Persians' ships got in the way of each other and rammed and sank their own boats.

And so the Persian fleet was completely beaten, and the proud and boastful Xerxes, with most of his army and all the navy that was left, made a hasty retreat back to Persia the way they had come.

And this was the last time the Persians ever tried to conquer little Greece.

If Themistocles had not had his way and built such a strong fleet, what do you think would have become of Athens and Greece!

26

The Golden Age

WHEN we were talking about the Stone Age and the Bronze Age, I told you that later we should also hear of a Golden Age.

Well, we have come to the Golden Age now. This doesn't mean that people at this time used things made of gold, nor that they had a great deal of gold money. It means—well, let us see what sort of a time it was, and then you can tell what it means.

After the wars with Persia, Athens seemed to have been cheered up by her victory to do wonderful things, and the next fifty years after the Persians were driven out of Greece—that is, 480 to 430 B. C.—were the most wonderful years in the history of Greece and perhaps the most wonderful years in the history of the world.

Athens had been burned down by Xerxes. At the time it happened this seemed like a terrible misfortune. But it wasn't. The people set to work and built a much finer and much more beautiful city than the old one had been.

Now, the chief person in Athens at this time was a man named Pericles. He was not a king nor a ruler, but he was so very wise and such a wonderful speaker and such a popular leader that he was able to make the Athenians do as he thought best. He was like the popular captain of a football team, who is a fine player himself and can make fine players of all the others on his team. Athens was his team, and he trained it so well that any one of the team would have been able to fill any position no matter how important it was. Some men became great artists. Some men became great writers. Some men became great philosophers. Do you know what philosophers are? They are wise men who know a great deal and love knowledge.

The artists built many beautiful buildings, theaters, and temples. They made wonderful statues of the Greek gods and goddesses and placed them on the buildings and about the city.

The philosophers taught the people how to be wise and good.

The writers composed fine poems and plays. The plays were not like those we have nowadays but were all about the doings of the gods and goddesses.

The theaters were not like those we have nowadays, either. They were always out of doors, usually on the side of a hill, where a "grand stand" could be built facing the stage. There was little or no scenery, and instead of an orchestra of musicians there was a chorus of singers to accompany the actors. The actors wore false faces or masks to show what their feelings were, a "comic" mask with a grinning face when they wanted to be funny and a "tragic" mask with a sorrowful face when they wanted to seem sad.

Perhaps you have seen pictures of these masks, for in the decorations of our own theaters these same comic and tragic masks are sometimes used.

Tragic and comic masks.

Athens had been named after the goddess Athene, who was supposed to watch out for and look after the city. So the Athenians thought she should have a special temple. Accordingly, they built one to her on the top of a hill called the Acropolis. This temple they called in her honor the Parthenon, meaning the "maiden," one of the names by which she was known.

The Parthenon is considered the most beautiful building in the world, though as you see by the picture, as it is to-day, it is now in ruins. In the center of this temple was a huge statue of Athene made of gold and ivory by a sculptor named Phidias. We are told that it was the most beautiful statue in the world as the Parthenon was the most beautiful building, but it has completely disappeared, and no one knows what became of it. One might guess, however, that the gold and ivory tempted thieves, who may have stolen it piece by piece.

The Parthenon.

Phidias made many other statues on the outside of the Parthenon, but most of these have been carried away and put in museums or have been lost or destroyed.

This statue of Athene and the other sculptures on the Parthenon made Phidias so famous that he was asked to make a statue of Jupiter to be placed at Olympia, where the Olympic Games were held. The statue of Jupiter was finer even than the one he had made of Athene and was so splendid that it was called one of the Seven Wonders of the World. You remember the pyramids of Egypt and the Hanging Gardens of Babylon were two others of the Seven Wonders.

Phidias is probably the greatest sculptor that ever lived, but he did a thing which the Greeks considered a crime and would not forgive. We do not see anything so terribly wrong in what he did, but the Greeks' idea of right and wrong was different from ours. This is what he did. On the shield of the statue of Athene that he had made, Phidias carved a picture of himself and also one of his friend Pericles. It was merely a part of the decoration of the shield, and hardly any one would have noticed it. But according to the Greek notion it was sacrilege to make a picture of a human being on a statue of a goddess. So when the Athenians found out what Phidias had done they threw him into prison, and there he died.

The Greeks used different kinds of columns on their buildings, and these columns are used in many public and in some private buildings to-day. I'll tell you what each kind is like; then see how many you can find.

The Parthenon was built in a style called Doric.

The top of the column is called the capital, and the capital of the Doric column is shaped like a saucer with a square cover on top of it. There was no base or block at the bottom of the column. It rested directly on the floor. As the Doric column is so plain and strong-looking it is called the man's style.

The second style is called *Ionic*.

The capital of the Ionic column has a base, and the capital has ornaments like curls underneath the square top, and the column has a base.

As this column is more slender and more ornamental than the Doric, it is called the woman's style.

The third style is called *Corinthian*.

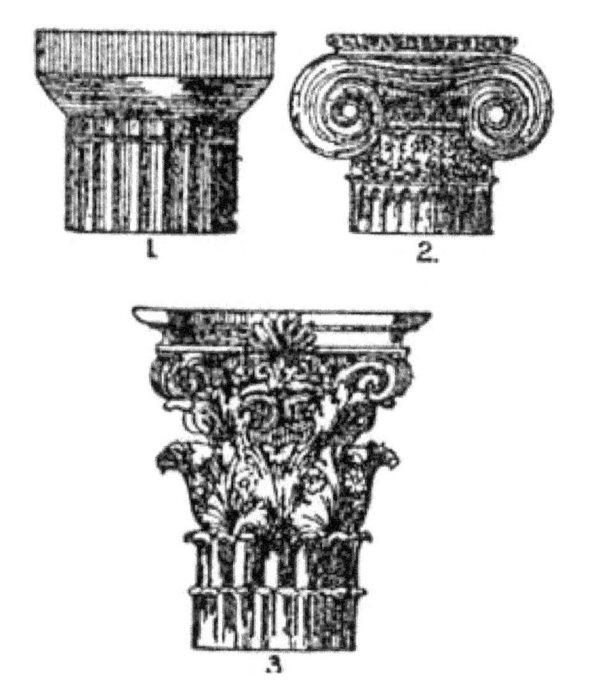

1. **Doric.**
2. **Ionic.**
3. **Corinthian.**

The capital of the Corinthian column is higher than either of the other two and still more ornamental. It is said that the architect who first made this column got his idea for its capital from seeing a basketful of toys that had been placed on a child's grave as was the custom instead of flowers. The basket had been covered with a slab, and leaves of the thistle called the acanthus had grown up around the basket. It looked so pretty that the architect thought it would make a beautiful capital for a column, and so he copied it.

I asked some boys which one could find the most columns. The next day one boy said he had seen two Ionic columns, one on each side of the door of his house. The second had seen ten Doric columns on the savings-bank. But the third said he had seen 138 Corinthian columns.

"Where on earth did you see so many?" I asked.

"I counted the lamp-posts from my house to the school," he said. "They were kind of Corinthian columns."

One of the friends of Pericles was a man named Herodotus. He wrote in Greek the first history of the world. For this reason Herodotus is called the Father of History, and some day if you study Greek you may read what he wrote in his own language. Of course, at that time there was very little history to write. What has happened since *hadn't* happened then, and before his time little was known of what had taken place. So Herodotus's history was chiefly a story of the wars with Persia, which I have just told you about. After that he had to stop; there was nothing more to write about.

In those days every once in a while a terrible contagious disease, called a plague, would break out, and people would be taken sick and die by the thousands, for the doctors knew very little about the plague or how to cure it. Such a plague came upon Athens, and the Athenians died like poisoned flies. Pericles himself nursed the sick and did all he could for them, but finally he, too, was taken sick with the plague and died. So ended the Golden Age, which has been called in honor of its greatest man the Age of Pericles.

27

When Greek Meets Greek

THE Golden Age, when Athens was so wonderful, lasted for only fifty years. Why, do you suppose, did it stop at all?

It stopped chiefly because of a fight.

This time, however, the fight was not between Greece and some one outside, as in the Persian Wars. The fight was between two cities that had before this been more or less friendly—mostly less—between Sparta and Athens. It was a family quarrel between Greeks. And the fight was all because one of these cities—Sparta—was jealous of the other—Athens.

The Spartans, as you know, were fine soldiers. The Athenians were fine soldiers, too. But ever since Themistocles with the ships he had built had beaten the Persians at Salamis, Athens had also a fine fleet, and Sparta had no fleet. Furthermore, Athens had become the most beautiful and most cultured city in the whole world.

Sparta did not care much about Athens's beautiful buildings and her education and culture and that sort of thing; that did not interest her. What did make her jealous was Athens's fleet. Sparta was inland, not on nor near the sea-shore as Athens was; so she could not have a fleet at all. Sparta did not intend, however, to let Athens get ahead of her, and so on one excuse or another Sparta with all of *her* neighbors started a war against Athens with all of *her* neighbors.

Sparta was in a part of Greece which was called by the hard name, the Peloponnesus. But in those days the boys did not think this a hard name, for they were as familiar with it as you are with such a name as Massachusetts, for instance, which would seem just as hard to a Greek as Peloponnesus does to you. This war between Athens and Sparta was therefore called the Peloponnesian War from the fact that it was not only Sparta but all of the Peloponnesus that fought against Athens.

We think a war lasts entirely too long if it lasts four or five years, but the Peloponnesian War lasted twenty-seven years! There is a saying, "When Greek meets Greek then comes a tug of war!" which means to say, "When two equal fighters such as Athens and Sparta, both Greek, meet each other in battle, who knows how it will end?"

I am not going to tell you about all the battles that took place during these twenty-seven years, but at the end of this long and bloody war both cities were tired and worn out, and the glory of Athens was gone. Although

Sparta was ahead, neither city ever amounted to much afterward. The Peloponnesian War ruined them both. That's the way war does!

All during the Peloponnesian War there was a man at Athens by the name of Socrates who, many think, was one of the wisest and best men who ever lived. He was called a philosopher and went about the city teaching the people what was right and what they ought to do. But instead of actually *telling* the people what he thought was right, he asked them questions which made them see what was right. In this way, chiefly by asking questions, he led people to find out for themselves what he wanted them to know. This kind of teaching, simply by asking questions, has ever since been called Socratic.

Socrates had a snub nose and was bald and quite ugly, and yet he was very popular with the Athenians, which may seem strange, for the Athenians loved beautiful faces and beautiful figures and beautiful things, and Socrates was anything but beautiful. It must have been the beauty of Socrates's character that made them forget his ugliness, as I know some boys and girls who think their teacher is perfectly beautiful just because she is so good and kind that they love her, although she is really not pretty at all.

Socrates had a wife named Xantippe. She had a bad temper and was the worst kind of a crosspatch. She thought Socrates was wasting his time, that he was a loafer, as he did no work that brought in any money. One day she scolded him so loudly that he left the house, whereupon she threw a bucket of water on him. Socrates, who never answered back, merely remarked to himself:

"After thunder, rain may be expected."

Socrates didn't believe in all the Greek gods, Jupiter, Venus, and the rest, but he was careful not to say so himself, for the Greeks were very particular that no one should say or do anything against their gods. Phidias, you remember, was thrown into prison for merely putting his picture on the shield of the goddess Athene, and one would have been put to death for teaching young men not to believe in the gods.

At last, however, Socrates, as he had feared he would be, was charged with not believing in the Greek gods and with teaching others not to believe in them. And so for this he was condemned to death. He was not hanged or put to death as prisoners are now, however. He was ordered to drink a cup of hemlock, which was a deadly poison. Socrates's pupils, or disciples, as they were then called, tried to have him refuse to drink the cup, but he would not disobey the order; and so, when he was nearly seventy years old, he drank the cup of hemlock and died with all his disciples around him.

Although this was four hundred years before Christ was born, and before, therefore, there were any such things as Christians or a Christian religion, yet

Socrates believed and taught two things that are just what Christians also believe.

One of these things he believed was that each of us has inside a conscience, which tells us what is right and what is wrong; we don't have to read from a book or be told by another what is right or what is wrong.

Another thing he taught was that there is a life after death and that when we die our souls live on.

No wonder he was not afraid himself to die!

28

Wise Men and Otherwise

HAVE you ever been playing in your yard when a strange boy who had been watching from the other side of the fence asked to be let into the game, saying he would show you how to play? You didn't want him around, and you didn't want him in, but somehow or other he got in and was soon bossing everybody else.

Well, there was a man named Philip who lived north of Greece, and he had been watching Sparta and Athens—not playing but fighting—and he wanted "to get into the game." Philip was king of a little country called Macedonia, but he thought he would like to be king of Greece, also, and it seemed to him a good time, when Sparta and Athens were "down and out" after the Peloponnesian War, to step in and make himself king of that country. Philip was a great fighter, but he didn't want to fight Greece unless he had to. He wanted to be made king peaceably, and he wanted Greece to do it willingly. So he thought up a scheme to bring this about, and this was his scheme.

He knew, as you do, how the Greeks hated the Persians whom they had driven out of their country over a hundred years before. Although the Persian Wars had taken place so long ago, the Greeks had never forgotten the bravery of their forefathers and the tales of their victories over the Persians. These stories had been told them over and over by their fathers and grandfathers, and they loved to read and reread them in Herodotus's history of the world.

So Philip said to the Greeks:

"Your ancestors drove the Persians out of Greece, to be sure, but the Persians went back to their country, and you didn't go after them and punish them as you should have done. You didn't try 'to get even' with them. Why don't you go over to Persia and conquer it now, and make the Persians pay for what they did to you?" Then he slyly added:

"Let me help you. I'll lead you against them."

No one seemed to see through Philip's scheme—nobody except one man. This man was an Athenian named Demosthenes.

Demosthenes, when he was a boy, had decided that he would some day be a great speaker or orator, just as you might say you are going to be a doctor, or an aviator, or a lawyer when you grow up.

But Demosthenes had picked the one profession which by nature he was worst fitted for. In the first place, he had such a very soft, weak voice that one could hardly hear him. Besides this, he st-st-stammered very b-b-badly and could not re-cite even a sh-sh-short p-p-poem without hesit-t-tating and st-st-stumbling so that people laughed at him. It seemed absurd, therefore, that he should aim to be a great speaker.

But Demosthenes practised and *practised* and *practised* by himself. He went down on the sea-shore and put pebbles in his mouth to make it more difficult to speak clearly. Then he spoke to the roaring waves, making believe that he was addressing an angry crowd, who were trying to drown the sound of his voice, so that he would have to speak very loud indeed.

So at last, by keeping constantly at it, Demosthenes did become the greatest speaker that ever lived. He spoke so wonderfully that he could make his audience laugh or make them cry whenever he wanted to, and he could persuade them to do almost anything he wished.

Now, Demosthenes was the man who saw through Philip's scheme for conquering Persia. He knew that Philip's real aim was to become king of Greece. So he made twelve speeches against him. These speeches were known as Philippics, as they were against Philip. So famous were they that even to-day we call a speech that bitterly attacks any one a Philippic.

The Greeks who heard Demosthenes were red-hot against Philip while they listened to him. But as soon as they got away from the sound of Demosthenes's words the same Greeks became lukewarm and did nothing to stop Philip.

So at last, in spite of everything that Demosthenes had said, Philip had his way and became king over all Greece.

Before, however, he could start out, as he had promised, to conquer Persia, he was killed by one of his own men, so that he was unable to carry out his plan.

But Philip had a son named Alexander. Alexander was only twenty years old, not old enough even to vote if he had lived in our country, but when his father died he became king of Macedonia and also of Greece.

When Alexander was a mere child, he saw some men trying without success to tame a young and very wild horse that shied and reared in the air so that no one was able to ride it. Alexander asked to be allowed to try to ride the animal. Alexander's father made fun of his son for wanting to attempt what those older than he had been unable to do, but at last gave his consent.

Now, Alexander had noticed what the others, although much older, had not noticed. The horse seemed to be afraid of its own shadow, for young colts are easily frightened by anything black and moving, as some children are afraid of the dark.

So Alexander turned the horse around facing the sun, so that its shadow would be behind, out of sight. He then mounted the animal and, to the amazement of all, rode off without any further trouble.

His father was delighted at his son's cleverness and gave him the horse as a reward. Alexander named the horse Bucephalus and became so fond of him that when the horse died Alexander built a monument to him and named several cities after him.

Now, Alexander was a wonderful boy, but he had such a wonderful teacher named Aristotle that some people think part, at least, of his greatness was due to the teacher.

Aristotle was probably the greatest teacher that ever lived. If there were more great teachers like Aristotle, it seems likely there would have been more great pupils like Alexander.

Aristotle wrote books about all sorts of things—books about the stars called astronomy, books about animals called zoölogy, and books on other subjects that you probably have never even heard of, such as psychology and politics.

For thousands of years these books that Aristotle wrote were the school-books that boys and girls studied, and for a thousand years they were the *only* school-books. Nowadays, a school-book is usually old-fashioned a few years after it is written and is then no longer used. So you see how remarkable it was that Aristotle's school-books should have been used for so long a time.

Aristotle had been taught by a man named Plato, who was also a great teacher and philosopher. Plato had been a pupil of Socrates, so that Aristotle was a kind of "grand-pupil" of Socrates. You have heard of the Wise Men of the East. These were the three Wise Men of Greece.

Socrates,
Plato,
Aristotle.

Some day you may read what they wrote or said over two thousand years ago.

29

A Boy King

WHEN you are twenty years old, what do you think you will be doing?

Will you be playing football on your college team?

Will you be working in a bank, or what?

When Alexander was twenty he was king of both Macedonia and Greece. But Macedonia and Greece were entirely too small for this wonderful young man. He wanted to own a much bigger country; in fact, he thought he would like to own the whole world; that was all—nothing more.

So Alexander went right ahead with his father's plan to conquer Persia. The time had come to pay back Persia for that last invasion one hundred and fifty years before.

He got together an army and crossed the Hellespont into Asia and won battle after battle against the first Persian armies sent out to stop him.

He kept moving on, for Persia was a vast empire.

Soon he came to a town where in a temple there was kept a rope tied into a very far-famed and puzzling knot. It was called the Gordian Knot, and it was very famous because the oracle had said that whoever should undo this knot would conquer Persia. But no one had ever been able to untie it.

When Alexander heard the story, he went to the temple and took a look at the knot. He saw at once that it would be impossible to untie it, so, instead of even trying, as others had done, he drew his sword and with one stroke cut the knot in two.

So now when a person settles something difficult, not by fussing with it as one untangles a snarl, but at a single stroke, cutting through all difficulties, we say he "cuts the Gordian Knot."

From that time on, Alexander conquered one city after another and never lost any battle of importance until he had conquered the whole of Persia.

A scroll, pens and ink.

Then he went into Egypt, which belonged to Persia, and conquered that country, too. To celebrate this victory, he founded a town near the mouth of the Nile and named it after himself, Alexandria. Then he started there a great library which later grew to be so big that there were said to be five hundred thousand books in it—that is, half a million—and was the largest library of ancient times. The books were not like those in the library of Assur-bani-pal nor the kind we have now, of course, because printing had not been invented. They were every one of them written by hand, and not on pages, but on long sheets which were rolled up on sticks to form a scroll.

In the harbor of Alexandria was a little island called Pharos, and on this island some years later was built a remarkable lighthouse named from the island, the Pharos, and its light could be seen for many miles. It was really a building more like a modern sky-scraper with a tower. It was over thirty stories high, which seemed most remarkable at that time when most buildings were only one or two stories high, and its light could be seen for many miles. So the Pharos of Alexandria was called one of the Seven Wonders of the World. You have already heard of three others, so this makes the fourth.

Alexandria grew in the course of time to be the largest and most important seaport of the ancient world. Now, however, the Pharos and the library and all the old buildings have long since disappeared.

But Alexander did not stay very long in any one place. He was restless. He wanted to keep on the move. He wanted to see new places and to conquer new people. He almost forgot his own little country of Macedonia and Greece. Instead of being homesick, however, as most any one would have been, he kept going farther and farther away from home all the time. We should call such a man an adventurer or an explorer, as well as a great general.

And so he kept on conquering and didn't stop conquering until he had reached far-off India.

There in India his army, which had stayed on with him all the way, became homesick and wanted to go back. They had been away from home for more than ten years and were so far off that they were afraid they would never get back.

Alexander was now only thirty years old, but he was called Alexander the Great, for he was ruler of the whole world—at least, all of it that was then known and inhabited by civilized people, except Italy, which was still only a collection of little, unimportant towns at that time. When Alexander found there were no more countries left for him to conquer, he was so disappointed that he wept!

And so at last, when there was nothing more to conquer, he agreed to do what his army begged him and started slowly back toward Greece.

He got as far as Babylon, the city once so large and so magnificent. There he celebrated with a feast, but while feasting and drinking he suddenly died. So he never reached Greece.

This was in 323 B.C. when he was but 33 years old. You can remember these figures easily, for they are all 3's except the middle figure in the date, which is one less than 3.

Alexander the Great had conquered the largest country that has ever been under the rule of one man, and yet this was not the only reason we call him the "Great."

He was not only a great ruler and a great general, but—this may surprise you—he was also a great teacher. Aristotle had taught him to be that.

Alexander taught the Greek language to the people whom he conquered so that they could read Greek books. He taught them about Greek sculpture and painting. He taught them the wise sayings of the Greek philosophers, Socrates and Plato and his own teacher, Aristotle. He trained the people in athletics as the Greeks did for their Olympic Games. And so we can say that he taught far more people than any other teacher who has ever lived.

Alexander had married a beautiful Persian girl named Roxana, but their only child was a baby, not born until after his father's death; so when the great king died there was no one to rule after him. He had told his generals before he died that the strongest one of them should be the next ruler; to fight it out among themselves, as we sometimes say, "May the best man win."

So his generals did fight to see who should win, and finally four of them, who were victorious, decided to divide up this great empire and each have a share.

One of his generals was named Ptolemy I, and he took Egypt as his share and ruled well; but the others did not amount to much, and after a while their shares became unimportant and went to pieces. Like a red toy balloon which stretches and stretches as you blow it up, Alexander's empire grew bigger and bigger until—all of a sudden—"*pop*"—nothing was left but the pieces.

30

Picking a Fight

"EVERY dog has his day."

A tennis or golf champion wins over the one who was champion before him and then has a few years during which he is unbeaten. Sooner or later, however, some younger and better man beats him and in turn takes the championship.

It seems almost the same way with countries as with people. One country wins the championship from another, holds it for a few years, and then, when older, finally loses it to some new-comer.

We have seen that

Nineveh was champion for a while; then
Babylon had her turn; then
Persia, had her turn; then
Greece; and, lastly,
Macedonia.

You may wonder who was to be the next champion after Alexander's empire went to pieces—who was to have the next turn.

When Alexander was conquering the world he went east toward the rising sun, and south. He paid little attention to the country to the west toward the setting sun. Rome, which we have not heard of for some time, was then only a small town with narrow streets and frame houses. It was not nearly important enough for Alexander to think much about. Rome herself was not thinking of anything then except keeping the neighboring towns from beating her.

Map of Mediterranean showing Carthage, Spain, etc.

It is usual to speak of a city as "her" or "she" as if a city were a girl, but Rome was more like a small boy whom all the other boys were "picking" on. In the course of time, however, Rome began to grow up and was not only able to take care of herself but could put up a very stiff fight. She was then no longer satisfied with just defending herself. So she fought and won battles with most of the other towns in Italy, until at last she found herself champion of the whole of the "boot." Then she began to look around to see what other countries there were outside of Italy that she might conquer.

Perhaps you have noticed that Italy, the "boot," seems about to kick a little island as if it were a football. This island is Sicily, and just opposite Sicily was a city called Carthage.

Carthage had been founded by the Phenicians many years before and had become a very rich and powerful city. As she was by the sea, she had built many ships and traded with all the other seaports along the Mediterranean, just as the old Phenician cities of Tyre and Sidon had done.

Carthage did not like to see Rome getting so strong and growing so big and becoming so powerful. In other words, Carthage was jealous of Rome.

Rome, on her side, was jealous of the wealth and trade of Carthage. So Rome anxiously looked around for some excuse to get into a fight with her.

Now, you know how easy it is to pick a quarrel and start a fight when you are "looking for trouble." One boy sticks out his tongue, the other gives him a kick, and the fight is on.

Well, two countries are at times just like little boys; they start a fight with just as little excuse, and though they call the fight "war" it is nothing but a "scrap." Only there are no fathers to come along and give them both a spanking and send them to bed without any supper.

So it didn't take long for Rome and Carthage to find an excuse, and a war was started between them. The Romans called this fight a Punic War, for "Punic" was their name for Phenician, and the Carthaginians were Phenicians.

As Carthage was across the water, the Romans could not get to her except in boats. But Rome had no boats. She was not on the sea-shore, and she knew nothing about making boats, nor about sailing them, if she had had them.

The Carthaginians, on the other hand, had many, many boats, and, like all the Phenicians, were old and experienced sailors.

But Rome happened to find the wreck of a Carthaginian ship that had been cast ashore, and she at once set to work to make a copy of it. In a remarkably short time she had built one ship, then another and another, until she had a great many ships. Then, though she was new at the game, she attacked the Carthaginian fleet.

It would seem that the Carthaginians could easily have won, for the Romans knew so little about boats. But in sea battles, before this, the fighting had been done by running into the enemy and ramming and sinking their ships.

The Romans knew they were no match for the Carthaginians in this sort of fighting. So they thought up a way in which they could fight them as on land.

To do this they invented a kind of big hook which they called a "crow." The idea was for a ship to run close alongside a Carthaginian ship and, instead of trying to sink her, to throw out this big hook or "crow," catch hold of the other ship, and pull both boats dose together. The Roman soldiers would then scramble over the sides into the enemy's boat and fight them the same way they would on land.

The scheme worked.

This new kind of fighting took the Carthaginians by surprise, and they were no match for the Romans at first.

But Rome did not have things all her own way by any means. The Carthaginians soon learned how to fight in this fashion, too. So Rome lost, as well as won, battles both on land and on sea. But at last she did win, and the Carthaginians were beaten. Thus ended the first Punic War.

31

The Boot Kicks and Stamps

But the Carthaginians were not beaten for good. They were only waiting for another chance to get even. As, however, they had been unsuccessful in attacking Italy from in front as they had been doing, they made up their minds to attack her from the back. Their scheme was to go the long way round through Spain and down into Italy from the north.

In order to do this, they had first of all to conquer Spain so that they could get through. They did this, however, rather easily, for the Carthaginians had a very great general named Hannibal. But then came the great difficulty, to get into Italy by this back way.

Across the top of the "boot," at the north of Italy, there are the great mountains called the Alps. They are miles high and covered even in summer with ice and snow. There are crags and steep cliffs along which any one passing who made a single misstep would be dashed to death thousands of feet below.

It was the Alps, therefore, that formed a bigger and better wall than any city or country could possibly build. Of course the Romans thought it impossible for any army to climb over such a terribly high and dangerous wall.

Time and again there have been things that people call impossible to do, and then some one has come along and done them.

People said it was impossible to fly.

Then some one did it.

People said it was impossible to cross the Alps with an army.

Then Hannibal came along, and before the Romans knew what had happened he had done it. He had crossed the Alps with his army and was in at the back door!

The Romans were unable to keep him from marching on toward their city, winning battle after battle as he came along. They were unable to prevent him marching up and down Italy, conquering other towns in Italy and doing pretty much as he pleased. It seemed as if Rome were beaten and she were to lose all of Italy.

Now, in some games, if you can't defend your own goal, it may be a good plan to try attacking your opponent's goal.

Rome thought she would try this plan. While Hannibal was attacking her, she herself would attack Carthage while its general was away and there was no strong goal-keeper to defend that city.

So the Romans sent a young man named Scipio with an army to do this.

First, however, Scipio went to Spain to cut Hannibal off from the way he had come, and this country Scipio reconquered.

Then he went over to Africa to attack Carthage itself.

The Carthaginians, frightened at being attacked with their general and his army far off in Italy, sent as fast as they could for Hannibal to come home. When at last he arrived, it was too late. Scipio fought a famous battle at Zama near Carthage, and the Carthaginians were beaten, beaten a second time by the Romans. Thus ended the second Punic War in 202 B.C. This is another easy name and easy date—just like a telephone number:

> Zama—two-O-two.

The Romans had won two wars against Carthage; you would think that they would now have been satisfied. But they weren't. They thought they had not beaten Carthage badly enough. They were afraid she was not quite dead or that she might come to life. They thought there might be a little spark left that might start a fire if it weren't trampled out.

Now, it is bad sport to pummel your opponent after he is beaten, and Carthage was beaten—beaten, black and blue—there was no hope of her "coming back." And yet a few years later the Romans attacked her again for the third and last time.

Carthage was unable to defend herself, and the Romans viciously burned the city to the ground. It is said they even plowed over the land so that no trace of the city should remain, and sowed it with salt which prevented anything growing there. After that Carthage was never rebuilt, and now it is hard to tell even where the old city once was.

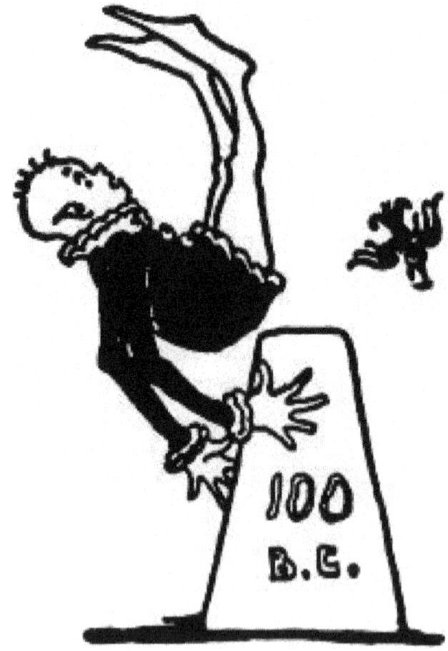
100
B.C.

32

The New Champion of the World

YOU can well imagine how proud all the Romans now were that they *were* Romans, for Rome was the champion fighter of the world. If a man could toss his head and say, "I am a Roman citizen," people were always ready to do something for him, afraid to do him any harm, afraid what might happen to them if they did. Rome was ruler not only of Italy but of Spain and Africa. Like other nations before her, once she had started conquering, she kept on conquering, until by 100 B.C. she in her turn was ruler of almost all the countries bordering the Mediterranean Sea—all except Egypt.

The New Champion of the World, who was to be champion for a great many years, was very businesslike and practical.

The Greeks loved beautiful things, beautiful buildings, beautiful sculpture, beautiful poems. The Romans copied the Greeks and learned from them how to make many beautiful things, but the Romans were most interested in practical and useful things.

For example, now that Rome ruled the world, she had to be able to send messengers and armies easily and quickly in every direction to the end of her empire and back again. So it was necessary for her to have roads, for of course there were no railroads then. Now, an ordinary road made by simply clearing away the ground gets full of deep ruts and in rainy weather becomes so muddy that it can hardly be used at all.

So Rome set to work and built roads. These roads were like paved streets. Large rocks were placed at the bottom for a foundation, smaller stones placed on top, and large, flat paving-stones laid over all. Thousands of miles of such roads she built to all parts of her empire. One could go from almost anywhere all the way to Rome on paved roads. We still have an expression, "All roads lead to Rome." So well were these roads made that many of them still exist to-day, two thousand years after they were built.

The Romans also showed their practical minds by making two very important city improvements. If you live in a city, you turn on a spigot and you get plenty of pure water whenever you want it. The people in cities at that time, however, usually had to get their water both for drinking and for washing from wells or springs near-by. These springs and wells often became dirty and made the people very sick. And so every once in a while because of such dirty water there were those terrible plagues, those terribly contagious diseases like the one I told you about in Athens when people died faster than they could be buried.

Roman Aqueduct.

The Romans wanted pure water, and so they set to work to find lakes from which they could get pure water. As oftentimes these lakes were many miles away from the city, they then built big pipes to carry the water all the way to the city. Such a pipe was not made of iron or terra-cotta as nowadays, but of stone and concrete, and was called an "aqueduct," which in Latin means "water-carrier." If this aqueduct had to cross a river or a valley, they built a bridge to hold it up. Many of these Roman aqueducts are still standing and in use to-day.

Now, up to this time waste water, after it had been used, and also every other kind of dirt and refuse, was simply dumped into the street. This naturally made the city or town filthy and unhealthy and was another cause of plagues. But the Romans built great underground sewers to carry off this dirt and waste water and empty it into the river or into some other place where it would do no harm and cause no sickness. Nowadays, every large city has aqueducts and sewers as a matter of course, but the Romans were the first to build them on a large scale.

One of the most important things that Rome did was to make rules that every one had to obey; laws, we call them. Many of these laws were so fair and just that some of our own laws to-day are copied from them.

All the cities and towns of the Roman Empire had to pay money or taxes to Rome. So Rome became the richest city in the world. Millions of this money, which was brought to her, was spent in putting up beautiful buildings in the city, temples to the gods, splendid palaces for the rulers, public baths and huge open-air places called amphitheaters where the people could be amused.

The amphitheaters were something like our football and baseball fields or stadiums. They did not have football or baseball, however. They had chariot-races, and deadly fights between men, or between men and animals. Chariots were small carts with large wheels drawn by two or by four horses and driven by a man standing up. Perhaps you have seen chariot-races in the circus.

But the sport that the Romans enjoyed most of all was a Fight of Gladiators. Gladiators were very strong and powerful men who had been captured in battle by the Romans. They were made to fight with one another or with wild animals for the amusement of the crowd. These gladiatorial fights were very cruel, but the Romans enjoyed seeing blood shed. They liked to see one man kill another or a wild animal. It was so amusing. The movies would not have interested them half so much. Usually the gladiators fought until one or the other was killed, for the people were not, as a rule, satisfied until this was done.

Sometimes, however, if a gladiator, who had been knocked out, had shown himself particularly brave and a good fighter or a good sport, the people seated all around the amphitheater would turn their thumbs *up* as a sign that his life was to be spared by the other gladiator. So the winning gladiator, before killing his opponent whom he had down, would wait to see what the people wished. If they turned their thumbs *down*, it meant he was to finish the fight by killing his man.

But although Rome had become such a fine and beautiful and healthy city in which to live, the rich people were getting most of the money that came there from all over the empire. They were getting richer and richer all the time, while the poor people, who got nothing, were getting poorer and poorer all the time. The Romans brought the people whom they conquered in battle to Rome and made them work for them without pay. These were slaves and they did all the work. It is said that there were more than twice as many slaves as Romans—two slaves for every Roman citizen.

Now, Scipio, who had conquered Hannibal in the Punic War, had a daughter named Cornelia Graccha, and she had two sons. They were very fine boys, and Cornelia was naturally very proud of them.

One day a very rich Roman woman was visiting Cornelia and showing off all her rings and necklaces and other ornaments, of which she had a great many and was very proud.

When she had shown off all she had, she asked to see Cornelia's jewels.

Cornelia called to her two boys, who were playing outside, and when they came in to their mother she put her arms around them and said:

"*These* are *my* jewels."

But boys who are jewels when they are young do not always turn out to be jewels when they grow up. So you may wonder how Cornelia's jewels tinned out.

When they grew up, the Gracchi, as they were called, saw such great extravagance among the rich and such great misery among the poor that they wanted to do something about it. They saw that the poor had hardly anything to eat and no place to live. This did not seem fair. So they tried to lower the price of food, so that the poor might be able to buy enough to eat. Then they tried to find some way to give the poor at least a small piece of land where they might raise a few vegetables. They were partly successful in bringing this about. But the rich people didn't like giving up anything to the poor, and they killed one of the Gracchus brothers, and later they killed the other one, also. These were Cornelia's jewels.

33

The Noblest Roman of Them All

HERE'S a puzzle for you:

A man once found a very old piece of money that had on it the date "100 B. C."

That couldn't be so. Why not? See if you can tell without looking at the answer at the bottom of the page.[1]

[1] People living 100 years before Christ was born could not have known when he was to be born and so could not put such a date on the coins they made.

In the year 100 B. C. was born in Rome a boy who was named Julius Cæsar.

If you had asked him when he was born, he would have said in the Year 653.

Why do you suppose?

Because Roman boys counted time from the founding of Rome in 753 B. C., and Cæsar was born 653 years after the city was founded. That makes it 100 years before Christ, doesn't it?

Pirates seemed to be everywhere in the Mediterranean Sea at that time— *Pirates*. Now that Rome was ruler of the world, there were many ships carrying gold from different parts of the empire to Rome. So the pirates sailed up and down, lying in wait to capture and rob these ships laden with gold.

When Cæsar grew to be a young man, he was sent off to sea to fight these pirates, and he was captured by them. The pirates kept Cæsar a prisoner and sent to Rome saying they would not let him go unless Rome sent them a great deal of money. Cæsar knew that he would be killed if the money was not sent. He knew, too, that he might be killed, anyway. But he was not only not afraid but he told the pirates that if he lived to get back home he would return with a fleet and punish every one of them. When at last the money came they let him go, nevertheless. They thought Cæsar would not dare to do what he said. They thought he was just "talking big." At any rate, they did not believe he would be able to catch them. Cæsar, however, kept his word, came back after them as he said he would do, and took them prisoners. Then he had them all put to death on the cross, which was the Roman way of punishing thieves.

The far-off places of the Roman Empire were always fighting against Rome trying to get rid of her rule, and had to be kept in order by a general with an army. As Cæsar had shown such bravery in fighting the pirates he was given an army and sent to fight two of these far-off places—Spain and a country north of Spain then known as Gaul, which is now France.

Cæsar conquered these countries, and then he wrote a history of his battles in Latin, which of course was his own language. Nowadays this book, called "Cæsar's Commentaries," is usually the first book which those who study Latin read.

In 55 B. C. Cæsar crossed over in ships to the island of Britain, which is now England, conquered it, and went back again next year in 54 B. C.

Cæsar was becoming famous for the way he conquered and ruled over the western part of the Roman Empire. Besides this, he was very popular with his soldiers.

Now there was in Rome at this time another general named Pompey. Pompey had been successfully fighting in the eastern part of the Roman Empire while Cæsar had been fighting in the west. Pompey had been a great friend of Cæsar, but when he saw how much land Cæsar had conquered and how popular he was with his soldiers, he became very jealous of him. Notice how many quarrels and wars are caused simply by jealousy. You have heard of at least two already.

So while Cæsar was away with his army Pompey went to the Roman Senate and persuaded the senators to order Cæsar to give up the command of his army and return to Rome.

When Cæsar received the order from the Senate to give up his command and return to Rome, he thought over the matter for some time. Then at last he made up his mind that he would return to Rome, but he would *not* give up his command. Instead, he decided that he and his army would take command of Rome itself.

Now, there was a little stream called the Rubicon which separated the part of the country over which Cæsar was given charge from that of Rome. The Roman law forbade any general to cross this stream with an army ready to fight—this was the line beyond which he must not pass, for the Romans were afraid that if a general with an army got too close to Rome he might make himself king.

When Cæsar decided not to obey the Senate, he crossed this stream—the Rubicon—with his army and marched on to Rome.

People now speak of any dividing line from danger as "the Rubicon" and say that a person "crosses the Rubicon" when he takes a step from which there is no turning back, when he starts something difficult or dangerous which he must finish.

When Pompey heard that Cæsar was coming he took to his heels and fled to Greece. In a few days Cæsar had made himself head not only of Rome but of all Italy. Cæsar then went after Pompey in Greece and in a battle with his army beat him badly.

Now that Pompey was out of the way, Cæsar was the chief ruler of the whole of the Roman Empire.

Egypt did not yet belong to Rome. So Cæsar next went there and conquered that country. Now, in Egypt there was ruling a beautiful queen named Cleopatra. Cleopatra was so charming that she seemed able to make every one fall in love with her. Cleopatra flirted with Cæsar and so fascinated him that he almost forgot everything else except making love to her. So although he had won Egypt he made Cleopatra queen over that country.

Just at this time some people in the far eastern part of the empire started a war to get rid of the rule of Rome. Cæsar left Egypt, traveled rapidly to the place where the enemy were, made quick work of conquering them, then sent back the news of his victory to Rome in the most laconic (do you remember what that means?) description ever given of a battle. There were only three words in the message. Although the messenger could have carried three thousand as easily as three words, Cæsar sent a message that would have been short even for a telegram. He wrote, "Veni, vidi, vici," which means, "I came, I saw, I conquered."

When Cæsar at last got back to Rome, the people wanted to make him king, or said they did. Cæsar was already more than king, for he was head of the whole Roman Empire. But he wasn't called king, for there had been no kings since 509 B. C., when Tarquin was driven out. The Romans had been afraid of kings and hated them, or were supposed to hate them.

A few of the people thought that Cæsar was getting too much power and believed it would be a terrible thing to make him a king. They, therefore, decided on a plot to prevent such a thing happening. One of these plotters was a man named Brutus who had been Cæsar's very best friend.

One day when Cæsar was expected to visit the Roman Senate they lay in wait for him until he should appear—in the same way I have seen boys hide around the corner for some schoolmate, against whom they had a grudge, until he should come out of school.

Cæsar came along, and just as he was about to enter the Senate the plotters crowded around him, and one after another they stabbed him.

Cæsar, taken by surprise, tried to defend himself; but all he had was his stylus, which was a kind of pen he used for writing, and he could not do much with that, in spite of a famous saying, "The pen is mightier than the sword."

When at last Cæsar saw Brutus—his best friend—strike at him, his heart seemed broken and he gave up. Then, exclaiming in Latin, "Et tu, Brute!" which means, "And thou, O Brutus!" he fell down dead. This was in 44 B.C.

Antony, one of Cæsar's true friends, made a speech over Cæsar's dead body, and his words so stirred the crowd of people that gathered round that they would have torn the murderers to pieces if they could have caught them.

Shakspere has written a play called "Julius Cæsar," and the month of July is named after him.

Now whom do you suppose Antony called "The Noblest Roman of Them All"?

"Julius Cæsar"?

No, you're wrong. Brutus, the friend who stabbed Cæsar, was called, "The Noblest Roman of Them All."

Why, do you suppose?

You'll have to read Antony's speech at the end of the play to find out.

Cæsar was pronounced in Latin "Kaiser"; and in later years the rulers of Germany were called this, and those of another country by the shortened form, "Czar."

34

An Emperor Who Was Made a God

A MAN is famous who has a town or a street named after him.

Will you ever do anything great enough to have even an alley named after you?

But just suppose a month, one of the twelve months of the year, was given your name!

Millions upon millions of people would then write and speak your name forever!

But I'm going to tell you about a man who not only had a month named after him but who was made a god!

After Cæsar had been killed, three men ruled the Roman Empire. One of these three men was Antony, the friend of Cæsar, who made the famous speech over his dead body. The second was Cæsar's adopted son, who was named Octavius. The name of the third you don't need to know now, for Antony and Octavius soon got rid of him. Then no sooner had they forced him out than each of these two began to plot to get the share of the other.

Antony's share, over which he ruled, was the eastern part of the empire. The capital of this part was Alexandria in Egypt, and so Antony went there to live.

In Egypt Antony fell in love with Cleopatra, as Cæsar before him had done, and he finally married her.

Octavius, in the west, which was his share, then made war on Antony and Cleopatra together, and in the end beat them both. Antony felt so bad at being beaten by Octavius that he committed suicide.

His widow, Cleopatra, thereupon, flirted with Octavius as she had with Julius Cæsar and Antony, hoping to make him also fall in love with her and so win him in that way.

But it was no use. Octavius was a different kind of man from both Julius Cæsar and Antony. He was cold-blooded and businesslike. He had no heart for love-making. He would not let a woman charm him or turn him aside from his plan, which was to be the greatest man in the world!

Cleopatra saw that it was no use trying her tricks on him. Then she heard that she was going to be taken back to Rome and paraded through the streets, as was done with any other prisoners taken in battle. She could not stand such a shame as that, and so she made up her mind she would not be taken back to Rome.

Now, in Egypt there is a kind of snake called an asp, which is deadly poisonous. Taking one of these asps in her hand, she uncovered her breast and let it bite her, and so she died.

Octavius was now ruler over all the countries that belonged to Rome, and when he returned home to that city, the people hailed him "Emperor." He then gave up the name Octavius and had himself called "Augustus Cæsar," which is like saying, "His Majesty, Cæsar." This was in 27 B.C. Rome had got rid of her kings in 509. From now on she had emperors, who were more than kings, for they ruled over many countries.

Octavius, now with his name changed to Augustus Cæsar, was only thirty-six years old when he became sole master of the Roman world. Rome was the great capital of this vast empire. The city of Rome had probably as many people as New York City proper now has, and the Roman Empire had perhaps as many people as the United States has at present.

Augustus set to work to make Rome a beautiful city. He tore down a great many of the old buildings made of brick and put up in their place a remarkable number of new and handsome buildings of marble. And so Augustus always bragged that he found Rome brick and left it marble.

One of the finest buildings in Rome, the Pantheon, was built. Pantheon means the temple of all the gods. Do not mix this with the Parthenon in Athens, for the two buildings are quite different, and though the names look something alike and sound something alike, they mean quite different things; Parthenon is from the goddess Athene Parthenos; Pantheon is from the two words "Pan theon," which means "all gods."

The Pantheon has a dome built of concrete. This dome is shaped like a bowl turned upside down, and in the top of the dome is a round opening called an eye. Though this eye is uncovered, the height is so great above the floor that it is said that rain coming through the eye does not wet the floor beneath but evaporates before reaching it.

So magnificent did the city become with all these wonderful buildings, and so permanently did it seem to be built, that it was known as The Eternal City and is still so spoken of.

There was a public square in Rome called the Forum. Here markets were held and the people came together for all sorts of things. Around the Forum were erected temples to the gods, court-houses, and other public buildings. These court-houses were something like the temples that the Greeks built, only the columns were put on the inside of the building instead of on the outside.

Roman forum.

Triumphal arches also were erected to celebrate great victories. When a conquering hero returned from the war, he and his army passed through this arch in a triumphal parade.

There had been in Rome a great amphitheater that is supposed to have held more people than any structure that has ever been built—two hundred thousand, it is said, or more than all the people who live in some good-sized cities. This was called the Circus Maximus. It was at last torn down to make room for other buildings.

Another amphitheater was the Colosseum, but this was not built until some time after Augustus had died. It held about the same number as the largest stadium in this country does to-day. Here were held those fights between men, called gladiators, and wild animals that I have already told you about. It is still standing, and, though it is in ruins, you can sit in the same seats where the old Roman emperors did, see the dens where the wild animals were kept, the doors where they were let into the arena, and even bloody marks that are said to be the stains made by the slain men and beasts.

So many famous writers lived at the time of Augustus that this has been called the Augustan Age. Two of the best known Latin poets, whom every school-boy now reads after he has finished "Cæsar's Commentaries," lived at this time. These poets were Vergil and Horace. Vergil wrote the "Æneid," which told of the wanderings of Æneas, the Trojan, who settled in Italy, and was the great-great-great-grandfather of Romulus and Remus. Horace wrote many short poems called Odes. They were love-songs of shepherds and shepherdesses and songs of the farm and country life. People liked his songs, and many still name their sons after him.

When Augustus Cæsar died, he was made a god, because he had done so much for Rome; temples were built in which he was worshiped, and the month of August was named after him.

35

"Thine is the Kingdom, the Power, and the Glory"

AUGUSTUS CÆSAR had been Ruler of the World.

He had found Rome brick and left it marble.

He had had a month named after him, and

He had been made a god!

Surely no one could ever be greater than he! Yet a greater than he was living at the very same time—a greater ruler of a greater kingdom with greater power and greater glory, although Augustus himself knew nothing about Him and lived and died without ever having heard of Him. This Man was born in the eastern part of Augustus's empire in a tiny little village called Bethlehem, and His name was Jesus Christ.

For many, many years after Christ was born no one except His family and friends knew or cared anything about His birth or paid the slightest attention to it.

Christ was a Jew, the son of a carpenter. As a boy and young man He led a very simple and quiet life working in His father's shop. He did not begin to preach until He was more than thirty years old. Then He went about teaching the people what we learn to-day as the Christian religion.

He taught that there was one God over all.

He taught brotherly love, that one should love one's neighbor as oneself.

He taught the golden rule; that is, "do unto others as you would be done by."

He taught that there was a life after death for which this short life on earth was only a preparation; that therefore you should "lay up your treasures in heaven" by doing good works here.

The poorer Jews listened to Christ and believed what He taught them. But they thought He was going to set them free from the rule of the Romans, which they hated. The Jewish priests, however, were afraid of what Christ taught. He was teaching some things that were just the opposite of what they themselves taught. So they plotted to have Him put to death.

Now, the Jews could not put Christ to death without the permission of the Roman ruler of that part of the empire where Christ lived. This ruler was named Pilate. So they went to Pilate and told him that Christ was trying to make himself king. Christ of course meant and always said that He was a heavenly ruler and not an earthly king. The Jews knew that Pilate would not care at all what religion Christ taught. There were all sorts of religions in the Roman Empire—those that believed in mythological gods and those that believed in idols and those that believed in the sun, moon, and so on—one more new religion made little difference to the Romans, and Christ would not be put to death simply for teaching another. But the Jews knew if they could make Pilate believe that Christ was trying to make himself a king, that was a thing He could be crucified for. Pilate did not believe much in what the Jews said against Christ. It was a small matter to him, one way or the other, however. But he wanted to please the Jews, so he told them to go ahead and put Christ to death if they wanted to. So He was crucified.

Christ had chosen twelve men to teach what He told them. These twelve men were called apostles. After Christ was crucified these apostles went through the land teaching the people what Christ had taught them. Those who believed in and followed His teachings were called disciples of Christ or Christians. The apostles were teachers; the disciples were pupils.

The Romans thought these disciples of Christ were trying to start a new world empire, and that they were against Rome and the emperor and should be arrested and put in prison. So the Christians usually held their meetings in secret places, sometimes even underground, so that they would not be found and arrested.

But after a while the leaders of the Christians became bolder. They came out of their secret places and taught and preached openly, although they knew they would sooner or later be thrown into prison and perhaps killed. Indeed, so strongly did they believe in the teachings of Christ that they seemed even glad to die for His sake, as He had died on the cross for them.

In the first hundred years after Christ, there were a great many Christians put to death because they were thought traitors. Christians who died for Christ's sake were called martyrs. The first martyr was named Stephen. He was stoned to death about 33 A.D.

One of the men who helped in putting Stephen to death was a man named Saul. Saul was a Roman citizen and, like other Roman citizens, was proud of that fact. He thought the Christians were enemies of his country, and he did everything he could to have the Christians punished. Then, all of a sudden, Saul had a change of heart and came to believe in the religion of the very people whom he had been fighting. Whatever Saul did or whatever he believed he did or believed with his whole soul. Though he had never seen Christ, he became one of the chief Christians and then was made an apostle and was called by his Roman name, Paul.

Paul preached the new religion far and wide just as earnestly as he had fought against it at first. Then he, too, was condemned to death. Paul, however, was, as I have said, a Roman citizen, and a Roman citizen could not be put to death by the ordinary judges who were not Roman citizens nor in the ordinary way by crucifying. So Paul appealed to the emperor. Nevertheless, he was put in prison in Rome and afterward beheaded. And so he is called St. Paul.

Peter was another of the chief apostles. Christ had said to him, "I will give unto thee the keys of the kingdom of heaven."[2] Peter, too, was thrown into prison, and was sentenced to be crucified. But he asked to be crucified with his head downward. He thought it too great an honor to die in just the same way as his Lord. On this spot in Rome where Peter was put to death was built long afterward the largest church in the world, the Cathedral of St. Peter.

[2] Matthew, xvi, 19.

As everything before Christ's birth is called B.C. and everything since His birth is called A.D., you would naturally suppose that 0 would be the date of His birth.

But it was not until some five hundred years later that people began to date from Christ's birth. And then, when they did begin to date from this event, they made a mistake. It was found out that Christ was really born four years before He was supposed to have been born—that is, in 4 B.C.—but when the mistake was found out, it was then too late to change.

36

Blood and Thunder

I ONCE had a big Newfoundland dog, and he was one of the best friends a boy ever had. I don't know who it was that named him; he was named before I got him; but whoever it was must either have been ignorant of history or a bad chooser of names. He was called Nero, and even a dog would have hated such a name, had he known whose it once was.

Every good story usually has a villain to make it interesting. Nero is the prize villain of history. He was a Roman emperor who lived not long after Christ, and he is considered the most terribly cruel and wicked ruler that ever lived.

He killed his mother.

He killed his wife.

He killed his teacher, who was named Seneca. He was not a bad teacher, either.

We think that Nero ordered both St. Peter and St. Paul put to death, for they were executed at this same time.

Nero seemed to take great pleasure in making others suffer. He loved to see men torn to pieces by wild beasts; it amused him greatly. I have seen boys who liked to throw stones at dogs just to hear them yelp, or tear the wings off of butterflies. Such boys must have some Nero in them; don't you think?

If a man was a Christian, that gave Nero an excuse to torture him horribly. Nero had some of the Christians wrapped in tar and pitch, then placed around the garden of his palace and set fire to, as if they were torches. It is even said that Nero set Rome on fire just for the fun of seeing the city burn. Then he sat in a tower and, while he watched the blaze spreading, played on a harp. The saying is that "Nero fiddled while Rome burned"; but there were no fiddles at that time, and so we know it must have been a harp. The fire burned day and night for a whole week and destroyed more than half of the city. Then Nero laid the blame on the Christians, who, he said, started the fire. Did you ever blame another for something you had done?

Some think Nero really was crazy, and we hope he was, for it is hard to think any human being who was not crazy could act as he did.

Nero built himself an immense palace and overlaid it extravagantly with gold and mother-of-pearl. It was known as Nero's House of Gold. At its front door he put up a colossal statue of himself in bronze fifty feet high. Both the House of Gold and the statue were later destroyed, but the Colosseum, which was built a few years afterward, was named Colosseum from this "coloss-al" statue of Nero that was once there.

Nero was very conceited. He thought he could write poetry and sing beautifully. Although he did both very badly, he liked to show off, and no one dared to laugh at him. Had any one been so bold as to make fun of him or even to smile, he would have had that person put to death instantly.

Even the Roman people who were not Christians feared and hated Nero. So they voted to have him put out of the way. But before they had a chance to do anything, Nero heard what they were planning, and in order to save himself the disgrace of being put to death by his own people he decided to kill himself. He was such a coward, however, that he couldn't quite bring himself to plunge the sword into his heart. But as he hesitated, holding the sword to his breast and whimpering, his slave, impatient to finish the job, shoved the blade in. Thus was Rome rid of its worst ruler.

So much for the first part of this "blood and thunder" story. Here is the second part:

The Jews in Jerusalem didn't like to have Rome rule over them. They never had. But they were afraid to do much about it. But in the Year 70 A.D. they rebelled; that is, they said they would no longer obey Rome or pay her money. The emperor sent his son, who was named Titus, with an army to put an end to the rebellion, to punish them as if they were disobedient children.

The Jews crowded into their city of Jerusalem to make a last stand against the Romans. But Titus destroyed that city completely and the Jews in it, a million of them, it is supposed. Then he robbed the great temple of all its valuable ornaments and brought them back to Rome.

To celebrate this victory over Jerusalem an arch was built in the Forum at Rome, and through this arch Titus and his army marched in triumph. On this arch was carved a procession, showing Titus leaving the city of Jerusalem with these ornaments. Chief among these ornaments was a golden seven-branched candlestick he had taken from the temple. To-day we see many copies in brass of this famous seven-branched candlestick. Perhaps you may have one in your home on the mantelpiece.

The city was rebuilt later, but most of the Jews who were left have ever since been living in all the other countries of the earth.

Titus became emperor, but in spite of the way in which he had massacred so many Jews, he was not such a bad emperor as you might suppose. He thought he was doing right in killing these men because they had rebelled against Rome. But Titus had a rule of life, much like that the Boy Scouts now have. This rule was, "Do at least one good turn a day."

The third part of this story is the "thunder."

In Italy there is a volcano named Vesuvius. You remember that "volcano" came from the name "Vulcan," the blacksmith god, and people imagined that his forge in the heart of a volcano made the smoke and flame and ashes. From time to time this volcano, Vesuvius, thunders and quakes and spouts forth fire and throws up stones and gas and boils over with red-hot melted rock called lava. It is the hot inside of the earth exploding. Yet people build houses and towns near-by and live even on the sides of the volcano. Every once in a while their homes are destroyed when the volcano quakes or pours forth fire. Yet the same people go right back and build again in the same place!

Vesuvius erupting, Pompeii in foreground.

There was at the time of Titus a little town named Pompeii near the base of Vesuvius. Wealthy Romans used to go there to spend the summer. Suddenly, one day in the year 79 A.D., just after Titus had become emperor, Vesuvius began to spout forth fire. The people living in Pompeii rushed for their lives, but they hadn't time to get away. They were smothered with the gases from the volcano before they hardly had time to move and, falling down dead, were buried deep in a boiling rain of fire and ashes, just where they happened to be when the eruption, as it was called, took place.

The people and their houses lay buried beneath the ashes for nearly two thousand years, and in the course of time every one had forgotten there ever had been such a place. People came back as they had before and built houses over the spot where every one had forgotten there once was a city. Then one day a man was digging a well over the spot where Pompeii had once been. He dug up a man's hand—no, not a real hand, but the hand of a statue. He told others, and they set to work and dug and dug to see what else they could find until the whole town was dug out. And now one can go to Pompeii and see it very much as it was in 79 A.D., before it had ever been destroyed.

There are houses of the Romans who went there to spend their vacations. There are shops and temples and palaces and public baths and the theater and the market place or forum. The streets were paved with blocks of lava, once melted stone. They still show ruts which were worn into them by the wheels of the chariots that the Romans used to drive. Stepping-stones were placed at some crossings, so that in case of heavy rains, when the streets were full of water, one could cross on them from curb to curb. These stepping-stones are still there. The floors of the houses were made of bits of colored stone to form pictures. They are still there. In the vestibule of one house, there is in the floor a mosaic picture of a dog. Under it are the Latin words, "Cave canem." What does that mean? Can you guess? It means, "Look out for the dog!" That was a Roman's idea of a joke two thousand years ago!

The bones of the people who were caught and buried alive in the ashes were also found. There were also found bronze ornaments worn by the women, vases that decorated the home, lamps which they used to light the houses, pots and pans and dishes. Beds and chairs were found just as they had been buried. Still more remarkable, cakes were found on the table, a loaf of bread half eaten, meat ready to be cooked, a kettle on the fire with the ashes still underneath it—beans and peas and *one egg* unbroken—probably the oldest egg in the world!

37

A Good Emperor and a Bad Son

HAVE you ever said, "I don't care," when you really did care?

I have. Every one has.

Perhaps you have been naughty and have been told you could have no dessert or must go to bed early, and you tossed your head and said, "I don't care."

Well, once upon a time there was a society or club formed of grown-up people who said they weren't ever going to care what happened to them; whether it was good or whether it was bad would make no difference. I should call them the "Don't Care Club," but they called themselves "Stoics," and they thought the way to be good was "not to care."

If a Stoic's house burned down, he would say to himself and try to make himself believe, "I don't care; it doesn't matter."

If some one gave him a million dollars, he would say, "I don't care; it doesn't matter."

If he was told by the doctor he was going to die next week, he would say, "I don't care; it doesn't matter."

This Society of Stoics was started by a Greek philosopher named Zeno.

Zeno lived in Athens later than those philosophers, Socrates and Plato, whom you have already heard about. Zeno said that the only way to be good and the only way to be happy was not to care for pleasure and not to mind pain or suffering but calmly to put up with everything, no matter how unpleasant or disagreeable it was, and the Stoics believed him. Even to-day people who bear troubles and pain and hardships without a murmur are called stoics.

One of the chief members of the society was a Roman emperor.

Rome's worst emperor, Nero, had been dead a hundred years when there came to the throne this new emperor, who was just as good as Nero was bad. This emperor was named Marcus Aurelius. Although he was so very good and pious, he was not a Christian. Indeed, Marcus Aurelius treated the Christians terribly, as they had been treated terribly by the previous emperors, for he thought them traitors to the empire.

At this time most of the Romans had very little religion of any sort. They were not Christians, but neither did they put much faith in their own gods, Jupiter and Juno and the rest. They honored them because they were brought up to honor them and because they thought if they didn't honor them they might have bad luck, so they took no chances. But instead of believing in such gods, people usually believed in the teachings of some wise man or philosopher and obeyed more or less the rules he made. Zeno was one of these philosophers, and the Stoics were the members of this society.

Although Marcus Aurelius was an emperor, he would rather have been a Stoic philosopher or a priest. Although he had to be a soldier and a general, he would rather have been a writer. When he was off, fighting with his army, he carried his writing-materials with him, and he would go to his tent at night and write out his thoughts. These thoughts he called his "Meditations." Here is one of the things he wrote:

When you find you do not want to get up early in the morning, make this short speech to yourself. I am getting up now to do the business of a man. Was I made to do nothing but doze and keep warm under the covers?

That was written long years ago, yet your father might have told you the same thing this morning.

People read this book of Marcus Aurelius to-day, either in the Greek in which it was written or translated into English.

A great many of Marcus Aurelius' sayings seem almost as if they might have been in the Bible. Indeed, some people keep his book by their bedside as if it were a Bible.

One of his rules was, "Forgive your enemies," and he seemed almost glad to have enemies so that he might have a chance to forgive them. Indeed, he took such a special delight in forgiving his enemies that he even went out of his way to do so. Though Marcus Aurelius was not a Christian, nevertheless he was more Christian in the way he acted than some of the later emperors who were supposed to be Christians.

But like many people who are very good themselves, Marcus Aurelius was unable to bring up his son to be so. His son was named Commodus, and Commodus was just as bad as his father was good. He may have been bored when a child by too many of his father's instructions, for when he grew up and was able to choose for himself and do as he pleased, instead of following Zeno and joining the Stoics, he joined the society of another philosopher called Epicurus.

Epicurus had lived about the same time as Zeno. But he had taught what at first seems almost the opposite of what Zeno taught. Epicurus said that the chief end and aim of man and the only good in the world was pleasure; *but*, said he, the pleasure must be of the right kind. Nowadays people who are very fond of eating nice things, whose whole thought in life is the pleasure of eating, are called "epicures."

Commodus's one thought was pleasure, and the worst kind of pleasure at that. A friend of mine thought Marcus Aurelius was such a fine man that he named his son after him, "Marcus Aurelius Jones," but when the son grew up he was not at all like his namesake. The name "Commodus" would have suited him much better, for instead of being good and pious, he thought of nothing but pleasure and he was so bad that he ended in jail.

Commodus thought nothing of giving his people a good government; he only thought of giving himself a good time. He was an athlete and had beautiful muscles and a handsome figure, of which he was so proud that he had a statue made of himself. The statue showed him as the strong and muscular god Hercules. Commodus made the people worship him as if he were this god. Just to show off his muscles and his muscular ability, he himself took part in prize-fights—quite bad taste for an emperor. He poisoned or killed any one who found fault with or criticized him. He led a wild and dissipated life, but at last he met the end he deserved. He was strangled to death by a wrestler.

Lycurgus would have said again:

"I told you so."

38

I — H — — S — — — — V — — — — —

THE name of this story I'm going to put at the end, for you wouldn't know what it means, anyway, until you have heard the story, and so it's no use looking ahead.

All through the years since Christ was crucified, those who said they believed in Christ had been terribly treated—"persecuted," we call it—because they were Christians. They had been flogged; they had been stoned; they had been torn with iron hooks; they had been roasted and burned to death. Yet, strange as it may seem, in spite of this terrible treatment, more and more people were becoming Christians every day. They believed so strongly in life after death, and they believed that they would be so much happier after death if they died for Christ's sake, that they seemed even glad to suffer and to be killed. But at last the emperor himself put a stop to all these persecutions. This is how it happened.

About the year 300 A.D. Rome had an emperor by the name of Constantine. Constantine was not a Christian. His gods were the old Roman gods. He probably did not put much faith in them, however.

Well, once upon a time Constantine was fighting with an enemy when he dreamed one night that he saw in the sky a flaming cross. Beneath this cross were written the Latin words, "In hoc signo vinces." In English this is, "In this sign thou shalt conquer." Constantine thought this meant that if he carried the Christian cross into battle he would conquer. He thought it would at least be worth while to give the Christian God a trial. So he had his soldiers carry the cross, and he did win the battle. Then immediately he became a Christian himself and asked every one in the Roman Empire to become a Christian also. From that time on, all the Roman emperors who came after Constantine, all except one, were Christians.

To celebrate Constantine's victory the Roman Senate built a triumphal arch in the Forum of Rome and called it the Arch of Constantine. If has three openings; the Arch of Titus has only one.

Constantine's mother was named Helena. She was one of the very first to become a Christian and be baptized. Then she gave up her life to Christian works and built churches at Bethlehem and on the Mount of Olives. It is said that she went to Palestine and found the actual cross on which Christ had been crucified three hundred years before and sent part of it to Rome. When she died she was made a saint, and so she is now called St. Helena.

Constantine built a church over the spot where St. Peter was supposed to have been crucified. Many years later, this church was torn down so that a much larger and grander church to St. Peter might be built there.

But Constantine did not care for Rome. He preferred to live in another city in the Eastern part of the Roman Empire. This city was called Byzantium. So he moved from Rome to Byzantium and made that city his capital. Byzantium was called New Rome, and then the name was changed to Constantine's city. In Greek, the word for "city" is "polis." We see the word used in Anna*polis* and Indiana*polis*. So Constantine's City became Constantinepolis, and then shortened to Constantinople.

Hardly had the Roman Empire become Christian before a quarrel arose between those Christians who believed one thing and those who believed another. The chief thing they quarreled about was whether Christ was equal to God the Father or not equal to Him. Constantine called the two disagreeing sides together at a place called Nicæa to settle the question. There the leaders of each side argued the matter hotly. Finally, it was decided that the Christian Church should believe that God the Son and God the Father were equal. Then they agreed to put what they believed in words. This was called a creed, which means "believe," and because it was made at Nicæa it was known as the Nicene Creed, which many Christians still say every Sunday.

Before the time of Constantine, there were no weekly holidays. Sunday was no different from any other day. People worked or did just the same things on Sunday as they did on other days. Constantine thought Christians should have one day a week for the worship of God—a "holy day," or holiday, as we call it—so he made Sunday the Christian day of rest, a "holy day" such as Saturday was for the Jews.

But although Constantine was head of the Roman Empire, there was another man whom all Christians throughout the world looked to as their spiritual head. This man was the Bishop of Rome. In Latin he was called "papa," which means the same thing in Latin that it does in English, "father." So the bishop of Rome was called "papa," and this became "pope." St Peter was supposed to have been the first Bishop of Rome. For many centuries the pope was the spiritual ruler of all Christians everywhere, no matter in what country they lived.

As now you know what the name of this story means I'm putting it here:

In Hoc Signo Vinces

39

Our Tough Ancestors

BUT Rome with the Roman Empire had had her day. She had risen as high as she could. It was her turn to fall. She had become as large as she ever was to be. It was her turn to be conquered. But you cannot guess what people were to do the conquering and to be next in power.

When I was a boy there was a gang of toughs who lived down by the gashouse and railroad tracks. They were ragged, unwashed, unschooled, but terrible fighters. Their leader was known to us as Mug Mike, and the very mention of him and his gang struck terror to our souls. Every now and then they paid our neighborhood a visit. Once we had offered fight, but with such terrible results that ever after at word of their approach the alarm would be sounded and we would hide indoors.

For ages there had been such a gang of half-civilized toughs living on the northern borders of the Roman Empire. Every now and then they tried to cross over the border into the Roman lands, and the Romans had to be constantly fighting them to keep them back where they belonged. Julius Cæsar had fought with them. So had Marcus Aurelius and so had Constantine. These wild and warlike people were called Teutons and—you may be shocked to hear it, but—they are the ancestors of most of us!

They had light hair and blue eyes; that is, they were what we call blonds. The Greeks and Romans and other people who lived around the Mediterranean Sea had black hair and dark eyes. They were what we call brunettes. If you have light or brown hair, you are probably a Teuton. If you have black hair, you are probably not.

The Teutons were white people, and they were Aryans, but they were uneducated toughs and could neither read nor write.

They wore skins of animals instead of clothes made of cloth. They lived in huts made of wood, sometimes of branches woven together—like a large basket. The women raised vegetables and took care of the cows and horses. The men did the hunting and fighting and blacksmithing. Blacksmithing was very important, for the blacksmith made the swords and spears with which they fought and the tools with which they worked. That is why the name "Smith" was so honored among them.

When the men went to battle they wore the heads of animals they had killed, an ox's head, horns and all, or the head of a wolf or bear or fox. This was to make themselves look fierce and to frighten the enemy.

Teuton warrior.

Bravery was the chief thing the Teuton thought good. A man might lie, he might steal, he might even commit murder, but if he was a brave warrior, he was called a "good" man.

The Teutons did not have a king. They elected their chiefs, and of course they always chose the man who was the bravest and strongest. But he could not make his son ruler after him. So he was more like a president than a king.

The Teutons had an entirely different set of gods from those of Greece and Rome. Their chief god, as you might guess, was the god of war, and they called him Woden. Woden was also the god of the sky. He was like the two Greek gods, Jupiter and Mars, put together. Woden was supposed to live in a wonderful palace in the sky called Valhalla, and many tales are told of the wonderful things he did and of the adventures he had. Wednesday, which was once Wodensday, is named after him. That is why there is a letter "d" in this word, although we don't pronounce it.

After Woden, Thor was the next most important god. He was the god of thunder and lightning. He carried a hammer with which he fought great giants who lived in the far-off cold lands and were called "ice-giants." Thursday, which was once Thorsday, is named after him.

Another god was named Tiu, and from his name we get Tuesday, and another Freya, from whom we get Friday, so that four out of seven of our days are named after Teuton gods, in spite of the fact that we are—most of us—Christians and no longer believe in these gods.

Of the other three days of the week, Sunday and Monday of course are named after the sun and moon, and Saturday is named after a Greek god, Saturn.

From these wild people all fair-haired people to-day are said to be descended—the English, French, German, and such of us whose forefathers are English or French or German.

About the Year 400 A.D. these Teuton toughs were becoming particularly troublesome to the Romans. They began to push their way down into the northern part of the Roman Empire, and after a few years the Romans could hold them back no longer. Two of these Teuton gangs, or tribes, as they were called, went over into Britain, and the Romans who were living there found it wisest to get out, go back to Rome, and leave the country to the Teutons.

These tribes who settled in Britain were known as Angles and Saxons. So the country came to be called the land of the Angles, or, for short, "Angle-land." After the words "Angle-land" were said over for many years, they became "England," which is what we call the country to-day. The people of England are still known by the full name "Anglo-Saxons," and this is the name by which we call everything descended from these old Teuton tribes of Angles and Saxons who settled in Britain about 400 A.D.

Another gang or tribe called the Vandals went into Gaul. Gaul is where France is now. Then they kept on down into Spain, stealing, smashing, and burning like Mug Mike's gang of toughs on Hallowe'en. They crossed over by boats into Africa. They injured or destroyed everything they came upon. So to-day when any one damages or destroys property wickedly, we call him a vandal. If you cut up your desk, tear your books, or scratch names on walls or fences, you, too, are a vandal.

A tribe called the Franks followed the Vandals into Gaul, and there they stayed, giving the name "France" to that country.

The Teutons north of Italy were the Goths. They had a leader by the name of Alaric. He was the "Mug Mike" of the gang of Goths. Alaric and his Goths crossed over the mountains into Italy and robbed or destroyed everything of value they could lay their hands on. They then entered Rome and carried away whatever they wanted, and the Romans could not stop them. But the worst was yet to come.

40

White Toughs and Yellow Toughs Meet the Champions of the World

THE Teutons were wild toughs but they were white.

Farther north of the Teutons and to the east was a tribe of people who were still more savage and fierce. They were called Huns. They lived far off in the forests and wilds way beyond the Teutons, in a part of the country that no one then knew much about.

The Huns were, we think, not white as the Teutons were, but yellow. Even the Teutons themselves, fierce fighters though they were, feared the Huns, and it was chiefly because they were afraid of them and wanted to get away from them as far as they could that the Teutons went over the borders into the Roman Empire. It was much easier to fight the Romans than it was to fight the Huns.

The Huns seemed more like wild beasts than human beings. Their leader was a dreadful creature named Attila. He boasted that nothing ever grew again where his horse had trod. He and his Huns had conquered and laid waste the country all the way from the East almost to Paris. At last the Teutons made a stand against them and fought a great battle at a place not so very far from Paris, a place called Châlons.

The Teutons fought desperately; they fought madly. It was white toughs against yellow toughs, and the Huns were beaten. It was lucky they were beaten, for if they had won, these dreadful wild, yellow people might have conquered and ruled the world. The white toughs were bad enough, but the yellow would have been worse. So the battle of Châlons, 451 A.D., is written in history in capital letters and large figures—CHÂLONS 451.

After Attila and his Huns had been beaten at Châlons they left the Teutons alone, but they then went after the Romans. Turning back they went down into Italy, where there was no one able to stop them. They destroyed everything as they moved on. The people of the country didn't even attempt to fight. They thought the Huns were monsters and simply fled before them. So on to Rome the Huns went.

Now, there was at Rome at this time a Pope named Leo I, which means Lion. Leo, of course, was neither a soldier nor a fighting man, but he and his cardinals and bishops went out from Rome to meet Attila. They were not clad in armor, and none of them carried any weapons with which to fight. The pope and those with him were dressed in gorgeous robes and richly colored garments. It seemed as if they must be slaughtered by Attila and his Huns like lambs before wolves.

But something strange happened when Attila and the pope met; exactly what no one knows. Perhaps Attila was awed by the pomp and splendor of those Christians. Perhaps he feared what Heaven might do to him if he destroyed those holy beings who had come out to meet him as if from heaven. At any rate, he did not destroy them, nor did he enter Rome, but turned about and left Italy, left it for good and all, and he and his Huns returned to the unknown land to the north from which they had come.

Now that the dreaded Attila was out of the way, the Vandals in Africa saw their chance to attack Rome. Attila had barely left Italy before the Vandals crossed over from Africa and sailed up the Tiber to Rome. They captured the city without any difficulty, helped themselves to everything they wanted, and carried away all Rome's treasures.

Poor old Rome! She was at last beaten, beaten for good! She had been the Champion for a great many years. But now all her strength was gone. She was old and weak and no longer able to defend herself against these gangs of toughs. Rome's last emperor had the high-sounding name "Romulus Augustulus," the same name as the first king, Romulus, with the addition of Augustulus, which means the little Augustus. But in spite of his high-sounding name, Romulus Augustulus could do nothing. He was like the little boy living in the marble house on the avenue, the little boy with curls and a velvet suit, whom Mug Mike caught out one day and—you can guess the rest. "Great Cæsar's ghost!" How Cæsar's ghost must have felt!

It was the Year 476 that Rome was beaten. The western half of the empire, of which Rome had been the capital, broke up into pieces, and the pieces were ruled over by Teutons. Like Humpty Dumpty, Rome had had a great fall, and all the king's horses and all the king's men couldn't put it together again. Only the eastern part, of which Constantinople was the capital, still went on. This eastern half was not conquered by the barbarians, and it still kept going for nearly a thousand years longer until—but wait till we come to that time in history.

People speak of this date, 476, as the end of Ancient History. After Ancient History, there was a time over five hundred years long which was known as the Dark Ages—the Night-time of History. The Dark Ages lasted from 476 to about 1000 A.D. These centuries are called the Dark Ages, because during that long time the Teutons, those uneducated toughs who were unable even to read and write, were the chief people in Europe, and they ruled over those who had once been the educated and cultured people.

The Teutons, though such rough toughs, barbarians as they were called, were, strange to say, quick to learn many things from the Romans whom they had conquered. Even before they had conquered Rome, most of the Teutons had already become Christians.

Of course they had to learn the Latin language in order to talk to their subjects. But they changed the Latin a good deal and mixed it with their own language. This mixture of their own language with the Latin at last became Italian. The Teutons who went to Spain in a like way mixed their language with the Latin, and this mixture was Spanish. In France the mixture of the two languages became French.

In Britain, however, the Anglo-Saxons would have nothing to do with the Romans and would not use the Roman language but kept their own language. After a while this language of the Anglo-Saxons was called English. The Anglo-Saxons also kept their own religion, and they worshiped Thor and Woden and their other gods until about one hundred years later, or about 600 A.D.

At that time some English slaves were being sold in the slave-market at Rome. They were very handsome. The pope saw them and asked who they were.

"They are Angles," he was told.

"Angles!" exclaimed he; "they are handsome enough to be 'angels,' and they should certainly be Christians."

So he sent some missionaries to England to convert the English; to change Angles to Angels. So at last the English, too, became Christians.

41

Nightfall

It was 500 o'clock by History Time.

Night was coming on.

The Dark Ages had begun.

At least, that is what people call it now. But people didn't call it so then.

Crazy people don't think they are crazy.

Ignorant people don't think they are ignorant.

So the Dark Ages didn't think they were dark.

The ignorant Teutons were ruling over the pieces of the Western Empire.

They couldn't read; they couldn't write.

They didn't know much except to fight.

They didn't know 'twas dark as night.

At Constantinople, however, a Roman was still ruling over the Eastern Empire. This Roman was named Justinian. Now, up to this time there had been a great many rules or laws by which the people were governed. But there were so many of these rules and they were so mixed up that one law would tell you you could do one thing and another would tell you you couldn't. It was as if your mother said you could stay up till nine o'clock to-night and your father said you must go to bed at eight. It was hard for people to tell, therefore, what one must do and what one must not do.

In order to untangle this snarl, Justinian had a set of laws made for the government of his people, and many of these were so good and so just that they are still the law to-day. If you notice that Justinian begins with "Just," this will help you to remember that he was the one who made *just* laws.

Another thing Justinian did that has lasted to the present time. He built in Constantinople a very beautiful church called Santa Sophia. Though it is no longer a church, it is still standing after all these years and is a beautiful sight to see. Still another thing he did which you could never guess. It had nothing to do with war or law or buildings.

Travelers from the Far East, where China now is, had brought back tales of a wonderful caterpillar that wound itself up with a fine, thin thread over a mile long, and they told stories of how the Chinese unwound this thread and wove it into cloth of the finest and smoothest kind. This thread, as you might guess, was called silk, and the caterpillar that made it was called the silkworm. People in Europe had seen this beautiful silk cloth, but how it was made had been a mystery—a secret. They thought it so wonderfully beautiful that it was supposed to have been made by fairies or elves or even sent down from heaven. Justinian found out about these caterpillars and had men bring these silkworms into Europe so that his people also might make silk cloth and have silk ribbons and fine silk garments, and therefore we give him the honor of starting the manufacture of silk in Europe.

Outside of Justinian's empire the ignorant Teutons were living. It took them nearly a thousand years to learn as much as any school-boy now knows, and the first thing they learned was not reading, nor writing, but the Christian religion.

About the same time that Justinian lived there was a king in France named Clovis. Clovis, of course, was a Teuton and belonged to the tribe called the Franks, which gave the name "France" to that country. Clovis believed in Thor and Woden as all of his people did. Clovis had a wife named Clotilda, whom he loved very dearly. Clotilda, though a Teuton, thought all the fighting and cruelty which her people seemed to like was wrong. She had heard about the religion of Christ, which did not believe in quarreling and fighting, and she thought she would like to be a Christian. So she was baptized. Then she tried to persuade her husband, Clovis, to become a Christian, also.

Clovis was just then going to war—the very thing the Christians preached against. But, just to please his wife, he promised her, if he won the battle, he would become a Christian. He did win, and he kept his word and was baptized and had his soldiers baptized, also. Clovis made Paris his capital, and Paris is still the capital of France.

It was about this same time, also, that a king named Arthur was ruling in England. Many stories and poems have been written about him, which, however, we know are fairy-tales and not history. But although we know these stories are not true, they are, nevertheless, interesting—like those tales that are told about the heroes of the Trojan War.

It was said that there was a sword called Excalibur stuck so fast in a stone that no one could draw it out except the man who should be king of England. All the nobles had tried without success to draw the sword, when one day a young boy named Arthur pulled it out with the greatest ease, and he was accordingly proclaimed king.

King Arthur chose a company of the nobles to rule with him, and as they sat with him at a Round Table, they were known as the Knights of the Round Table. Tennyson, the great English poet, has written in verse an account of all the doings of King Arthur and his knights in a long poem called "The Idylls of the King," which you will have to read yourself, for we must go on to the next story.

42

"Being Good"

WHAT do you mean by "being good"?

The Teutons thought "being good" meant being brave.

The Athenians thought whatever was beautiful was "good."

The Stoics thought "not caring" was "being good."

The Epicureans thought having a good time was "being good."

The martyrs thought "being good" meant suffering and dying for Christ's sake.

Ever since the time of the martyrs, Christians who wanted to be very, very good indeed, went off into the wilderness and lived by themselves. They wished to be far away from other people, so that they could spend all their time praying and thinking holy thoughts. This, they believed was "being good."

One of the strangest of these men who wanted to get away from others was named St. Simeon Stylites. He built for himself a pillar or column fifty feet high, and on the top of it he lived with room only to sit but not to lie down. There on the top he lived for many years, day and night, winter and summer, while the sun shone on him and the rain rained on him, and he never came down at all. He could be reached only by a ladder, which his friends used to bring him food. High up out of the world, he thought he could best lead a holy life. That was his idea of "being good" although we should think such a person simply crazy.

In the course of time, however, men who wanted to lead holy lives, instead of living alone as they had done at first, gathered in groups and built themselves homes. These men were called monks, and the house where they lived was known as a monastery or abbey. The head monk of such an abbey was called an abbot, and he ruled over the other monks like a father over his children, giving them orders and punishing them when he thought they needed it.

In the five hundreds there lived an Italian monk named Benedict. He believed very strongly that one must work if he was to be holy, that work was a necessary part of being holy. He thought, also, that monks should have no money of their own, for Christ had said in the Bible, "If thou wilt be perfect, go and sell that thou hast, and give to the poor." So Benedict started a club or order of monks for those people who would agree to three things:

The first thing they were to agree to was to have no money.

The second thing was to obey.

The third thing was not to marry.

Monks who joined this club were called Benedictines.

Now, you might think there would have been hardly any one who would promise for life three such things as to have no money, to obey the abbot—no matter what he told them to do—and never to marry. Nevertheless, there were a great many men in every country of Europe who did become Benedictines.

Usually the monks lived in little bare rooms like prison cells, and ate their very simple meals together at a single table in a room called the refectory. They prayed at sunrise and sunset, and many times during the day besides, and they even woke up at midnight to say their prayers. But praying was not all they had to do. Work of every kind they were obliged to do, and they did it joyfully, whether the work was scrubbing floors or digging in the garden.

Oftentimes the monastery was situated in a barren or swampy spot on land that had been given the monks because it was no good, or even worse than no good, dangerously unhealthy. But the monks set to work and drained off the water, tilled the soil, and made the waste places bloom like the rose. Then they raised vegetables for their table, fodder for their horses and cattle and sheep. Everything they ate or used or needed, they raised or made.

But they did not only the rougher hand-work; they did fine hand-work, too. Printing had not been invented at this time; all books had to be written by hand, and the monks were the ones who did this. They copied the old books in Latin and Greek. Sometimes one monk would slowly read the book to be copied, and several other monks at one time would copy what he dictated. In this way a number of copies would be made.

Monk writing a manuscript.

The pages of the books were not made of paper but of calfskin or sheepskin, called vellum, and this vellum was much stronger and lasted much longer than paper.

These old books which the monks wrote were called "manuscripts," which means "hand-written." Many of these may now be seen in museums and libraries. Some of these manuscripts have been beautifully hand-printed with loving care and the initial letters and borders ornamented with designs of flowers and vines and birds and pictures in red and gold and other colors. If the monks hadn't done this copying, many of the old books would have been lost and unknown to us.

The monks also kept diaries, writing down from day to day and year to year an account of the important things that happened. These old diaries, or chronicles, as they were called, tell us the history of the times. As there were then no newspapers, if these chronicles had not been written we should not know what went on at that time.

The monks were the best educated people of those days, and they taught others—both young and old—the things they themselves knew. The monasteries were also inns for travelers, for any one who came and asked for lodging was received and given food and a place to sleep, whether he had any money to pay or not.

The monks helped the poor and needy. The sick, too, came to the monastery to be treated and taken care of, so that a monastery was often something like a hospital, too. Many people who had received such help or attention made rich gifts to the monasteries, so they became very wealthy, although the monks could own not so much as a spoon for themselves.

So you see the monks were not merely holy men; they were most useful citizens. They were in many ways more nearly everything that Christ would have wished than perhaps any one large group of men has ever been since. They were really "GOOD FOR SOMETHING."

43

A Camel-Driver

EVERY hundred years is called a century, but a thing that seems a little strange is this—the hundred years from 500 to 600 is called the *sixth* century, not the fifth; the hundred years from 600 to 700 is called the *seventh* century, not the sixth; and so on. Thus 615, 625, 650, and so on are all *seventh* century.

Well, we have now reached the seventh century—the six hundreds, and we are to hear of a man who was to make a change in the whole world. He was neither a Roman nor a Greek nor a Frank nor a Goth nor a Briton. He was neither a king nor a general, but only a—

What do you suppose?

A CAMEL-DRIVER!

and he lived in a little town called Mecca in far-off Arabia. His name was Mohammed. Mohammed went on an errand for a wealthy Arabian lady, and the lady fell in love with him. Although he was a poor camel-driver and only a servant and she was rich, they were married. They lived happily together, and nothing remarkable happened until Mohammed was forty years old.

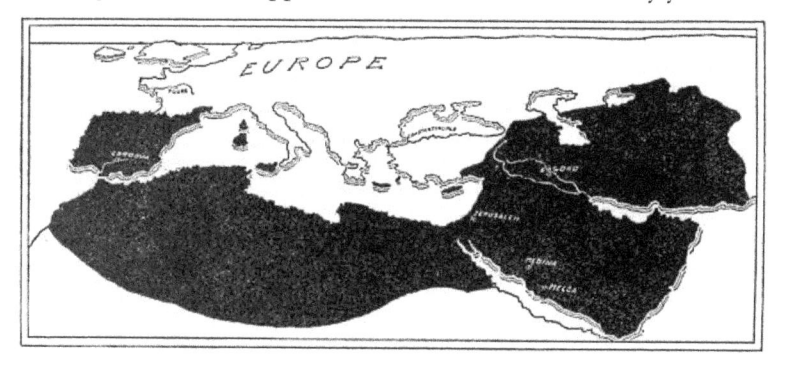

Map of Saracenic empire showing Mecca, Medina, Constantinople, Tours, Cordova, Bagdad, Jerusalem, also Europe.

Mohammed had been in the habit of going out to a cave in the desert to study and think. One day when he visited this cave he had a dream, or a vision, as it is called when such things happen in the daytime when one is awake. In this vision, so Mohammed said, the angel Gabriel had appeared and told him that God, whom the Arabs called Allah, said he must go forth and teach the people a new religion.

So Mohammed went home to his wife and told her what had happened, and she believed his story and became his first follower. Mohammed then went forth as he had been directed and taught his relatives and friends what he said Allah had told him, and they, too, believed what he said and became his followers.

But when he set out to teach others, who were not his friends nor relatives, they simply thought him crazy and perhaps dangerous. So they got together and planned to get rid of him—even kill him if necessary. But he heard what they were planning, and so he packed up all his belongings and, with his wife and those who believed in him, left the city of Mecca and fled to the town of Medina, a little way off. This was in 622—Six-Two-Two—and was called the Hegira, which in the Arabic language means "flight."

I have told you this exact date, for later as you will see this religion, which Mohammed started, grew bigger and bigger, and now at this very day there are one third as many people who believe in Mohammed and the religion he started as there are who believe in Christ and the religion He started; that is, there are now one third as many Mohammedans in the world as there are Christians. The Mohammedans began to count from the Hegira, 622, calling it the Year 1 as the Christians did from the Birth of Christ, as the Greeks did from the First Olympiad, as the Romans did from the Founding of Rome. So the Greeks, the Romans, the Mohammedans, and the Christians each had a different Year 1.

This new religion was called Islam. From time to time Mohammed received messages which he said came from God. Mohammed himself could neither read nor write, and so he had some one else write down these messages on palm-leaves. There were so many of these messages that when they were finally gathered together they made a big book. This book is called the "Koran," and it is the Mohammedan Bible and tells what Mohammedans must do and what they must not do.

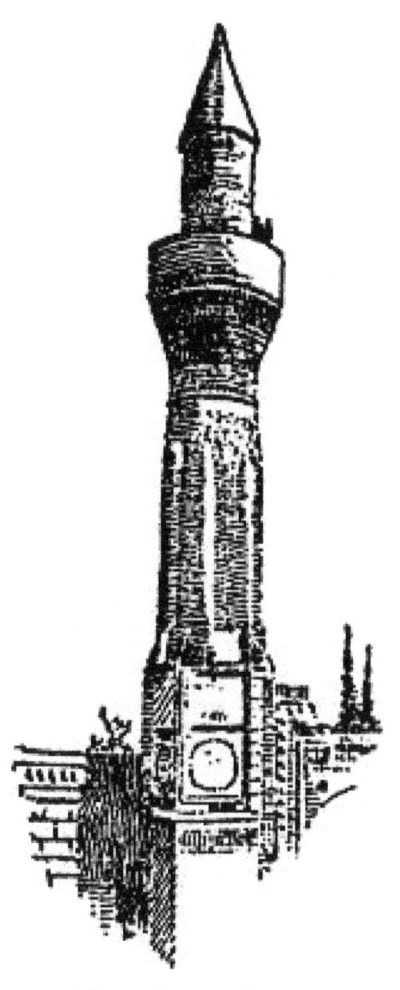

**Muezzin on minaret
calling to prayer.**

As Mohammed was born in Mecca, Mecca is the sacred city of the Mohammedans. To Mecca each good Mohammedan tries to go at least once in his lifetime, no matter how far off from it he may live; and toward Mecca he always faces when he prays. There are always pilgrims, as such travelers are called, wending their way to Mecca. The Mohammedans worship in a temple called a *mosque*, but they also pray five times each day wherever they may be. A man called a muezzin cries out this time for prayer. He goes out on a little balcony on the minaret of the mosque and calls aloud: "Come to prayer; come to prayer. There is but one god and he is Allah." Then, no matter who the Mohammedan is, no matter where he may be or what he may be doing, even though he is in the street or market-place, whether he is working or playing, he faces toward Mecca, falls on his knees, bows his head and hands to the ground and prays. Sometimes he carries a small rug called a prayer-rug with him so that he may have something holy to kneel on when he prays.

Many people liked this new religion. Those who believed in Islam were known as Moslems, and before long, as I have told you, there were as many Moslems or Mohammedans as there were Christians. At first the Moslems tried to persuade others to join simply by talking to them and telling them how fine their religion was, and how much better than what they had already had. But very soon they began to *force* others to become Moslems whether they wanted to or not. Like the highway robber who says, "Money or your life," they gave every one a choice. "Money or your life, or be a Moslem!" This may seem a strange way for people to make others believe their religion, but the Moslems said that Allah wanted all people to be Mohammedans, and didn't want any one who was not.

Mohammedan praying.

Mohammed only lived for ten years after the Hegira; that is, until 632. But those who came after Mohammed went on with the new religion and kept on conquering and making people Mohammedans with the sword.

The new leaders and rulers of the Mohammedans were called caliphs. The second caliph was named Omar. Omar went on to Jerusalem and built a Mohammedan mosque in the place where the temple of Solomon had stood. This mosque which Omar built still stands to-day in the same place in Jerusalem.

The Arabs, or Saracens, as they are also called, kept on northward toward Europe and conquered and converted every one to Islam as they went along. Those they could not convert they put to death. At last they reached the City of Constantine, Constantinople, where the people were Christians. This was the gateway from Asia to Europe, and the Arabs tried to get by. But the Christians poured down red-hot tar and burning oil from the walls of the city, and the Moslems had to stop. They could get no farther. Again and again the Moslems tried to capture the city, but without success. Finally, they had to give up trying to get into Europe by this way.

Then they tried the opposite direction from Mecca, the long, long, way round to Europe. Across Egypt they went with little difficulty, converting every one to Islam. Further on still they kept going, along the coast of Africa, conquering everything before them until they reached the ocean. Then they turned north, took boats, and crossed over the Strait of Gibraltar and marched on up into Spain. Farther and farther on they went up into France. It seemed as if they would soon conquer all of Europe and make the whole civilized world Mohammedan. But finally, near the town of Tours in France, they met their match. The king of France had a right-hand man named Charles who had been nicknamed Charles the Hammer because he could strike such terrific blows. Charles was called Mayor of the Palace, which merely meant that he was the chief servant of the king, but he was much more able than the king himself. In fact, the king was of very little account.

Charles the Hammer, with his French soldiers, went forth to meet the Moslems, and near Tours he beat them so badly that they never attempted to go farther. So Europe at last was saved from Islam and the Saracens. This battle of Tours was in 732, just 110 years from the time of the Hegira. The Mohammedan religion had only been started 110 years before; yet in this short time the Mohammedans had conquered and converted the whole of the country bordering the Mediterranean from Constantinople all the way round the southern edge and as far up into France as Tours. The people south and east of the Mediterranean are still Mohammedans to-day.

44

Perhaps you have read the "Arabian Nights." This is the story of

Arabian Days

THE Moslems had tried to get into Europe by the front gate and failed.

They had then tried the back gate and failed.

Burning tar and oil had stopped them at Constantinople.

Charles the Hammer had stopped them at Tours.

So Europe was saved from the Moslems and from the Moslem religion of Islam. Yet we may wonder what Europe would have been like if the Moslem Arabs had conquered, for the Arabs were in many ways a great people, and we have learned many things from them. Here are some of the things.

The Phenicians invented our alphabet, but the Arabs invented the figures which we use to-day in arithmetic. 1, 2, 3, 4, and so on are called Arabic figures. The Romans used letters instead of figures, V stood for 5, X for 10, C for 100, M for 1000, and so on. Think how difficult it must have been for a Roman boy to add such numbers as

　IV

　XII

+ MC

　CXII

　VII

　―――

They could not be added up in columns as we do. And when you think of multiplying and dividing with Roman numbers, it seems almost impossible, for example:

$$\text{MCMCXVII} \\ \times \text{XIX}$$

Occasionally you may see Roman figures still used—on clock-faces, for instance—but all the figures that you use every day in your arithmetic and that your father uses at the bank or store or office are Arabic figures.

Another thing:

The Arabs built many beautiful buildings; but these buildings look quite different from those that the Greeks and Romans and Christians built. The doors and window-openings, instead of being square or round, were usually horseshoe-shaped. On the top of their mosques they liked to put domes shaped something like an onion, and at the corners they put tall spires or minarets from which the muezzin could call aloud the hour for prayer. They covered the walls of their buildings with beautiful mosaics and designs. The Mohammedans, however, were very careful that these designs were not copies of anything in nature, for they had a commandment in the "Koran" something like the Christian commandment, "Thou shalt not make ... any likeness of anything that is in heaven above, or that is in the earth beneath, or that is in the water under the earth." Because of this commandment they never made drawings or pictures of any living thing, neither of plants nor flowers nor animals. They thought they would be breaking the commandment if they did. So they made designs out of lines and curves without copying anything from nature. These designs were called Arabesques, and although they were not like anything in nature, they were often very beautiful.

Still another thing:

In Arabia there grew a little bush on which were small berries with seeds inside. The sheep seemed to like these berries and, when they ate them, became very lively. The Arabs themselves tried eating the seeds of these berries with the same effect. Then they made a drink out of these seeds by roasting and grinding them and boiling them in water. This was coffee—which the Arabs had discovered and which is now drunk all over the world.

Still another thing:

The Arabs found out that when the juice of grapes or other fruits or grains spoiled, or fermented, as we call it, a peculiar change took place. Any one who drank this changed juice became greatly excited and even crazy. They called the new thing to which these juices changed, "alcohol," and they were so much afraid of it and what it did to those who drank it that they forbade every Mohammedan to drink anything containing alcohol, such as wine, beer, or whisky. So the Moslems not only discovered alcohol, but, believing it to be poison, they prohibited its use. They have been prohibitionists, therefore, for more than a thousand years, while all the rest of the world has been using wine and beer and other drinks containing alcohol until the United States only recently forbade their use in this country.

Still another thing:

Woolen cloth which people used for clothes was made from the hair of sheep or goats. As it took the hair of a great many such animals to make a very little cloth, woolen cloth was expensive. The Arabs found out a way of making cloth from a plant, the cotton plant, which of course was much cheaper. Then in order to decorate the cloth and make it pretty and attractive, they stamped the plain cloth with wooden blocks shaped in different forms and dipped in color. This printed cloth that the Arabs had invented was called calico.

Still another thing:

The Arabs made swords and knives of such wonderful steel that the blades could be bent double without breaking. The blades were said to be so keen they could cut through the finest hair if floated on water, a thing that only the sharpest razor will do, and yet at the same time so strong that they could cut through a bar of steel. Such swords were made in the East at a place called Damascus, which is in Arabia, and in the West at a place called Toledo, which is in Spain; and these swords and knives were known as Damascus or Toledo blades. Unfortunately, no one now knows the Arab's secret for making such marvelous blades. It is what is called a lost art.

Near where Babylon once was the Arabs built a city named Bagdad. You have heard of it if you have ever read any of the "Arabian Nights," for most of these stories were told about Bagdad. It was the eastern capital of the Moslems. There at Bagdad the Arabs built a great school that was famous for many, many years. At Cordova in Spain was the western capital of the Moslems, and there they built another great school.

Mohammedan veiled woman standing by Saracenic ornamented arch.

I might tell you many other things these people did—how they invented the game of chess, of all games the one that needs the most thought; how they made clocks with pendulums to keep time—people had no real clocks before; how they started wonderful libraries of books; and so on—but this is enough for the present to show you what intelligent people they were.

The Arabs were not Aryans. They belonged to the Semite family, the same family to which the Phenicians and Jews belong. The Arabs were as clever as their cousins the Phenicians, who, you remember, were very clever, but they were also as religious as their other cousins the Jews, who, you remember, were very religious.

But the Moslems had peculiar ideas about women. They thought it was immodest for a woman to show her face to men, and so every woman had to wear a thick veil which hid her face all except her eyes whenever she went out where there were men. With such a veil she could see but not be seen.

But here are their two most peculiar ideas: they believed women were only fit to be slaves to the men, and they thought that a man might have as many wives as he wished all at one time!

So we may wonder, then, what Europe would really have been like if the Moslems had conquered all the rest of the world at that time—if they had left no country Christian—*if we were all of us Moslems to-day instead of Christians!*

45

A Light in the Dark Ages

EUROPE had been "dark" for three hundred years. You know what I mean.

There were not enough "bright" people to make it light. Ignorant Teutons had been ruling over the pieces of the old Roman Empire.

The Arabs were bright, but they were not in Europe.

But in 800 there was a very "bright light"—a man—a king—who by his might and power was able to join the pieces of Europe together once again to form a new Roman Empire. He was not a Roman, however, but a Teuton, as you can tell from his name, which was Charles. He was a grandson of that Charles the Hammer who had stopped the Moslems at Tours, and he was called by the French name Charlemagne, which means Charles the Great.

Charlemagne at first was king of France alone, but he was not satisfied to be king of that country only, and so he soon conquered the countries on each side of him, parts of Spain and Germany. Then he moved the capital of his empire from Paris to a place in Germany called Aix-la-Chapelle, which was more convenient than Paris to this larger empire, and besides at Aix-la-Chapelle there were warm springs which made fine baths, and Charlemagne was very fond of bathing and was a fine swimmer.

Italy was then ruled over by the pope. But the pope was having a good deal of trouble with some tribes in the north of Italy, and he asked Charlemagne if he wouldn't come down and conquer them. Charlemagne was quite ready and willing to help the pope, so he went over into Italy and easily settled those troublesome tribes. The pope was grateful to Charlemagne for this and wished to reward him.

Now, Christians everywhere used to make trips to Rome in order to pray at the great Church of St. Peter, which had been built over the spot where St. Peter had been crucified. Well, at Christmas-time in the Year 800 Charlemagne paid such a visit to Rome. On Christmas day he went to the Church of St. Peter and was praying at the altar when suddenly the pope came forward and put a crown on his head. The pope then hailed him "Emperor," and as the pope at that time could make kings and emperors, Charlemagne became emperor of Italy added to the other countries over which he already ruled. These countries together were really about the same as the western part of the old Roman Empire. So Charlemagne's empire was now like a new Roman Empire, but with this big difference: it was ruled over not by a Roman, but by a Teuton.

Charlemagne started out an ignorant uneducated Teuton, but he was not like most other Teutons who didn't know they were ignorant and didn't care whether they were ignorant or not. He was anxious to know everything there was to be known. He wanted to be able to do everything any one could do.

In those days when the Teutons were ruling, few people had any education, and hardly any one could read or write. Charlemagne wanted an education, but there was no one in his own country who knew enough or was able to teach him. In England, however, there was a very learned monk named Alcuin. He knew more than any one of that time, and so Charlemagne invited Alcuin to come over from England and teach him and his people. Alcuin taught Charles about the sciences; he taught him Latin and Greek poetry; he taught him the wisdom of the Greek philosophers.

Charlemagne learned all these things very easily, but when it came to the simple matter of learning to read and write he found this too hard. He did learn to read a little, but he seemed unable to learn to write. It is said that he slept with his writing-pad under his pillow and practised whenever he awoke. And yet he never learned to write anything more than his name. He did not begin to study until he was a grown man, but he kept on studying all the rest of his life. Except for reading and writing, he became, next to his teacher, Alcuin, the best-educated man in Europe.

In spite of the fact that Charlemagne's daughters were princesses, he had them taught how to weave and sew and make clothes and cook just as if they had to earn their own living.

Although Charlemagne was such a rich and powerful monarch and could have everything he wanted, he preferred to eat plain food and dress in plain clothes. He did not like all the finery that those about him loved. One day, just to make his nobles see how ridiculously dressed they were in silks and satins, he took them out hunting in the woods while a storm was going on, so that he could laugh at them. That was his idea of a good joke. You can imagine how their silk and satin robes looked after being soaked with rain, covered with mud, and torn by briers. Charlemagne thought it was very funny.

But although his tastes were simple in matters of dress, he made his home a magnificent palace. He furnished it with gold and silver tables and chairs and other gorgeous furniture. He built in it swimming-pools and a wonderful library and a theater and surrounded it with beautiful gardens.

At this time and all through the Dark Ages people had a strange way of finding out whether a person had stolen or committed a murder or any other crime. The person suspected was not taken into court and tried before a judge and a jury to see whether he was telling the truth and had done the thing or not. Instead he was made to carry a red-hot iron for ten steps, or to dip his arm into boiling water, or to walk over red-hot coals. If he was not guilty it was thought no harm would come to him, or if he were burned it was thought that the burn would heal right away. This was called *trial by ordeal*. It probably started from the story told in the Bible of Shadrach, Meshech, and Abednego, who, you remember, in the time of Nebuchadnezzar, had walked through the fiery furnace unharmed because they had done no wrong. Strange to say, though Charlemagne was so intelligent, he believed in the trial by ordeal. To-day we have no such cruel and unfair way of finding out whether one is guilty or not. Yet we say of a person who has a lot of trouble that seems to be a test of his character, "He is going through an ordeal."

While Charlemagne was living, there was a caliph in far-off Bagdad named Haroun, which is the Moslem spelling of Aaron. You may have heard of him if you have read any of the "Arabian Nights," for the "Arabian Night" stories were written at this time, and Haroun is described in them. Although Haroun was a Mohammedan, not a Christian, and though he was ruler of an empire that hated the Christians, nevertheless he admired Charlemagne very much. To show how much he thought of him, he sent him valuable presents; among other things, a clock which struck the hours, which you remember, was an invention of the Arabs. This was a great curiosity, for there were then no clocks in Europe. People had to tell time by the shadow the sun cast on a sun-dial, or else by the amount of water or sand that dripped or ran out from one jar to another.

Haroun was a very wise and good ruler over the Moslems, and so he came to be called "al Rashid," which means "the Just." Do you remember what Greek was also called "the Just"?[3] Haroun used to disguise himself as a workman and go about among his people. He would talk with those he met along the street and in the market-place, trying to find out how they felt about his government and about things in general. He found they would talk freely to him when dressed in old clothes, for then they did not know who he was but thought him a fellow-workman. In this way, Haroun learned a great deal about his people's troubles and what they liked or didn't like about his rule. Then he would go back to his palace and give orders to have rules and laws made to correct anything that seemed wrong or unjust.

[3] Aristides.

After Charlemagne died there was no one great enough or strong enough to hold the new Roman Empire together, and once again it broke up into small pieces, and "all the king's horses and all the king's men could not put it together again."

46

Getting a Start

I ONCE knew a boy who had a red birthmark on his arm. It was just the shape of England on the map, and he used to call it "My England."

England is just a little island.

It was quite an unimportant little island in 900 A.D.

England is still just a little island.

But it is now the most important island in the world!

About one hundred years after Charles the Great—that is, 900—there was a king of England named Alfred. When Alfred was a boy he had a hard time learning to read, for he did not like to study. In those days many of the hand-written books made by the monks had pretty drawings and letters made in bright colors and even in gold. One day Alfred's mother showed such a book to her children and promised to give it to the one who could read it first. That was a game. Alfred wanted to win the book, and so, for the first time in his life, he really tried. He studied so hard that in a very short time he had learned to read before his brothers and so he won the book.

When Alfred grew up, England was being troubled by pirates. These pirates were cousins of the English—a tribe of Teutons called Danes. The English had long ago become Christians and civilized, but their cousins, the Danes, were still rough and wild. They came over from their own country across the water, landed on the coast of England, robbed the towns and villages, and then sailed back to their homes, carrying off everything valuable they could lay their hands on—like bad boys who climb a farmer's fence and steal apples from his orchard. At last the Danes became so bold that they didn't even run away after robbing the country; they were like the bad boys who stick out their tongues and throw stones at the farmer who comes after them. The king's armies went out to punish these pirates, but, instead of beating, they were beaten. It began to look as if these Danes, who were able to do pretty much as they pleased, might conquer England and rule over the English.

Once when things looked pretty black for England, King Alfred was without an army. Alone, ragged, tired out, and hungry, he came to the hut of a shepherd and asked for something to eat. The shepherd's wife was baking some cakes by the fire, and she told Alfred he should have one if he watched them while she went out to milk the cow. Alfred sat down by the fire, but in thinking about what he could do to beat the Danes he forgot all about the cakes, and when the shepherd's wife returned they were all burned. Thereupon she scolded him roundly and drove him off, not knowing that it was her king that she was treating in this way, for he never told her who he was.

Alfred decided that the best way to fight the Danes was not on land but on the water, and so he set to work to build boats bigger and better than those the Danes had. After a while he had something of a fleet, and the boats he built were bigger than those of the Danes, but they were so big that they could not go into shallow water without running aground. The Danes' boats, on account of their small size, could go safely close in to shore. In deep water, however, Alfred's fleet was very strong and powerful. This was the first navy that England ever had. England's navy is now the largest in the world, and Alfred the Great was the one who started it more than a thousand years ago.

After fighting with the Danes for many years, Alfred finally thought it best to make an agreement with them and give them a part of England to live in if they would promise to stop stealing and live peaceably. So the Danes did agree to this, and they settled down peaceably on the land that Alfred gave them—and then became Christians. After that there was no further trouble.

Alfred made very strict laws and severely punished those who did wrong. Indeed, it is said that the people of England were so careful to obey the law in his reign that one might leave gold by the roadside, and no one would steal it.

Alfred also brought over learned men from Europe to show his people how to make things and to teach the boys and girls and the older people how to read and write. He is also said to have started a school that is now one of the greatest places of learning in the world, a university called Oxford that is now more than a thousand years old.

But Alfred not only built a navy and made wise laws and started schools and colleges which the English had not had before; he did many other useful things, besides.

He invented, for instance, a way of telling time by a burning candle. You have heard how wonderful the clock, that which Haroun-al-Rashid sent to Charlemagne one hundred years before was thought to be. Although striking clocks are, of course, very common nowadays, it was an extraordinary thing then when there were no clocks nor watches at all in England. Alfred found out how fast candles burned down and marked lines around them at different heights—just the distance apart that they burned in one hour. These were called time-candles.

Candles were also used for lighting, but when they were carried outdoors they were very likely to be blown out by the wind. So Alfred put the candle inside of a little box, and in order that the light might shine through the box, he made sides of very thin pieces of cow's-horn, for glass then was very scarce. This box with horn sides was called a horn lamp or "lamphorn," and after a while this word when said rapidly became "lanthorn," and finally "lantern," which we still call such a thing to-day, although horn is, of course, no longer used, but glass. This is one explanation of the word as the old spelling was "lanthorn," but it seems more likely that lantern came from the Latin word "lanterna."

Such inventions may seem very small and unimportant, and they are when you think of the marvelous inventions and wonderful machines that are made by the thousands nowadays. These inventions of Alfred were no more than the household ideas for which some magazines now offer only a dollar apiece. But I have told you about them just to show you how ignorant and almost barbarian the English, as well as other Teuton tribes of Europe, were in those days. How much superior were the Arab thinkers with their striking clocks. The English were just "getting a start."

47

The End of the World

WHAT would you do if you knew the world was coming to an end next week, or even next year?

The people who lived in the tenth century thought the Bible said[4] something that meant that the world was coming to an end in the Year 1000—which was called the millennium from the Latin word meaning a thousand years.

[4] Book of Revelations, chapter xx.

Some people were glad that the world was coming to an end. They were so poor and miserable and unhappy here that they were anxious to go to heaven, where everything would be fine and lovely—if they had been good here. So they were particularly good and did everything they could to earn a place for themselves in heaven when this old world should end.

Others were not so anxious to have the world come to an end. But, they thought, if it were coming to an end so soon, they might as well hurry up and enjoy themselves here while they still had a chance.

Well, the Year 1000 came, and nothing happened. At first people simply thought that a mistake had been made in counting the years—that there had not really been one thousand years since Christ's birth. The years went by, and still people waited for the end. They re-read their Bibles and thought perhaps it meant a thousand years after Christ's *death*, instead of his birth. As time went on, without any change, they began to think the end was delayed for some reason they could not explain. But it was not for many years after the millennium that people came at last to realize that the world was not going to stop after all.

Every once in a while some one who thinks he knows more than others says the end of the world is not far off, but we may be quite sure that the world will keep on going and that it will keep on going long after we have all grown up and died and our children have done the same.

At this time, when people were looking for the end of the world there was in the north of Europe a tribe of Teutons who were not Christians and knew and cared nothing about what the Bible said as to the end of the world. They belonged to the same family as the Danes who had come to England in the time of King Alfred. They were called Norsemen or Vikings. They were bold seafaring men, even more hardy and unafraid than the Phenician sailors of old. Their boats were painted black and had prows carved with figures of sea-monsters or dragons. They sailed the northern seas and went farther westward toward the setting sun than any sailors had ever gone. They had discovered Iceland and Greenland, and at last under their chief who was named Leif Ericson they reached the shores of America. So about the same year that the Christians in Europe were expecting the end of the world—the Year 1000—the Vikings had gone to what they thought was "the end of the world."

They called the new country Vineland or Wineland, because they found grapes, from which wine is made, growing there. They did not go far on shore, however, and they thought this new land was only another small island. They had no idea it was a new world. But it was too far away from their own country, and they found wild savages there who made it so uncomfortable for them that they sailed back home leaving the country for good. The Vikings did nothing more about their discovery, and people forgot all about this new country until nearly five hundred years later.

48

Real Castles

YOU may think that castles belong only in fairy-tales of princes and princesses.

But about the Year 1000 there were castles almost everywhere over Europe, and they were not fairy-castles but real ones with real people in them.

After the downfall of Rome in 476, the Roman Empire was broken to pieces like a cut-up puzzle-map, and people built castles on the pieces, and they kept on building castles up to the fourteen hundreds. And this is why and how people built them and why they at last stopped building them.

Whenever any ruler, whether he was a king or only a prince, conquered another ruler, he gave to his generals, who had fought with him and helped him to win, pieces of the conquered land as a reward instead of paying them in money. The generals in turn gave pieces of their land to the chief men who had been under them and helped them in battle. These men who were given land were called lords or nobles, and each lord was called a vassal of him who gave the land. Each vassal had to promise to fight with his lord whenever he was needed. He could not make this promise lightly in an offhand way, however. He had to do it formally so that it would seem more binding. So the vassal had to kneel in front of his lord, place his folded hands between the folded hands of his lord, and make the solemn promise to fight when called upon. This was called "doing homage." Then once a year, at least, thereafter, he had to make the same promise over again. This method of giving away land was known as the Feudal System.

Castle, drawbridge, moat and knights.

Each of these lords or nobles then built himself a castle on the land that was given him, and there he lived like a little king with all his work-people about him. The castle was not only his home, but it had to be a fort as well to protect him from other lords who might try to take his castle away from him. So he usually placed it on the top of a hill or a cliff, so that the enemy could not reach it easily, if at all. It had great stone walls often ten feet or more thick. Surrounding the walls there was usually a ditch called a moat filled with water to make it more difficult for an enemy to get into the castle.

In times of peace when there was no fighting the men farmed the land outside of the castle; but when there was war between lords, all the people went inside the castle walls, carrying all the food and cattle and everything else they had, so that they could live there for months or even years while the fighting was going on. A castle, therefore, had to be very large to hold so many people and animals for so long a time, and often it was really like a walled town.

Inside the walls of the castle were many smaller buildings to house the people and animals and for cooking and storing the food. There might even be a church or chapel. The chief building was, of course, the house of the lord himself and this was called the *keep*.

The main room of the keep was the hall, which was like a very large living-room and dining-room combined. Here meals were served at tables which were simply long and wide boards placed on something to hold them up. These boards were taken down and put away after the meal was over. That is where we get the names "boarding" and "boarding-house." There were no forks nor spoons nor plates nor saucers nor napkins. Every one ate with his fingers and licked them or wiped them on his clothes. Table manners were more like *stable* manners. The bones and scraps they threw on the floor or to the dogs, who were allowed in the room. Itchy-scratchy! At the end of the meal a large bowl of water and towels were brought in so that those who wished might wash their hands.

After dinner the household was entertained during the long evenings with songs and stories by men called minstrels, who played and sang and amused the company.

Shut up within the castle walls, it seemed as if the lord and his people would be absolutely safe against any attacks of his enemies. In the first place, any enemy would have had to cross the moat or ditch which surrounded the castle. Across this moat there was a drawbridge to the entrance or gate of the castle. In the entrance itself was an iron gate called a portcullis, which was usually raised like a window to allow people to pass. In time of war the drawbridge was raised. But in case an enemy was seen approaching and there was no time to raise the drawbridge, this portcullis could be dropped at a moment's notice. When the drawbridge was raised there was no way of getting into the castle except by crossing the moat filled with water. Any one trying to do this would have had stones or melted tar thrown down on him. Instead of windows in the wall of the castle there were only long slits through which the fighters could shoot arrows at the enemy. At the same time, it was very difficult for any one on the outside to hit the small crack-like opening with an arrow.

And yet attacks *were* made on castles. Sometimes the enemy built a tall wooden tower on wheels. This they would roll up as closely as they could get to the walls, and from its top shoot directly over into the castle.

Sometimes they built tunnels from the outside right under the ground, under the moat, and under the castle walls into the castle itself.

Sometimes they built huge machines called battering-rams, and with these they battered down the walls.

Sometimes they used machines like great slingshots to throw stones over the walls. Of course there were no cannons nor cannon-balls nor guns nor gunpowder then.

The lord and his family were the society people; all the others were little better than slaves. In times of peace most of the common people lived outside the castle walls on the land called the *manor*. The lord gave them just as little as he could and took from them just as much as he could. He had to feed and take some care of them so that they could fight for him and serve him, just as he had to feed and take care of his horses that carried him to battle, and the cattle that provided him with milk and meat. But he didn't treat them as well as he did his domestic animals. The common people had to give their time and labor and a large part of the crops they raised to the lord. They themselves lived in miserable huts more like cow-sheds, with only one room, and that had a dirt floor. Above this was perhaps a loft reached by a ladder where they went to bed. But bed was usually only a bundle of straw, and they slept in the clothes they wore during the day.

These work-people were called serfs. Sometimes a serf could stand this kind of life no longer, and he would run away. If he was not caught within a year and a day, he was a free man. But if he was caught before the year and a day were up, the lord might whip him, brand him with hot irons, or even cut off his hands. Indeed, a lord could do almost anything he wished with his serfs—except kill them, or sell them.

So what do you think of the Feudal System?

49

Knights and Days of Chivalry

THOSE *years* in history which I have been telling you about are known as the *days* of chivalry—which means the times of ladies and gentlemen. The lord and his family were the gentlemen and the ladies. All the other people, by far the greater number, were just common people.

There were no schools for these common people. Little was done for them. They were taught to work and nothing else. The sons of a lord of a castle, however, were very carefully taught. But even they were taught only two things, how to be gentlemen and how to fight. Reading and writing were thought of no importance; in fact, it was usually considered a waste of time to learn such things.

And this is the way the son of a lord was brought up. He stayed with his mother until he was seven years old. When he reached the age of seven he was called a page; and for the next seven years—that is, until he was fourteen, he remained a page. During the time he was a page his chief business was to wait on the ladies of the castle. He ran their errands, carried their messages, waited on table, etc. He also learned to ride a horse and to be brave and courteous.

When he was fourteen years old he became a squire and remained a squire for the next seven years; that is, until he was twenty-one. During the time he was a squire he waited on the men, as he had waited on the ladies when he was a page. He attended to the men's horses, went to battle with them, led an extra horse, and carried another spear or lance, in case these should be needed.

When he was twenty-one years old, if he had been a good squire and had learned the lessons that he was taught, he then became a knight. Becoming a knight was an important ceremony like graduating exercises, for the grown boy was now to take up the business of a man.

To get ready for this ceremony, first, he bathed. This may not seem worth mentioning, but in those days one very rarely took a bath, sometimes not for years. He was then dressed in new clothes. Thus washed and dressed, he prayed all night long in the church. When day came he appeared before all the people and solemnly swore always to do and to be certain things:

To be brave and good;
To fight for the Christian religion;
To protect the weak;
To honor women.

These were his vows. A white leather belt was then put on him and gold spurs fastened on his boots. After this had been done he knelt, and his lord struck him over the shoulders with the flat side of a sword, saying as he did so, "I dub thee knight."

A knight went into battle covered with a suit of armor made of iron rings or steel plates like fish-scales, and with a helmet or hood of iron. This suit protected him from the arrows and lances of the enemy. Of course if they had had any shot or shell, armor would have been no use at all, but they had no such things then.

Knights were so completely covered by their armor that when sides became mixed up in fighting, they could not tell one another apart. It was impossible to know which were friends and which were enemies.

So the knights wore, on the outside of the coat that went over their armor, a design of an animal, such as a lion, or of a plant or a rose or a cross or some ornament, and this design was known as a coat of arms. Perhaps your father may use a coat of arms on his letter-paper to-day, and if so he has inherited it from some great-great-grandparent who was a knight.

A knight, as I told you, was first of all taught to be a gentleman, and so we still speak of one who has good manners and is courteous, especially to ladies, as knightly or chivalrous. When a knight came into the presence of a lady he took off his helmet. It meant, "You are my friend, and so I do not need my helmet." That is why gentlemen raise their hats nowadays when they meet ladies.

But the most important thing the knights had to learn was to fight. Even their games were play fights.

Each country and each age has had its own games or sports in which it has taken special delight. The Greeks had their Olympic Games. The Romans had their chariot-races and gladiatorial contests. We have football and baseball. But the chief sport of the knights was a kind of sham battle called the tournament.

Lady with falcon.

The tournament was held in a field known as the *lists*. Large crowds with banners flying and trumpets blowing would gather around the lists to watch the sham fight, as crowds nowadays flock to a big football game waving pennants and tooting horns. The knights on horseback took their places at opposite ends of the lists. They carried lances, the points of which were covered so that they would not make a wound. At a given signal, they rushed toward the center of the field and tried with their lances to throw each other off their horses. The winner who succeeded in throwing the other knights was presented with a ribbon or a keepsake by one of the ladies, and a knight thought as much of this trophy of victory as the winner of a cup in a tennis tournament nowadays.

Knights were very fond of hunting with dogs. But they also hunted with a trained bird called a falcon, and both lords and ladies delighted in this sport.

The falcon was trained like a hunting-dog to catch other birds, such as wild ducks and pigeons and also small animals. The falcon was chained to the wrist of the lord or lady, and its head was covered with a hood as it was carried out to hunt. When a bird was seen the hood was removed, and the falcon, which was very swift, would swoop upon its prey and capture it. Thereupon the hunter would come up, take the captured animal, and put the hood on the falcon again. The men, however, usually preferred hunting the wild boar, which was a kind of pig with sharp tusks, for this was more dangerous and therefore supposed to be more of a man's sport.

50

A Pirate's *Great* Grandson

WHEN Alfred was king the Danes had raided England.

At the same time their cousins the Norsemen had raided the coast of France.

King Alfred at last had to give the Danes a part of the English coast, and they then settled down and became Christians.

The French king likewise did the same thing. In order to save himself from further raids, he gave the Norsemen a part of the French coast. Then the Norsemen, as the Danes had done, settled down and became Christians.

These Norsemen who raided France were led by a very bold and brave pirate named Rollo. In return for this gift of land Rollo was supposed to do homage by kissing the king's foot. But Rollo thought it beneath him to kneel and kiss the king's foot, so he told one of his men to do it for him. His man did as he was told, but he didn't like to do it, either, and so as he kissed the king's foot he raised it so high that he tipped his Majesty over backward.

That part of France which was given the Norsemen came to be called Normandy, and it is so called to-day, and the people were known thereafter as Normans.

In 1066 there was a very powerful duke ruling over Normandy. His name was William, and he was descended from Rollo the pirate. Perhaps your name may be William. Perhaps you may even be descended from this William.

William was strong in body, strong in will, and strong in rule over his people. He could shoot an arrow farther, straighter, and with more deadly effect than any of his knights. No one else was strong enough even to bend the bow he used.

William and his people had become Christians, but according to their idea the Christian God was more like their old god Woden under a new name. William believed that "might made right," for he was descended from a pirate, and he still thought and acted like a pirate. So whatever he wanted he went after and took, even though he was supposed to be a Christian.

Now, William was only a duke, not a king, and he wanted to be a king. In fact, he thought he would like to be king of England, which was just across the channel from his own dukedom.

It so happened that a young English prince named Harold was shipwrecked on the coast of Normandy and was found and brought before William. Now, it seemed likely that some day Harold would be king of England, and William thought this a good chance to get England for himself. So before he would let Harold leave, he made the young man promise that when his turn came to be king he would give him England just as if that country were a horse or a suit of armor that could be given away. Then, in order that this promise should be solemnly binding, William made Harold place his hand on the altar and swear, just as people place a hand on the Bible nowadays, when they take an oath. After Harold had sworn on the altar, William had the top lifted and showed Harold that below it were the bones of some of the Christian saints. Swearing on the bones of a saint was the most solemn kind of an oath one could possibly take. It was thought one would not dare to break such an oath for fear of the wrath of God.

Then Harold returned to England. But when the time came that he should be king the people naturally would not let him give England to William. Besides that, Harold said that such an oath, which he had taken against his will, an oath which had been forced on him by a trick, was not binding. So Harold became king.

When William heard that Harold had been made king, he was very angry. He said that he had been cheated and that Harold had broken his oath. So at once he got ready an army and sailed over to take the country away from Harold.

As William landed from his boat he stumbled and fell headlong on the shore. All his soldiers were shocked and greatly worried by this, for they thought it very bad luck—a bad omen, the Greeks would have called it. But William was quick-witted, and as he fell he grabbed up some of the earth in both hands. Then, rising, he made believe he had fallen on purpose and, lifting his hands in the air, exclaimed that he had taken up the ground as a sign that he was going to have *all* the land of England. This changed the bad omen into good luck.

The battle started, and the English fought furiously to defend themselves against these foreigners who were trying to take their country away from them. Indeed, they had almost won the battle when William gave an order to his men to pretend they were running away. The English then followed, wildly rejoicing, and running pell-mell after the Normans. Just as soon, however, as the English were scattered and in disorder, William gave another signal, and his men faced about quickly. The English were taken by surprise, and before they could get into fighting order again, they were defeated, and Harold, their king, was shot through the eye and killed. This was the battle of Hastings, one of the most famous battles in English History.

Harold had put up a brave fight. But luck was against him. Only a few days before this, he had had to fight a battle with his own brother, who in a traitorous way had got together an army against him. We are sorry for Harold, and yet it was probably better for England that things turned out as they did—yet who can tell?

William marched on to London and had himself crowned king on Christmas day, 1066. Ever since then he has been known as William the Conqueror, and the event is called the Norman Conquest. After this England had a new line of kings—a Norman family and a pirate family—to rule over her.

William divided England up among his nobles as if it were a pie, and gave each a share in the feudal way. They had to do homage to him as his vassals and promise to fight for him and to do as he said. Each of William's nobles built a castle on the property he was given. William himself built a castle in London by the Thames River. On the same spot Julius Cæsar had built a fort, but it had disappeared; and Alfred the Great had built a castle there, but it, too, had disappeared. But the castle William built is still standing to-day. It is known as the Tower of London.

William was a splendid boss and very businesslike. He set to work and had a list made of all the land in England, a list of all the people and of all the property they had. This record was called the Domesday Book and was something like the *census* now taken in this country every ten years. This list gave the name of every one in England and everything each owned, even down to the last cow and pig. If your ancestors were living in England then you can look in the Domesday Book and find their names, how much land they owned, and how many cows and pigs they had.

In order that no mischief might take place at night, William started what was called the *curfew*. Every evening at a certain hour a bell was rung. Then all lights had to be put out, and every one had to go indoors—supposedly to bed.

One thing, however, that William did made the English very angry. He was extremely fond of hunting, but there was no good place where he could hunt near London. So in order to have a place for hunting, he destroyed a large number of village houses and farms and turned that part of the country into a forest. This was called the New Forest, and though it is now nearly nine hundred years *old* it is still called New to this day.

But on the whole, William, although descended from a pirate, gave England a good government and made it a much safer and better place in which to live than it ever had been under its former rulers. So 1066 was almost like the Year 1 for the English.

We think it is remarkable when children of low-bred immigrants become society leaders, when, as we say, they rise from overalls to dress-suits, but here we have the son's son of a pirate rising to be king of England, and those living now who find they are descended from him brag of it!

51

A Great Adventure

HAVE you ever played the game called "Going to Jerusalem" in which every one scrambles to get a seat when the music stops playing?

Well, all during the Dark Ages "Going to Jerusalem" was not a game but a real journey which Christians everywhere in Europe wanted to take and did take if they could. They wanted to see the actual spot where Christ had been crucified, to pray at the Holy Sepulcher, and to bring back a palm-leaf as a souvenir, which they could show their friends, hang on the wall, and talk about all the rest of their lives.

So there were always some good Christians—and also some bad ones—"going to Jerusalem." Sometimes they went all by themselves, but more often they went with others. As of course there were no such things as trains in those days, poor people had to walk nearly the whole way from France and from England, from Spain and from Germany, and so it took them many months and sometimes years to reach Jerusalem. These travelers were called *pilgrims*, and their trip was called a *pilgrimage*.

Jerusalem at that time belonged to the Turks, who were Mohammedans. The Turks did not like these Christian pilgrims who came to see Christ's tomb, and they didn't treat them very well. Indeed, some of the pilgrims on their return told frightful stories of the way they had been treated by the Turks and the way the holy places in Jerusalem were also treated.

Just before the Year 1100 there was a pope at Rome named Urban. He was the head of all the Christians in the world. Urban heard these tales that the pilgrims told, and he was shocked. He thought it was a terrible thing, anyway, for the Holy City, as Jerusalem was called, and the Holy Land, where Jerusalem was located, to be ruled over by Mohammedans instead of by Christians. So Urban made a speech and urged all good Christians everywhere to get together and go on a pilgrimage to the Holy Land, with the idea of fighting the Turks and taking the city of Jerusalem away from them.

Now, there lived at that same time a monk whom people called Peter the Hermit. A hermit is a man who goes off and lives entirely by himself, usually in a cave or hut where no one can find him or go to see him, where he can spend all day in prayer. Peter the Hermit thought such a life was good for his soul, that it made him a better man to be hungry and cold and uncomfortable.

Peter the Hermit had made a pilgrimage to Jerusalem and was very angry at what he saw there. So he, too, began to tell people everywhere he went how disgraceful it was for them to allow Christ's tomb to belong to the

Mohammedans and called on every one to start on a pilgrimage with him to save Jerusalem. He talked to people in the churches, on the street-corners, in the market-places, on the roadside. He was such a wonderful orator that those who heard him wept at his descriptions and begged to go with him.

Before long, thousands upon thousands of people, old and young, men and women, and even some children had pledged themselves to join a band to go to Jerusalem and take it away from the Mohammedans. As Christ had died on the cross, they cut pieces of red cloth in the form of a cross and sewed them on the fronts of their coats as a sign that they were soldiers of the cross. So these pilgrims were called *Crusaders*, which is the Latin word for a cross-bearer. As they knew they would be gone a long time and perhaps never return, they sold all they had and left their homes. Not only poor people but lords and nobles and even princes joined the army of the Crusaders, and there were, besides the crowds on foot, large companies of those who rode on horseback.

The plan was to start in the summer of 1096, four years before 1100, but a great many were so anxious to get started that they didn't wait for the time that had been set. With Peter the Hermit and another pious man named Walter the Penniless as their leaders, they started off before things were really ready.

They had no idea how very far off Jerusalem was. They hadn't studied geography nor maps. They had no idea how long it would take, no idea how they would get food to eat on their journey, no idea where they would sleep. They simply trusted in Peter the Hermit and believed that the Lord would provide everything and show them the way.

Onward they marched, "Onward, Christian Soldiers," thousands upon thousands, toward the east and far-off Jerusalem. Thousands upon thousands of them died from disease and from hunger on the way. Every time they came within sight of another city, they would ask, "Is this Jerusalem?" so little did they know of the long distance that still lay between them and that city.

When the Mohammedan army in Jerusalem heard that the Crusaders were coming they went forth to meet the Christians and killed almost all of those who had started out with Peter ahead of the rest. But those Crusaders that had started out later, as had been planned at the beginning, marched on.

Finally, after nearly four years, only a small band of that vast throng that had set out so long before reached the walls of the Holy City. When at last they saw Jerusalem before them, they were wild with joy. They fell on their knees and wept and prayed and sang hymns and thanked God that he had brought them to the end of their journey. Then they furiously attacked the city. The

Christians fought so terribly that at last they beat the Mohammedans and captured Jerusalem. Then they entered the gates and killed thousands, so that it is said the streets of the Holy City ran with blood. This seems strange behavior for the followers of Christ, who preached against fighting and commanded, "Put up thy sword, for he that taketh the sword shall perish by the sword."

The Crusaders then made one of their leaders named Godfrey ruler of the city. Most of the other Crusaders that were left then went back home. So ended what is known as the First Crusade.

52

Tit-Tat-To; Three Kings in a Row

HERE are three kings:

Richard of England,
Philip of France, and
Frederick Barbarossa of Germany.

If you say their names over several times, they keep ringing through your mind and you cannot seem to stop thinking them whether you want to or not.

Jerusalem was captured. But it did not stay captured very long.

The Mohammedans attacked and won it back again.

So the Christians started a Second Crusade. Then about once in a lifetime during the next two hundred years there was one Crusade after another—eight or nine in all. Sometimes these later Crusades won back Jerusalem for a while, but for a while only. Sometimes they did not succeed at all.

The Third Crusade took place about a hundred years after the First; that is, nearly 1200 A. D. These three kings—Richard of England, Philip of France, and Frederick Barbarossa—started on the Third Crusade. But they didn't all finish. I will tell you about them in three-two-one order.

Richard of England, Philip of France, and Frederick Barbarossa

Frederick's name, Barbarossa, meant Red Beard, for in those days it was the custom to give kings nicknames that described them. Frederick's capital was in Aix-la-Chapelle, as Charlemagne's had been, but Frederick was king only of Germany. When a young man he had tried to make his country as large and powerful as the new Roman Empire that Charlemagne had made. But he was not a great enough man, and so was unable to do what Charlemagne had done. Frederick was quite old when he started out on the Third Crusade with the other two kings. But he never reached Jerusalem, for in crossing a stream on the way he was drowned. So much for Frederick, the third king.

The second king, Philip of France, was jealous of the first king, Richard, because Richard was so very popular and well liked by the Crusaders. So Philip finally gave up the Crusade and went back to France.

Richard of England was then the only king left on the Crusade. It would have been better if he, too, had gone back to his country instead of gallivanting off on a Crusade. But he thought going on a Crusade was much better sport than staying at home and working over the difficult business of governing his people.

But although he had his faults, Richard was the kind of a man that all men like and all women love. He was kind and gentle, yet strong and brave. Richard the Lion-Hearted they called him. He was hard on wrongdoers but fair and square. So people loved him, but they feared him, too, for he punished the wicked and those who misbehaved. Even long, long after he had died, mothers would try to quiet a naughty and crying child by saying: "Hush! If you don't be good, King Richard will get you!"

SOHNOFFGOBBELLUM!

Even Richard's enemies admired him. The Mohammedan king of Jerusalem at the time of this Third Crusade was named Saladin. Saladin, though being attacked by Richard, admired him very much and even became his friend. And so Saladin, instead of fighting Richard, finally made a friendly agreement with him to treat the Holy Sepulcher and the pilgrims properly. As this arrangement was satisfactory to every one, Richard left Jerusalem to Saladin and started back home.

On his way home Richard was captured by one of his enemies and put in prison and held for a large ransom from England. Richard's friends did not know where he was and did not know how to find him.

Now, it so happened that Richard had a favorite minstrel named Blondel. Blondel had composed a song of which Richard was very fond. So when Richard was taken prisoner, Blondel wandered over the country singing everywhere this favorite song in the hope that Richard might hear it and reveal where he was. One day he happened to sing beneath the very tower where Richard was imprisoned. Richard heard him and answered by singing the refrain of the song. His friends then knew where he was, the ransom was paid, and Richard was allowed to go free.

When, at last, Richard did reach England, he still had adventures. This was the time when Robin Hood was robbing travelers. Richard planned to have himself taken prisoner by Robin Hood, so that he might capture him and bring him to justice. So Richard disguised himself as a monk and was captured as he had planned. But he found Robin Hood such a good fellow after all that he forgave him and his men.

Richard's coat of arms was a design of three lions, one above the other; and this same design of three lions now forms part of the shield of England.

After Richard's Crusade there was a Fourth Crusade, and then in the year 1212—which is an easy date to remember, because it is simply the number 12 repeated—one, two, one, two—there was a crusade of children only. This was known therefore as the Children's Crusade. It was led by a French boy about twelve years old named Stephen, who was named after the first Christian martyr.

Children from all over France left their homes and their mothers and fathers—it seems strange to us that their mothers and fathers let them start off on such a trip—and marched south to the Mediterranean Sea. Here they expected the waters of the sea would part and allow them to march on dry land to Jerusalem, as they had read in the Bible the waters of the Red Sea had done to allow the Israelites to leave Egypt. But the waters did not part.

Some sailors, however, offered to take the children to Jerusalem in their ships. They said they would do it for nothing, just for the love of the Lord. But it turned out that these sailors were really pirates, and as soon as they got the children on board their ships they steered them straight across the Mediterranean to Africa into the very land of their enemies, the Mohammedans. Here, it is said, the pirates sold the children as slaves. This is not a Grimm's Fairy-Tale, and the pirates were not trapped by the children, so I cannot make a happy ending, for it was not.

The last or Eighth Crusade was led by a king of France called Louis. He was so pious and so devoted to the Lord that he was made a saint and ever after has been called St. Louis. Yet this Crusade failed, and ever since Jerusalem has been ruled by the Mohammedans until just recently, when, in 1918, it was captured by the English, and this, then, was really the Last Crusade.

Not all the Crusaders were good Christians. Like some people nowadays, a great many were Christian only in name. In fact, though strange to say, quite a number of the Crusaders were nothing but scalawags, looking for excitement and adventure, and they went on a Crusade merely as an excuse to rob and plunder.

The Crusades did not succeed in their object, which was to keep Jerusalem for the Christians. Yet in spite of that, they did a great deal of good. When the Crusades first started, the Crusaders were not nearly as civilized as the people they went to conquer. But travel sometimes teaches people more than books, and it taught the Crusaders. They learned the customs of the other lands through which they went. They learned languages and literature. They learned history and art.

There were then no public schools. Only a very, very few people had any education at all. So the Crusades did what schools might have done. They taught the people of Europe and put an end to the Dark Ages of ignorance.

53

Bibles Made of Stone and Glass

HOW often do you go to church?

Probably not more than once a week—on Sundays.

But in the Middle Ages people usually went to church every day and often several times a day. They did not go only when there was a church service. They went to say their prayers by themselves; they went to tell their troubles to the priest, to get advice from him, to burn a candle to the Virgin Mary, or simply to chat with their friends.

All during the Crusades, and immediately after the Crusades, the chief thing that people thought about was their church.

There was only one church in a neighborhood, and every one went to the same church for there were no Baptists, nor Episcopalians, nor Methodists; all were just Christians.

The church was every one's meeting-house, and so people naturally gave as much money and time and labor as they could to make their church the best that could be built. That is why there were built in France and other parts of Europe at this time many of the finest churches and cathedrals in the world. These churches and cathedrals are still standing, and, because they are so beautiful, people go long distances to see them.

Do you know what a cathedral is? A cathedral is not just a large church. It is the church of a bishop. In the chancel of this church there is a special chair for the bishop. This bishop's chair is called in Latin a "cathedra," and so his church is named a cathedral after this chair.

These churches and cathedrals were nothing like the old Greek and Roman temples; they were not like anything that had ever been built before.

If you have ever built a house out of blocks, you probably did it this way: first you stood two blocks upright, and then you laid another block across the top of these for a roof. This is the way the Greeks and Romans built.

But the Christians throughout Europe at that time did not build in this way at all.

When you were building toy-houses, instead of laying a single block across the two standing ones, you may perhaps have tried leaning two blocks together like the sides of a letter A for a roof? If you did, you know what happened: the two leaning blocks pushed over the sides, and *crash!* everything tumbled. Well, these churches were built somewhat in this way, with stones arched across the standing stone columns. But to keep the stone arches from pushing over the standing stone columns the builders put up props or braces. These props or braces were made of stone, too, and these props of stone were called *flying buttresses.*

Flying buttresses—Apse of Notre Dame.

The people in Italy thought this a crazy way of building. They thought such buildings must be shaky and might easily topple over—like a house of cards. The Goths who had conquered Italy in 476 were wild and ignorant and after that people called anything wild and ignorant "Gothic." So people called all buildings such as I have just described "Gothic," although the Goths had nothing to do with the buildings, for they had all died long years before.

Indeed, from my description you, too, may think such buildings propped up by flying buttresses must have been tottering and ugly, but they were neither. They were not rickety, for though occasionally one that was not carefully built did collapse, the largest and best are still standing to-day. And although there were old-fashioned people who thought no building was beautiful that was not built in the Roman or Greek style, we have come to admire the great beauty of these so called Gothic buildings.

But there were other ways in which the Gothic churches were different from the Greek and Roman temples. Before a Gothic church was started, a very large cross was first drawn on the ground with its head towards the east, because that is the direction of Jerusalem. On this cross-shaped plan, the church was built so that if you looked down from above on the finished building, it was shaped like a cross with the altar always toward the east.

Gothic churches had beautiful spires or *arrows*, which have been likened to *fingers pointing to heaven*. The doorways and windows were not square or round at the top, but pointed, like hands placed together in prayer.

Nearly the whole side of a Gothic church was made of glass. These large windows were not, however, plain white glass, but beautiful pictures made of colored glass. Small pieces of different colors were joined together at their edges with lead to make what looked like wonderful paintings. But these pictures were much finer than ordinary paintings, for the light shone through the stained glass and made the colors brilliant as jewels—blue like the clear sky, yellow like sunlight, red like a ruby. These pictures in glass told stories from the Bible. They were like colored illustrations in a book. So the people who could not read, and very few could read, were able to know the Bible stories just by looking at these beautiful illustrations.

Statues of saints and angels and characters in the Bible were carved in the stonework of the church. So the churches were like Bibles of stone and glass.

Besides these holy beings, strange, grotesque beasts were also made in stone—monsters like no animal that has ever been seen in nature. These creatures were usually put on the outside edge or corner of the roof or they were used for waterspouts and called *gargoyles*. They were supposed to scare away evil spirits from the holy place.

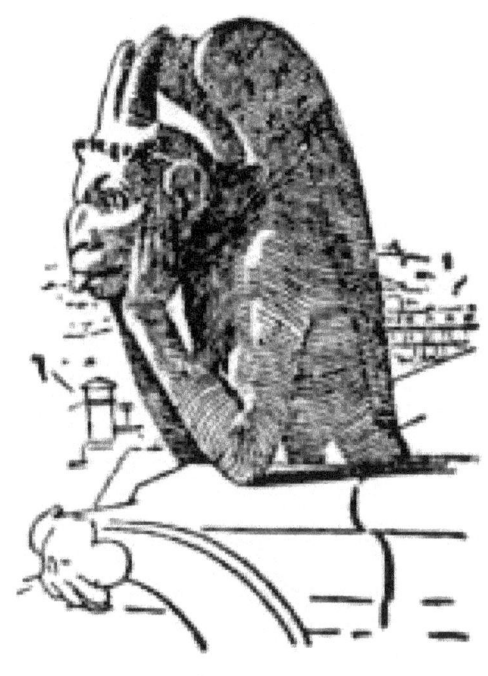

Gargoyle.

No one now knows who were the architects or the builders of these Gothic churches or who were the sculptors or artists. Almost every one did some work on the church, for it was *his* church. Instead of giving money he gave his time and labor. If he had any skill, he carved stone or made stained glass. If he had no skill he did the work of a common laborer.

Some of these Gothic churches took hundreds of years to build, so that the workmen who started them never lived to see them finished. Some of the most famous cathedrals are Canterbury Cathedral in England, the Cathedral of Notre Dame in Paris, and Cologne Cathedral in Germany.

Cologne Cathedral took the longest of all to build, as it was not entirely finished until about seven hundred years after it was begun! The beautiful Cathedral of Rheims in France was almost destroyed by the gun-fire of the Germans in the Great War only a few years ago.

Gothic churches were built, with loving care, of stone and jeweled glass. Nothing but the best was thought good enough. To-day almost all churches are still built with spires, pointed doors and some stained glass windows, and often the altar is toward the east. But although they imitate the Gothic style in these things, they seldom have stone ceilings, as Gothic churches had, nor flying buttresses, nor walls of stained glass. The ceilings are usually of wood, the spire often of wood, also, and even the whole building of wood or some cheap material. Real Gothic was enormously expensive and difficult, and nowadays people haven't the time, the money, nor the interest to build in such a way.

And that is the story of Gothic churches that the Goths had nothing to do with.

54

John, Whom Nobody Loved

RICHARD, the Lion-Hearted, whom everybody loved, had a brother named John, whom nobody loved.

This brother John became king, but he turned out to be a very wicked king.

He is another one of the villains in history, whom we do not like, but like to hear about, and like to clap when he gets what he deserves.

John was afraid that his young nephew named Arthur might be made king in his place, and so he had him murdered. Some say he hired others to do the killing; some say he murdered him with his own hands. This was a very bad beginning for his reign, but things got worse and worse as time went on.

John got into a quarrel with the pope in Rome. The pope at that time was head of all Christians in the world and said what should be done and what should not be done in all churches everywhere. The pope ordered John to make a certain man bishop in England, and John said he wouldn't do it. He wanted another man, a friend of his, to be bishop. The pope then said he would close up all the churches in England if John didn't do as he was told. John said he didn't care. Let the pope go ahead and close up all the churches if he wanted to. So the pope ordered all churches in England to be closed until John should give in. Nowadays this might not have made much difference, but then, as I have told you, the church was the one most important thing in every one's life; in fact, nothing else mattered so much. The closing of the churches meant that no services could be held in any church. It meant that children could not be baptized, and so, if they died, it was believed they could not go to heaven. It meant that couples could not be married. It meant that the dead could not be given a Christian burial.

The people of England were shocked. It was as if Heaven had put a curse on them. They were afraid that terrible things would happen to them. Of course the people blamed John, for he was the cause of the churches' being closed. They were so angry at him that he became scared—afraid what his people might do to him. When at last the pope threatened to make another man king of England in his place—yes, the pope had as much power as that— John in fear and trembling gave in and agreed to do everything that at first he had said he would not do and more besides. But John was pig-headed. He was always doing the wrong thing and sticking to it.

John had an idea that the world was made for the king and that people were put upon the earth simply so that the king might have servants to work for him, to earn money for him, to do what he wished them to do. Many of the kings of olden days felt the same way, though they did not go as far as John did. John would order people who were rich to give him whatever money he wanted. If they refused to give him all he asked, he would put them in prison, have their hands squeezed in an iron press until the bones cracked and the blood ran, or he would even put them to death.

John got worse and worse until at last his barons could not stand his actions any longer. So they made him prisoner and took him to a little island in the Thames River called Runnymede. Here they forced John to agree to certain things which they had written down in Latin. This was in the Year 1215; and 1215 was a bad date for John, but a good date for the English people. This list of things which the barons made John agree to was called by the Latin name for a great agreement, which is Magna Carta, or Charta.

John did not agree to Magna Carta willingly, however. He was as angry and furious as a spoiled child, who kicks and screams when forced to do something he does not want to do. But he had to agree, nevertheless.

John was unable to write his name, and so he could not sign the agreement as people sign contracts nowadays. But he wore a seal-ring which was used by people who could not sign their names, and this seal he pressed into a piece of hot wax which was dropped on the agreement where one would have signed.

John agreed in Magna Carta to give the barons some of the rights that we think every human being should have anyway, without an agreement. For instance, a person certainly has the right to keep the money that he earns, and he has the right not to have it taken away from him unlawfully. A person also has the right not to be put in prison or be punished by the king or any one else unless he has done something wrong and unless he has had a fair trial. These are two of the rights that John agreed to in Magna Carta. There were quite a number of others.

John didn't keep his agreement, however. He broke it the very first time he had a good chance, as a person usually does when he is forced to agree to something against his will. But John died pretty soon; and so, as far as he was concerned, Magna Carta didn't matter much. But kings who came after him were made to agree to the same things. So ever after 1215 the king in England was supposed to be the servant of the people, and not the people servants of the king as they had been before that time.

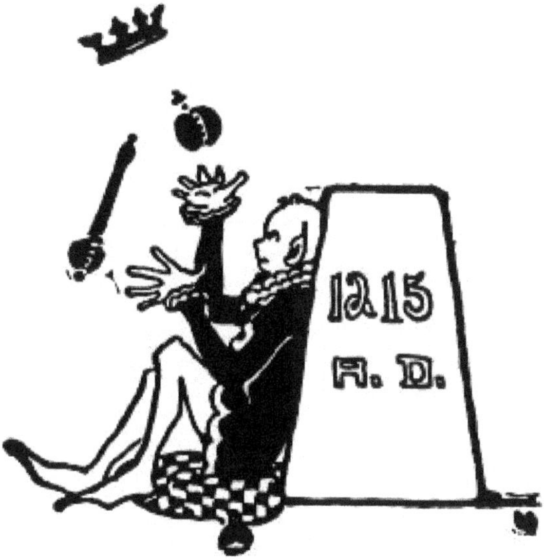
1215
A. D.

55

A Great Story-Teller

FAR away from England,

Far off in the direction of the rising sun,

'Way beyond Italy and Jerusalem and the Tigris and Euphrates and Persia and all the other places we have so far heard about, was a country called Cathay—C-A-T-H-A-Y.

If you looked down at your feet, and the world were glass, you would see it on the other side.

Cathay is the same place we now call China. The people in Cathay belonged to the yellow race, the same race to which the Chinese belong.

There had been people living in Cathay, of course, all through the centuries that had passed, but little was known of this land or of its people.

But in the thirteenth century or twelve hundreds, one of these tribes of yellow people called Mongols or Tartars, arose out of the East, like a black and terrifying thunderstorm, and it seemed for a while as if they might destroy all the other countries whose histories we have been hearing about. The ruler of these people was a terrible fighter named Genghis Khan. Genghis Khan had an army of Tartar horsemen who were terrific fighters. Genghis and his Tartars were a good deal like Attila and his Huns—only worse. Indeed, some people think Attila and his Huns were Tartars also.

Genghis usually found some excuse for making war on others, but if he couldn't find a good excuse he made up one, for he was bent on conquering. He and his Tartars thought no more of killing than would tigers or lions let loose.

So Genghis and his horsemen swept over the land from Cathay toward Europe. They burned and destroyed thousands upon thousands of towns and cities and everything in their way. They slew men, women, and children by the million. No one was able to stop them. It seemed as if they were going to wipe off of the face of the earth all white people and everything that white people had built.

Genghis Khan had conquered the whole land from the Pacific Ocean to the eastern part of Europe. But at last he stopped. With this kingdom he seemed to be satisfied. And he might well have been satisfied, for it was larger than the Roman Empire or that of even Alexander the Great.

Even when Genghis died, things were no better, for his son was just as frightful as his father and conquered still more country.

But the grandson of Genghis Khan was much less ferocious than his grandfather had been. He was named Kublai Khan, and he was quite different from his father and grandfather. He made his capital at a place in China now called Peking and ruled over this vast empire that he had inherited from his father. Kublai's chief interest was in building magnificent palaces and surrounding himself with beautiful gardens, and he made such a wonderful capital for himself that Solomon in all his glory did not live in such splendor as did Kublai Khan.

Now, far, far off from Peking and the palace of Kublai Khan, in the north of Italy was a city built on the water. Its streets were of water, and boats were used instead of carriages. This city was called Venice. About the Year 1300 there were living in Venice two men named Polo. The Polos got an idea in their heads that they would like to see something of the world. So these two Venetians, and the son of one of them named Marco Polo, started off toward the rising sun looking for adventure, just like boys in story-books who go off to seek their fortunes. After several years of travel, always toward the east, they at last came to the gardens and to the magnificent palace of Kublai Khan.

When Kublai Khan heard that strange white men from a far-off place and an unknown country were outside the palace, he wanted to see them. So they were brought into his presence. They told Kublai Khan all about their own land. They were good story-tellers, and they made it interesting. They told him also about the Christian religion and many other things that he had never heard of.

The emperor was so much interested in the Polos and in the stories they told about their country that he wanted to hear more. So he persuaded them to stay with him and tell him more. He gave them rich presents. Then he made them his advisers and assistants in ruling his empire. So the Polos stayed on for years and years and years and learned the language and came to be very important people in Cathay.

At last after they had spent about twenty years in Cathay the Polos thought it was about time to go home and see their own people again. So they begged leave to return. Kublai Khan did not want them to go. They were so useful to him and helped him so much in ruling that he didn't want to lose them. But in the end he did let them go, and they started back to what once had been their home.

When they at last arrived in Venice, they had been away so long and had been traveling so far that no one knew them. They had almost forgotten how to speak their own language, and they talked like foreigners. Their clothes had become worn out and ragged by their long trip. They looked like tramps, and not even their old friends recognized them. No one would believe that these ragged, dirty strangers were the same fine Venetian gentlemen who had disappeared almost twenty years before.

The Polos told their townspeople all about their adventures and the wonderfully rich lands and cities that they had visited. But the townspeople only laughed at them, for they thought them story-tellers.

Then the Polos ripped open their ragged garments, and out fell piles of magnificent and costly jewels, diamonds and rubies and sapphires and pearls—enough to buy a kingdom. The people looked in wonder and amazement and began to believe.

Marco Polo told his stories to a man who wrote them down and made a book of them called "The Travels of Marco Polo." This is an interesting book for you to read even to-day, although we cannot believe all the tales he told. We know that he exaggerated a great many things, for he liked to amaze people.

Marco Polo described the magnificence of Kublai Khan's palace. He told of its enormous dining-hall, where thousands of guests could sit down at the table at one time. He told of a bird so huge that it could fly away with an elephant. He said that Noah's Ark was still on Mount Ararat, only the mountain was so high and so dangerous to climb on account of the ice and snow with which it was covered that no one could go to see if the ark really were there.

56

"Thing-a-ma-jigger" and "What-cher-may-call-it" or a Magic Needle and a Magic Powder

ABOUT this same time that Marco Polo returned from his travels, people in Europe began to hear and talk about a magic needle and a magic powder that did remarkable things, and some say that Marco brought them back from Cathay, but this we doubt. The little magic needle when floated on a straw or held up only at its middle would always turn towards the north no matter how much you twisted it. Such a needle put in a case was called a compass.

Now, you may not see why such a little thing was so remarkable. But strange as it may seem, this little thing really made it possible to discover a new world.

Perhaps you have played the game in which a child is blindfolded, twisted around several times in the center of the room, and then told to go toward the door or the window or some other point in the room. You know how impossible it is for one who has been so turned round to tell which way to go, and you know how absurd one looks who goes in quite the opposite direction when he thinks he is going straight.

Well, the sailor at sea was something like such a blindfolded child. Of course, if the weather were fine he could tell by the sun or the stars which way he should go. But when the weather was cloudy and bad there was nothing for him to go by. He was then like the blindfolded child. He might easily become confused and sail in just the opposite direction from the way he wanted to go without knowing the difference.

This was perhaps one of the chief reasons why sailors, before the compass was used, had not gone far out of sight of land. They were afraid they might not be able to find their way back. So only that part of the world was known which could be reached by land or without going far out of sight of land.

But, with the compass, sailors could sail on and on through storm and cloudy weather and keep always in the direction they wanted to go. They simply had to follow the little magnetic needle suspended in its box. No matter how much the boat turned or twisted or tossed, the little needle always pointed to the north. Of course sailors did not always want to go north, but it was very easy to tell any other direction if they knew which was north. South was exactly opposite, east was to the right, and west was to the left. So all they had to do was to steer the boat on the course in whatever direction they wished.

It was a long while, however, before sailors would use a compass. They thought it was bewitched by some magic, and they were afraid to have anything to do with such a thing. Sailors are likely to be superstitious, and they were afraid that if they took the compass on board it might bewitch their ship and bring them bad luck.

The other magic thing was gunpowder.

Never before 1300 had there been such things in Europe as guns or cannons or pistols. All fighting had been done with bows and arrows or swords or spears or with some such weapons. A sword can only be used on a man a few feet away, but with guns an enemy may be killed and walls battered down miles away. But after gunpowder was invented the armor which the old knights wore was of course no longer of any use, for it could not protect them from shot and shell. So gunpowder has changed fighting completely and made war the terrible thing it has become.

Although Marco Polo was supposed to have told about gunpowder and its use in cannons as he had seen it in the East, most people think that an English monk named Roger Bacon knew about gunpowder and also about the compass and perhaps invented them. The monk Bacon knew about so many things which people at that time thought were magic that he was supposed to be in league with the devil, and so he was put in prison. Bacon was the wisest man of his time, but he was ahead of his time. If he were living now he would be honored as a great scientist and inventor. But people thought he knew *too* much—that any one who knew as much as he did was wicked—that he was prying into God's secrets, which God did not want any one to know.

Others, however, give the credit or the blame for the invention of gunpowder to a German chemist named Schwarz. They say that one day Schwarz was mixing some chemicals in an iron bowl with an iron mixer called a *pestle*, such as druggists use, when, all of a sudden, the mixture exploded and shot the iron pestle right up through the ceiling. Schwarz was much surprised; he had had a narrow escape from being killed; but this gave him an idea. Immediately he set to work to think out a way to use the same mixture in battle to shoot iron pestles at the enemy. Some people think it would have been far better if the pestle had struck and killed Mr. Schwarz at the time, and if his secret had been destroyed with him. We might then never have had the terrible wars and the killing of millions of human beings which have resulted from this discovery. It was quite a while, however, before gunpowder was made strong enough to do much damage. In fact, it was over a hundred years before fighting with guns entirely took the place of fighting with bows and arrows.

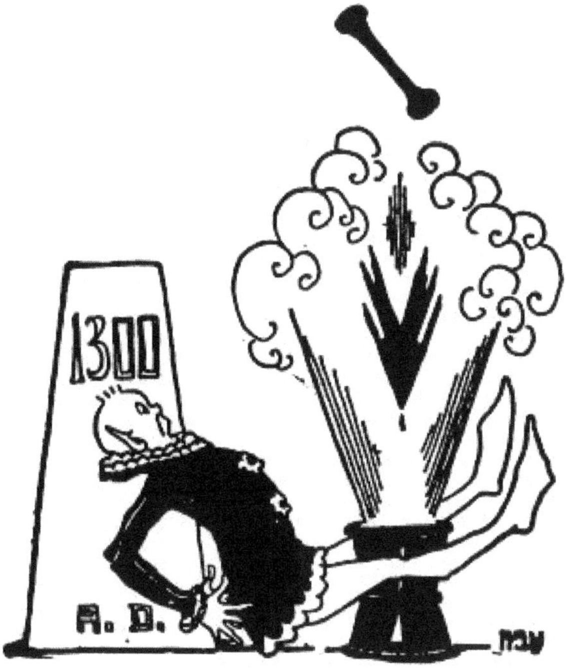
1300
A. D.

57

Thelon Gest Wart Hate Verwas

IS THIS another Latin heading?

No, it's English.

Don't you understand English?

It was 1338, and Edward III was king of England. Edward III wanted to rule France as well as England. He said he was related to the former king of France and had a better right to the country than the one who was ruling. So he started a war to take France, and the war he started lasted more than a hundred years. So this is known as the Hundred Years' War and it is:

The Longest War that Ever Was!

The English army sailed over from England and landed in France. The first great battle was fought at a little place called Crécy. The English army was on foot and was made up chiefly of the common people. The French army were mostly knights clad in armor on horseback—the society people.

The French knights on horseback thought themselves much finer than the common English soldiers who were on foot, as a man in a motor-car is likely to look down on the man who is walking.

The English soldiers, however, used a weapon called the *longbow*, which shot arrows with terrific force, and they completely whipped the French knights in spite of the fact that the knights were nobles, were trained to be fighters, rode on horses, and were protected by armor.

Cannon were used by the English in this battle for the first time. The cannon, however, did not amount to much nor do very much harm. They were so weak that they simply tossed the cannon-balls at the enemy as one might throw a basketball or football. They scared the horses of the French but did little other damage. But this was the beginning of what was before long to be the end of knights and armor and feudalism.

The battle of Crécy was only the beginning of the Hundred Years' War. The next year after the battle of Crécy a horribly contagious disease called the Black Death attacked the people of Europe. It was like the plague in Athens in the Age of Pericles, but the Black Death did not attack just one city or country. It was supposed to have started in Cathay, but it spread westward until it reached Europe. There was no running away from it. It spread far and wide over the whole land and killed more human beings than any war that has ever been. It was called Black Death because black spots came out all over the body of any one who caught it, and he was certain to die within a few hours or a day or two. There was no hope. No medicine had any effect. Many people committed suicide just as soon as they found they had the disease. Many died just from fright, actually "scared to death."

It lasted two years, and millions upon millions caught the disease. Half of the people of Europe died of it. Whole towns were wiped out, and in many places no one was left to bury the dead. Dead bodies lay where they had fallen—on the street, in the doorway, in the market-place.

The crops in the fields went to waste, for there was no one to gather them. Horses and cows roamed over the country at will, for there was no one to care for them. The plague attacked even sailors at sea, and ships were found drifting about on the water with not a soul alive left on board, with not even one left to steer the ship.

What if it had killed every last man, woman, and child in the world! What then would have been the future history of the world?

But, as if there were not enough people dead already, the Hundred Years' War still went on year after year. The soldiers who had fought at Crécy had been dead for years. Their children had grown up, fought, and died; their grandchildren had grown up, fought and died, and their great-grandchildren had done the same; and the English army was still fighting in France. The French prince at that time was very young and weak, and the French were almost in despair—hopeless—because they had no strong leader to help them drive out the English after all these many years.

Now, in a little French village there was living a poor peasant girl, a shepherdess, called Joan of Arc. As she watched her flocks of sheep, she had wonderful visions. She heard voices calling to her, telling her she was the one who must lead the French armies and save France from England. She went to the prince's nobles and told them her visions. But they did not put any faith in her or her visions, and they did not believe she was able to do the things she thought she could.

To test her, however, they dressed up another man as the prince and put him on the throne while the prince stood at one side with the nobles. Then they let Joan into the room. When Joan entered the royal hall, she gave one look at the man who was seated on the throne and dressed up as prince. Then without hesitating she walked directly past him and went straight to the *real* prince. Before him she knelt and said, "I have come to lead your armies to victory." The prince at once gave her his flag and a suit of armor, and she rode out at the head of all the army and had him crowned king.

Joan of Arc at the stake.

The French soldiers took heart again. It seemed as if the Lord had sent an angel to lead them, and they fought so hard and so bravely that they won many battles.

The English soldiers, however, thought that it was not the Lord but the devil who had sent Joan and that she was not an angel but a witch, and they were very much afraid of her. At last, the English made her prisoner. The French king, whom she had saved, in spite of all she had done for him, didn't even try to save her. Now that things were going his way, he didn't like to have a woman running things, and the soldiers didn't like to have a woman ordering them around, and they were glad to be rid of her.

The English tried her for a witch, judged her guilty of being a witch, and then they burned her alive at the stake.

But Joan seemed to have brought the French good luck, to have put new life into their armies, for from that time on, France increased in strength, and after more than a hundred years of fighting at last drove the English out of the country. In one hundred years of fighting hundreds of thousands of people had been wounded and crippled and blinded and killed, and after it all England was no better off, just the same as when she started—all the fighting all for nothing.

58

Print and Powder
or
Off with the Old
On with the New

UP TO this time there was not a printed book in the whole world. There was not a newspaper. There was not a magazine. All books had to be written by hand. This, of course, was extremely slow and expensive, so there were very few of even these handwritten books in all the world. Only kings and very wealthy people had any books at all. Such a book as the Bible, for instance, cost almost as much as a house, and so no poor people could own such a thing. Even when there was a Bible in a church, it was so valuable that it had to be chained to keep it from being stolen. Think of stealing a Bible!

But about 1440 a man thought of a new way to make books. First he put together wooden letters called type, and then smeared them with ink. Then he pressed paper against this inky type and made a copy. After the type was once set up, thousands of copies could be made quickly and easily. This, as you of course know, was printing. It all seems so simple, the wonder is that no one had thought of printing thousands of years before.

**Gutenberg at his press.
Comparing a printed sheet with a manuscript.**

It is generally believed that a German named Gutenberg made the first printed books about 1440, so he is called the inventor of printing. And what do you suppose was the first book ever printed? Why, the book that people thought the most important book in the world—the Bible. This Bible was not printed in English, however, nor in German, but in Latin!

The first book printed in English was made in England by an English man named Caxton, and you would never guess what the English book was. It was a description of the game of chess, the game that the Arabs had invented.

Before this time few people, even though they were kings and princes, knew how to read, because there were no books to teach them how to read and few books for them to read if they had learned, and so what was the use of learning.

You can see how difficult it must have been for people throughout the Middle Ages, without books or newspapers or anything printed, to learn what was going on in the world, or to learn about anything that one wanted to know.

But, now that printing had been invented, all that was changed. Story-books and school-books and other books could be made in large numbers and very cheaply. People who never before were able to have any books could now own them. Every one could now read all the famous stories of the world and learn about geography, about history, about anything he wanted to know. So the invention of printing was soon to change everything.

The Hundred Years' War had at last come to an end soon after the invention of printing.

At the same time something else that was a thousand years old came to an end.

The Mohammedans whom we haven't heard of for a long time, had tried to capture Constantinople in the seventh century, but had been stopped, as I told you, by tar and pitch that the Christians poured down on them.

But in 1458 the Mohammedans once again attacked Constantinople. This time, however, the Mohammedans were Turks, and they didn't try to batter down the walls of the city with arrows. They used gunpowder and cannon. Cannon had been used at Crécy more than a hundred years before, but they had done little damage. Since that time, however, they had become greatly improved. Against the power of this new invention the walls of Constantinople could not stand, and finally the city fell. So Constantinople became Turkish, and the magnificent Church of Santa Sophia, which Justinian had built a thousand years before, was turned into a Mohammedan mosque. This was the end of all that was left of the old Roman Empire—the other half of which had fallen in 476.

Ever after the downfall of Constantinople in 1453, wars were fought with gunpowder. No longer were castles of any use. No longer were knights in armor of any use. No longer were bows and arrows of any use—against this new kind of fighting. There was a new sound in the world, the sound of cannon-firing: "Boom! boom! boom!" Before this, battles had not been very noisy except for shouts of the victors and the moans of the dying. So 1453 is called the end of the Middle Ages, and the beginning of the New Ages that were to follow.

Gunpowder had put an end to the Middle Ages. The invention of printing and that little magic needle, the compass, did a great deal to start the New Ages.

59

A Sailor Who Found a New World

WHAT book do you like best?

"Alice in Wonderland"?

"Gulliver's Travels"?

One of the first books to be printed and one that boys at that time liked best was

"The Travels of Marco Polo"

One of the boys who loved to read these stories of those far-away countries of the East with their gold and precious jewels was an Italian named Christopher Columbus. Christopher Columbus was born in the city of Genoa, which is in the top of the "boot." Like a great many other boys who were born in seaport towns, he had heard the sailors on the wharves tell yarns of their travels, and his greatest ambition in life was to go off to sea and visit all the wonderful lands of which he had read and been told. At last the chance came, and, though only fourteen years old, he made his first voyage. After that, Columbus made many other voyages and grew to be a middle-aged man, but he never got to these countries he had read about in "The Travels of Marco Polo."

Many sea-captains of that time were trying to find a shorter way to India than the long and tiresome one that Marco Polo had taken. They felt sure there was a shorter way by sea and now that they had the compass to guide them they dared to go far off searching for such a waterway.

By this time many books had already been printed. Some of these books on travel were written by the old Greeks and Romans and declared what was thought to be a crazy notion that the world was not flat but round. Columbus had read these books and he said to himself that if the world is really round, one should be able to reach India by sailing toward the west. It should be much easier and shorter that way than if one took a boat to the end of the Mediterranean Sea and then went over land for thousands of miles the way Marco Polo had gone.

The more Columbus thought of the idea, the surer he was that this could be done and the more eager he was to get a ship to try out his idea. But every one laughed at him and his notion as foolish. Of course, being only a sailor, he had no money to buy or hire a ship in which to make the trial and he could find no one to help him.

So first Columbus went to the little country called Portugal. Portugal was right on the ocean's edge. It was to be expected then that the people of Portugal would be famous sailors, and they *were*—as famous as the Phenicians had been of old. So Columbus thought they might be interested and help. Besides, the king of Portugal was extremely interested in discovering new lands.

But the king of Portugal thought, as the others did, that Columbus was foolish and would have nothing to do with him. The king wanted to make quite sure, however, that there was nothing in Columbus's idea. Furthermore, if there were any new land, he wanted to be the first to discover it himself. So he secretly sent some of his sea-captains off to explore. After a while they one and all returned and stated that they had been as far as it was safe to go and that positively there was nothing at all to the west but water, water, water.

So Columbus in disgust then went to the next country—Spain—which at that time was ruled by King Ferdinand and his queen Isabella. King Ferdinand and Queen Isabella were just then too busy to listen to Columbus. They were fighting with the Mohammedans, who had been in their country ever since 732, when, you remember, they got as far north as France. But at last Ferdinand and Isabella succeeded in driving the Mohammedans out of their country, and then Queen Isabella became very much interested in Columbus's ideas and plans and finally promised to help him. She even said she would sell her jewels, if necessary, to give him the money to buy ships. But she didn't have to do this. So Columbus with her help was able to buy three little ships named the *Niña*, *Pinta*, and *Santa María*. So small were these three boats that nowadays we would have been afraid to go even out of sight of shore in them.

At last everything was ready, and Columbus set sail from the Spanish seaport of Palos with about a hundred sailors. Many of the sailors were criminals, who had been given a choice between prison and this dangerous voyage. They chose to risk their lives rather than to stay in prison. Directly toward the setting sun into the broad Atlantic, Columbus steered. Past the Canary Islands he sailed, on and on, day and night, always in the same direction.

See if you can get this idea—the idea that every one had at that time—that all there was of the world was what we have so far been studying about. Try to forget that you ever heard of North and South America. They, of course, knew of no such lands. Try to think of Columbus on deck scanning the waves in the daytime or peering off in the darkness at night, hoping sooner or later to sight, not a new land—he wasn't looking for a new land—but for China or India.

Columbus arguing with his crew.

Columbus had been out for over a month, and his sailors began to get worried. It seemed impossible that any sea could be so vast, so endless, with nothing in sight before, behind, or on either side. They began to think about returning. They began to be afraid they would never reach home. They begged Columbus to turn back. They said it was crazy to go any farther; there was nothing but water ahead of them, and they could go on forever and ever, and there would never be anything else.

Columbus argued with them, but it was no use. Finally he promised to turn back if they did not reach something very soon. As the days went on still with nothing new, the sailors plotted to throw Columbus overboard at night and so get rid of him. They would then sail home and tell those back in Spain that Columbus had fallen overboard by accident.

At last, when all had given up hope except Columbus, a sailor saw a branch with berries on it floating in the water. Where could it have come from? Then birds were seen flying—birds that never get very far away from shore. Then one dark night, more than two months after they had set sail, they saw far off ahead a twinkling light. Probably no little light ever gave so much joy in the world. A light meant only one thing—human beings—and land, land—land at last! And then on the morning of October 12, 1492, the three boats ran ashore. Columbus leaped out, and falling on his knees, offered up a prayer of thanks to God. He then raised the Spanish flag, took possession of the land in the name of Spain, and called it "San Salvador," which means in Spanish, "Holy Saviour."

Now, Columbus thought this land was India that he had at last reached, though of course we know now that a great continent, North and South America, blocked his way to India. In fact, it was only a little island off the coast of America where he had landed.

Strange men were the human beings he saw there. Their bodies and faces were painted, and they had feathers in their hair. As Columbus thought they must be people of India, he called them Indians, the name they still bear.

Columbus went on to other islands near-by; but he did not find any gold nor precious stones such as he had expected, or the wonders that Marco Polo had described; and as he had been away so long, he started back again to Spain the way he had come. With him he took several Indians to show the people at home, and also some tobacco, which he found them smoking and which no one had even seen or heard of before.

When he at last reached home safely again, people were overjoyed at seeing him and hearing of his discoveries. Everyone was wildly excited—but only for a while. People soon began to say it was nothing for Columbus to have sailed westward until land was found, that anyone could do that.

One day when Columbus was dining with the king's nobles, who were trying to belittle what he had done, he took an egg and, passing it around the table, asked each one if he could stand it on end. No one could. When it came back to Columbus, he set it down just hard enough to crack the end slightly and flatten it. Of course, *then* it stood up. "You see," said Columbus, "it's very easy if you only know how. So it's easy enough to sail west until you find land after I have done it once and shown you how."

Columbus made three other voyages to America, four in all, but he never knew he had discovered a new world. Once he landed in South America, but he never reached North America itself.

As Columbus did not bring back any of the precious jewels or wonderful things that those in Spain expected him to, people lost interest in him. Some were so spiteful and jealous of his success that they even charged him with wrongdoing, and King Ferdinand sent out a man to take his place. Columbus was put in chains and shipped home. Although he was promptly set free, Columbus kept the chains as a reminder of men's ingratitude and asked to have them buried with him. After this, Columbus made one other voyage, but when at last he died in Spain he was alone and almost forgotten even by his friends. What an end for the man who had given a new continent to the world and changed all history!

Of all the men of whom we have heard, whether kings or queens, princes or emperors, none can compare with Columbus. Alexander the Great, Julius Cæsar, Charlemagne, were all killers. They took away. But Columbus *gave*. He gave us a new world. Without money or friends or luck, he stuck to his ideas through long years of discouragement. Although made fun of and called a crank and even treated as a criminal he never

gave up,
gave out, nor
gave in!

60

Fortune-Hunters

THE New World had no name.

It was simply called the "New World," as one might speak of the "new baby."

It had to have a name, but what should it be?

Of course if we could have chosen the name, we should have called it "Columbia" after Columbus. But another name was selected, and this is how it happened.

An Italian named Americus made a voyage to the southern part of the New World. Then he wrote a book about his travels. People read his book and began to speak of the new land that Americus described as Americus's country. And so the New World came to be called America after Americus, although in all fairness it should have been named after Columbus; don't you think so? Children sometimes have names given them which they would like to change when they grow up. But then it is too late. So we often speak and sing of our country as Columbia, although that is not the name on the map. And that is why we call a great many cities and towns and districts and streets Columbus or Columbia.

After Columbus had shown that there was no danger of falling off the world and that there really was land off to the west, almost every one who had been hunting for India now rushed off in the direction Columbus had taken. "Copy cats!" A genius starts something; then thousands follow—imitate. Every sea-captain who could do so now hurried off to the west to look for new countries, and so many discoveries were made that this time is known as the Age of Discovery. Most of these men were trying to get to India. They were after gold and jewels and spices, which they thought they would find in India in great quantities.

Now we can understand why people might go long distances in search of gold and precious stones, but they also went after spices—such as cloves and pepper—and you may wonder why they were so eager to get spices? You yourself may not like pepper very much, and you may dislike cloves. But in those days they didn't have refrigerators filled with ice, and meats and other foods were often spoiled. We would have thought such food unfit to eat. But they covered it with spices to kill the bad flavor, and then food could be eaten that otherwise one could not have swallowed. Spices didn't grow in Europe—only in the far east. So people paid big prices to get them, and that is why men made long journeys after them.

A Portuguese sailor named Vasco da Gama was one of those who were trying to get to India all the way by water. He did not, however, sail *west* as Columbus had done, but *south* down around Africa. Others had tried before to get to India by going south and around Africa, but none had gone more than part way. Many frightful stories were told by those who had tried but had at last turned back. These stories were like the tales of "Sindbad the Sailor." They said that the sea became boiling hot; they said that there was a magnetic mountain which would pull out the iron bolts in the ship, and the ship would then fall to pieces; they said that there was a whirlpool into which a ship would be irresistibly drawn—down, down, down to the bottom; they said there were sea-serpents, monsters so large that they could swallow a ship at one gulp. The southern point of Africa was called the Cape of Storms, and the very name seemed to be bad luck, so that it was changed to Cape of Good Hope.

In spite of all such scary stories, Vasco da Gama kept on his way south. Finally, after many hardships and many adventures, he passed round the Cape of Good Hope. Then he sailed on to India, got the spices that then were so highly prized, and returned safely home. This was in 1497, five years after Columbus's first voyage, and Vasco da Gama was the first one to go to India by water. Spain had the honor of discovering a new land. Portugal had the honor of first reaching India by water.

15th Century Map of Africa

England also was to have the honor of making discoveries. In the same year that Vasco da Gama reached India, a man named Cabot set sail from England on a voyage of discovery. His first trip was a failure, but he tried again and finally came to Canada and sailed along the coast of what is now the United States. These countries he claimed for England, but he returned home, and England did nothing more about his discoveries until about a hundred years later.

Another Spaniard named Balboa explored the central part of America. He was on the little strip of land that joined North and South America which we now call the Isthmus of Panama. Suddenly he came to another great ocean. This strange new ocean he named the South Sea, for although the Isthmus of Panama connects North and South America, it bends so that one looks *south* over the ocean.

Then came the longest trip of all. A Portuguese named Magellan wanted to find a way to India *through* the New World, for he thought there must be some opening through which he might pass this new land that blocked the way. He tried to get his own country to help him. But again Portugal made the same mistake she had made in the case of Columbus. She would not listen to Magellan. So Magellan went to Spain, and Spain gave him five ships.

With these five ships Magellan sailed off across the sea. When he reached South America he sailed south along the shore trying to find a passage through the land. One place after another seemed to be the passage for which he was looking, but each one turned out to be nothing but a river's mouth. Then one of his ships was wrecked, and only four were left.

With these four ships he still kept on down the coast until he finally reached what is now Cape Horn. Through the dangerous opening there, since called after him the Straits of Magellan, he worked his way. One ship deserted and went back home the way it had come. Only three were then left.

With these three ships he at last came into the great ocean on the other side, the same ocean that Balboa had called the South Sea. This Magellan named the "Pacific," which means "calm," because after all the storms they had had it seemed so calm and quiet. But food and water became scarce and finally gave out. Magellan's men suffered terribly from thirst and hunger and even ate the rats that are always to be found on shipboard. Many of his men were taken sick and died. Still he kept on, though he had lost most of the crew with which he had set out. At last he reached what are now the Philippine Islands, where the people were savages. Here he and his men got into a battle with the natives, and Magellan was killed. There were now not enough men left to sail three ships, and so one of these was burned, and only two were then left.

**Magellan's Victoria.
(From an old print.)**

Two of the ships, however, out of the five with which Magellan had started out, still kept on. Then one of these was lost, disappeared, and was never heard of again, and only a single ship named the *Victoria*, remained. It seemed as if not one ship, not one man, would be left to tell the tale.

Around Africa the *Victoria* struggled. Magellan's men, worn out with hunger and cold and hardships, still battled against wind and storm. At last a leaky and broken ship with only eighteen men sailed into the harbor from which it had set out more than three years before. And so the *Victoria—Victory!—*Magellan's ship, but without the heroic Magellan—was the first ship to sail completely round the world. This voyage settled forever the argument that had been going on for ages, whether the earth was round or flat, for a ship had actually sailed around the world! And yet in spite of this proof for many more years thereafter there were people who still would not believe the world was round, and even to-day there are people who say the world is flat, but now we call them *cranks*.

61

The Land of Enchantment or the Search for Gold and Adventure

ALL sorts of marvelous tales were told about the wealth and wonders of the New World.

It was said that somewhere in the New World there was a *fountain of youth*, and that if you bathed in it or drank of its water, you would become young again.

It was said that somewhere in the New World there was a city called El Dorado built of solid gold.

So every one who liked adventure and could get enough money together went off in search of these things that might make him famous or healthy, wealthy or wise, or forever young.

One of these men was Ponce de León. Ponce de León was looking for the *fountain of youth*. While searching for this life-giving water, he discovered Florida. But instead of finding the fountain of youth, he lost his life in fighting with the Indians.

Another one of these men was de Soto. He was searching for El Dorado, the city of gold. While doing so he discovered the longest river in the world—the Mississippi. But instead of finding El Dorado, de Soto was taken sick with fever and died. Now, the Spaniards, to make the Indians fear them, had said that de Soto was a god and could not die. So in order to cover up the fact that de Soto had actually died his men buried him at night in the river he had discovered. They then told the Indians that he had gone on a trip to heaven and would presently return.

The central part of America was called Mexico. Here lived at that time a tribe of Indians known as Aztecs. These Aztecs were more civilized than the other Indians that the explorers had come across. They did not live in tents but in houses. They built fine temples and palaces. They made roads and aqueducts, something like those of the Romans. They had enormous treasures of silver and gold. And yet the Aztecs worshiped idols and sacrificed human beings to them. Their king was a famous chief named Montezuma.

A Spaniard named Cortés was sent to conquer these Aztecs. He landed on the shore of Mexico and burned his ships so that his sailors and soldiers could not turn back. The Aztecs thought these white-faced people were gods who had come down from heaven and that their ships with their white sails were white-winged birds that had borne them. They had never seen horses, some of which the Spaniards had brought over across the water, and they were astonished at what seemed to them terrible beasts that the white men rode. When the Spaniards fired their cannons, the Aztecs were terrified. They thought it was thunder and lightning that the Spaniards had let loose.

Cortés moved on toward the Aztec capital, the City of Mexico, which was built on an island in the middle of a lake. The natives he met on the way fought desperately, but as they had only such weapons as men used in the Stone and Bronze Ages, they were no match against the guns and cannons of the Spaniards.

Montezuma, their chief, wishing to make friends with these white gods, sent Cortés rich gifts, cart-loads of gold, and when Cortés reached the capital city Montezuma treated him as a guest instead of an enemy and entertained him and could not do enough for him. Cortés told Montezuma all about the Christian religion and tried to make him a Christian also, but Montezuma thought his own gods just as good as the Christian God, and he would not change. Then suddenly Cortés took Montezuma prisoner, and terrible fighting began. At last Montezuma was killed, and Cortés of course succeeded in conquering Mexico, for though the Aztecs fought desperately and bravely, shot and shell were too much for them.

In Peru in South America was still another tribe of civilized Indians even more wealthy than the Aztecs. They were called Incas, and it was said that their cities were paved with gold.

Another Spaniard named Pizarro went to Peru to conquer it as Cortés had conquered Mexico. Pizarro told the ruler, who was called the Inca, that the pope had given the country to Spain. The Inca had never heard of the pope and must have wondered what the pope had to do with Peru and how he could give it away. So naturally the Inca would not give up his country to Spain. Then Pizarro *took* it away. He had but a few hundred men, but he had cannon, and of course the Incas could not stand out against cannon.

France and other countries of Europe also sent out explorers to conquer parts of America, and then missionaries to teach the Indians the Christian religion, but these you will hear more about when you study American History.

Many of the explorers were really pirates, even worse pirates than the Norsemen who raided England and France, because they murdered people who were without equal weapons to fight back. The excuse they often gave for doing so was that they wanted to make the natives Christians. No wonder that the natives did not think much of the Christian religion if it taught murder of people who could not defend themselves. The Mohammedans made converts with the sword, but the Christians made converts with shot and shell.

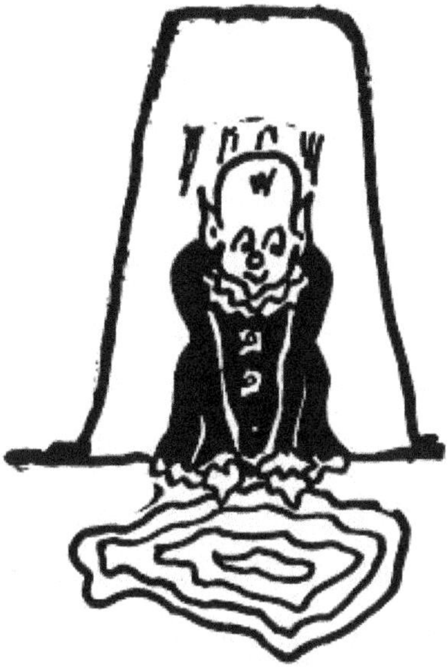

62

Born Again

HERE is a long word for you: it is Renaissance.

It means: born again.

Of course, nothing can be born again. But people call this time we have now reached the Renaissance, the born-again time. This is the reason why they call it that.

You remember the Age of Pericles, don't you? when such beautiful sculptures and buildings were made in Athens. Well, in the fifteen hundreds not every one was rushing off to the New World in search of adventure. While the discoveries that I have told you about were taking place, there were living and working in Italy some of the greatest artists the world has ever known.

Architects built beautiful buildings something like the old Greek and Roman temples. Sculptors made statues that were almost as beautiful as those of Phidias. People began to take an interest once more in the old Greek writers, whose books were now printed for every one to read. It seemed almost as if Athens in the Age of Pericles had been born again. So that is why people speak of this time as the Renaissance.

One of the greatest of these artists of the Renaissance was a man named Michelangelo. But Michelangelo was not just a painter; he was a sculptor, an architect, and a poet as well. Michelangelo thought nothing of spending years working on any statue or painting that he was doing. But when he had finished he had done something that people now go from all over the world to see.

Nowadays, sculptors first model a statue in clay and then copy it in stone or cast it in bronze, but Michelangelo did not do this. He cut his figures directly out of the stone, without making a model first. It was as if he saw the figure imprisoned in the stone and then cut away the part that closed the figure in.

A large block of marble had been spoiled by another sculptor. Michelangelo saw a figure of David *in* it, and, setting to work, he cut this young athlete *out*.

He made also a statue of Moses sitting down. It is now in a church in Rome, and when you walk up to it it is so lifelike that it seems as if you were in the presence of the prophet Moses himself. The guide tells you that when Michelangelo had finished this statue of Moses he was so thrilled by the figure he had created that, feeling it must come to life, he struck it on the knee with his hammer and commanded as he did so, "Stand Up"! And then the guide shows you a crack in the marble to prove that the story is true!

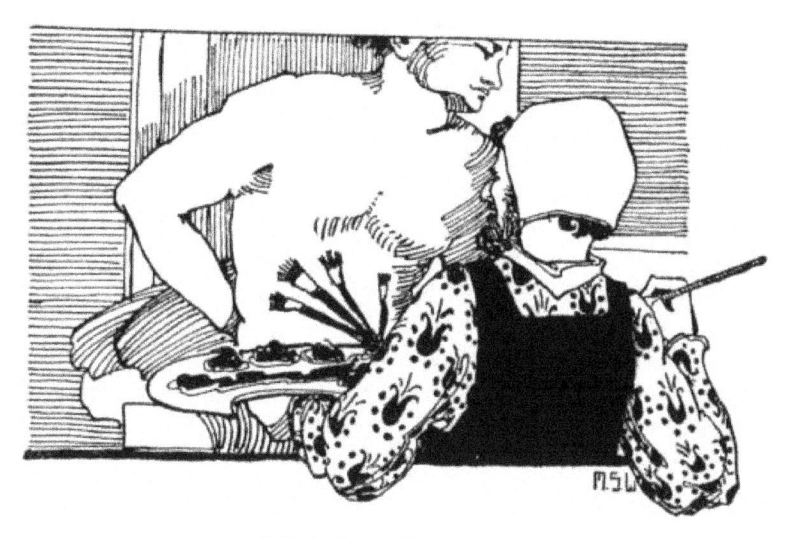

Michelangelo at work.

The pope wanted Michelangelo to paint the ceiling of his own private chapel in Rome. This was called the Sistine Chapel. At first Michelangelo didn't want to do the painting. He told the pope he was a sculptor and not a painter. But the pope insisted, and Michelangelo at last gave in. Once having agreed to do the work, however, Michelangelo gave himself heart and soul to it.

For four years he lived in this room—the Sistine Chapel—and hardly ever left it day or night. Beneath the ceiling, he built himself a platform, and, lying on this scaffold, he would read poetry and the Bible and work "as the spirit moved him." Locking himself in, he would let no one enter, not even the pope himself. He wanted to be alone and to be left alone.

The pope, however, felt that he was a privileged character, and one day, when he found the door left open, he came into the chapel to see how things were getting along. Michelangelo, thereupon, accidentally dropped some of his tools, and they just barely missed hitting the pope on the head. The pope was very angry, but he never returned uninvited again.

People now go from all over the world to see this ceiling, which only can be viewed comfortably by lying on the floor or by looking at it in a mirror.

Michelangelo lived to be nearly ninety years old, yet he had very little to do with people. He could not stand being bored by them. So he lived apart in the company of the gods and angels that he painted.

Raphael was another famous Italian artist. He lived at the same time as Michelangelo. Raphael, however, was just the opposite of Michelangelo in most ways. Michelangelo liked to be by himself. Raphael loved company. He was very popular and constantly surrounded by his friends and admirers, for everybody loved him on account of his genius and kindly nature. Young men swarmed about him, drinking in his words and humbly copying everything he did. He had fifty or more pupils studying and painting under him, and they went along with him whenever he went out even for a walk. They almost worshiped the ground he walked on.

Raphael painted many beautiful pictures of the Virgin Mary with the infant Jesus. These were called Madonnas. Madonnas were almost the only kind of pictures that artists painted at that time. Raphael painted one especially beautiful picture of Mary and the Christ-child called the "Sistine Madonna." This is considered one of the twelve greatest pictures in the world. It was painted for a little church, but it is now in a great picture-gallery, where it has a whole room to itself. No other pictures are thought worthy to have a place close by.

Raphael died when he was still a young man, but he worked so hard and so continuously that he has left a large number of pictures. He painted only the very important parts of his pictures himself—perhaps only the faces. The body and hands and clothing he usually left to be painted by his pupils. They were glad to be allowed to do even a finger of a painting on which their master had worked.

Michelangelo's paintings were strong and forcible as a man is supposed to be. Raphael's paintings were sweet and lovely and graceful, as a woman is supposed to be.

Leonardo da Vinci is another great artist who lived at this time. He was left-handed, yet he could do any number of things exceptionally well. He would be called a jack of all trades, but unlike most jacks of all trades, he was good at all. He was an artist, an engineer, a poet, and a scientist. It is said that he drew the first map of the New World that had the name of America on it. He made, however, very few paintings, because he did so many things beside, but these few pictures are extremely beautiful. One of these is "The Last Supper." It is considered, as is the "Sistine Madonna," one of the twelve greatest paintings in the world. Unfortunately, it was painted directly on a plastered wall, and in the course of time much of the plaster with the paint has peeled off, so that there is little now left of the original painting.

Leonardo usually painted his women smiling. One of his most famous paintings is the picture of a woman called "Mona Lisa." She has a smile that is called "quizzical." You can hardly tell whether she is smiling *at* you or *with* you.

63

Christians Quarrel

SOME people say young boys and girls can't understand this chapter. They say it is too difficult. But I want to see if it is.

Up to this time, as I have told you before, there had been only one Christian religion—the Catholic. There was no Episcopalian, nor Methodist, nor Baptist, nor Presbyterian, nor any other denomination. All were just Christians.

But in the sixteenth century some people began to think that changes should be made in the Catholic religion.

Others thought changes should not be made.

Some said it was all right as it was.

Others said it wasn't all right as it was. So a quarrel started.

This is the way the trouble began: The pope was building a great church called St. Peter's in Rome. It took the place of the old church that Constantine had built on the spot where St. Peter was supposed to have been crucified head down. The pope wanted it to be the largest and finest church in the world, for Christ had said, "Thou art Peter, and upon this rock [Peter means rock in Latin] I will build my church...." So the Church of St. Peter's was to be the Capitol of the Christian religion. Both Michelangelo and Raphael had worked on the plans for the new church. In order to get marble and stone and other materials for this Church of St. Peter, the pope did as others before him had done; he tore down other buildings in Rome and used their stone for the new church.

But besides all this the pope needed an enormous amount of money to build such a magnificent church as he had planned. So he started to collect from the people. Now, there was a man in Germany named Martin Luther who was a monk and a teacher of religion in a college. Martin Luther thought that not only this but also other things in the Catholic Church were not right. So he made a list of ninety-five things that he thought were not right and nailed them up on the church door in the town where he lived, and he preached against doing these things. The pope sent Luther an order, but Luther made a bonfire and burned it publicly. Many took sides with Luther, and before long there was a great body of people who had left the Catholic Church and no longer obeyed the pope.

The pope called on the king of Spain to help in this quarrel with Luther. The reason he called on him was this: The king of Spain was Charles V, the grandson of the Ferdinand and Isabella who had helped Columbus. He was not only a good Catholic but the most powerful ruler in Europe. The Spanish explorers had discovered different parts of America, and so Charles was owner of a large part of the New World. But he was emperor not only of these Spanish settlements in America but of Austria and of Germany as well. So it was quite natural that the pope should go to Charles for help.

Charles commanded Luther to come to a city named Worms to be tried. He promised Luther that no harm would be done him, and so Luther went. When Luther arrived at Worms, Charles ordered him to take back all he had said. Luther refused to do so. Some of Charles's nobles said Luther should be burned at the stake. But Charles, as he had promised, let him go and did not punish him for his belief. Luther's friends were afraid, though, that other Catholics might do him harm. They knew Luther would take no care of himself, and so they themselves took him prisoner and kept him shut up for over a year, so that no one could harm him. While Luther was in prison he translated the Bible into German; it was the first time that the Bible had been written in that language.

The people who protested against what the pope did were called Protestants, and those Christians who are not Roman Catholics are still called Protestants to-day. The time when these changes were made in the Catholic form of worship was called the Re-form-ation, as the old religion was *re-formed*.

Now, you may be a Catholic and your best friend may not be a Catholic, but that makes no difference in your friendship. But at that time those who were Catholics were deadly enemies of those who were not. Each side was sure it alone was right and the other side was wrong. Each side fought for the things it thought were right, fought the other side as furiously and madly and bitterly as if the other side were scoundrels and devils. Friends and relatives murdered each other because they thought differently about religion, and yet all were supposed to be Christians.

Charles was greatly worried and troubled by the religious quarrels and other difficulties in his vast empire. He became sick and tired of being emperor and of having to settle all the many problems he had to solve. He wanted to be free to do other things that he was more interested in. Being king did not mean being able to do whatever you wanted, as some people think. So Charles did what few rulers have ever done voluntarily: he resigned—"abdicated," as it is called—and gave up his throne to his son, who was named Philip II.

Then Charles, glad to be rid of all the cares of state, went to live in a monastery. There he spent his time doing what he liked—what do you suppose?—making mechanical toys and watches—until he died!

Now, the king of England at this time, when Charles was king of Spain, was Henry VIII. His last name was Tudor. So many kings had first names which were alike that such names were numbered to tell which Charles or Henry was meant and how many of the same name there had been before. Henry VIII was at first also a strong Catholic, and the pope had called him Defender of the Faith. But Henry had a wife whom he wanted to get rid of because she had no son. In order to get rid of her so that he might marry again, he had to have what was called a divorce, and the pope was the only one who could give Henry a divorce. Now, the pope at Rome was head of the Christian Church of the whole world and said what Christians could do or could not do, no matter whether they were in Italy or Spain or England. So Henry asked the pope to grant him this divorce. The pope, however, told him he would not give him a divorce.

Now, Henry thought it was neither right nor proper that a man in another country, even if he *were* pope, should say what could be done in England. He himself was ruler, and he didn't intend to let any foreigner meddle in his affairs or give him orders.

Henry VIII and his second wife Anne Boleyn.

So then Henry said that he himself would be head of all the Christians in England; then he could do as he wished without the pope's permission. So he made himself head, and then he divorced his wife. All the churches in England were now told by the king what they should do; the pope no longer had anything to say in the matter; the English churches obeyed the king, not the pope. This made the second big break in the Catholic Church.

After this Henry VIII had five other wives, six in all; not of course all at one time, for Christians could only have one wife at a time. His first wife he divorced, the second he beheaded, the third died. The same thing happened to his last three wives: the first he divorced, the second he beheaded, and the third died—but Henry died before she did.

Is this too difficult for you to understand?

64

King Elizabeth

KING Henry VIII had two daughters.

One was named Mary, and one was named Elizabeth.

Their last name was of course Tudor, the same as their father's, although we do not usually think of kings and queens as having last names.

King Henry had a son, also, and he was first to become king after his father died, for though he was younger than his sisters, a boy was supposed to be more fit to rule than a girl. But he didn't live long, and then Mary was the first of the two sisters to become queen.

"Mary, Mary, quite contrary" did not approve what her father had done when he turned against the pope and the Catholic Church. Mary herself was a strong Catholic and ready to fight for the pope and the Catholic Church. In fact, she wanted to have all who were not Catholics, all those who were Protestants, put to death. She thought that all those who did not believe as she did were wicked and should be killed. Like the queen in "Alice in Wonderland," she was always saying, "Off with his head!" This seems to us very unchristian, but in those days their ideas about such things were peculiar. Mary had the heads of so many people cut off that she was called Bloody Mary.

Mary married a man who was just as strong a Catholic as she and even "bloodier." He was not an Englishman, but a Spaniard, Philip II of Spain, son of Charles V, who had abdicated.

Philip II was much sterner than his father had been. Philip tried to make those who were Protestants, or who were supposed to be Protestants, confess and give up Protestantism. If they did not do so, they were tortured as the old Christian martyrs had been tortured. This was called the Inquisition. Those suspected of being Protestants were tormented in all sorts of horrible ways. Some were tied up in the air by their hands, like a picture hung on the wall, until they fainted from the pain or else confessed what they were told to confess. Some were stretched on a rack, their heads pulled one way and their legs the opposite way, until their bodies were nearly torn apart. Those who were found guilty of being Protestants were killed outright, burned to death, or put slowly to death, so that they would suffer longer.

The people whom Philip chiefly persecuted were the Dutch people in Holland. Holland then belonged to his empire, and a great many of the Dutch people had become Protestants.

Now, there was a Dutchman called William the Silent, because he talked little but did a great deal. William was furious at the way his people were treated. So he fought against Philip and at last succeeded in making his country free and setting up the Dutch Republic. But William the Silent was murdered by order of Philip.

And that's the kind of man Bloody Mary had for a husband.

After Mary Tudor died, her sister, Elizabeth Tudor, became queen, though she ruled like a king. Elizabeth had red hair and was very vain and loved to be flattered. She had many lovers but she never married, and as a woman who never marries is called a virgin she was known as the Virgin Queen.

Elizabeth was a Protestant and was just as bitter against the Catholics as her sister and her sister's husband had been against the Protestants.

A relative of Elizabeth was queen of Scotland. Scotland was a country north of England, but at that time it was not a part of England, and its queen was named Mary Stuart. Mary Stuart, Queen of Scots, was young, beautiful, and fascinating; but she was a Catholic, and so Elizabeth and she were enemies.

Elizabeth heard that Mary Stuart was trying to become queen of England as well as Scotland, so she had her, although a relative, put in prison. In prison Mary Stuart stayed for nearly twenty years and was then at last put to death by Elizabeth's orders. It is hard for us to understand how any one could have his own relatives killed in this cold-blooded way, especially any one who pretended to be a Christian, but in those times it was a very common custom, as we see when we hear of so many murders committed by the rulers of the people. Philip II, the great champion of the Catholics, made up his mind to punish Elizabeth, his sister-in-law, for killing such a good Catholic as Mary Stuart.

So he got together a large navy of very fine ships called the Spanish Armada. All Spain was very proud of this fleet. It was boastfully called the Invincible Armada; "invincible" means "unconquerable."

This Invincible Armada set forth in 1588 to conquer the English navy. Lined up in the shape of a half-moon, the ships sailed grandly toward England.

The English fleet was composed only of little boats. But instead of going out to meet the Armada in regular sea-battle as the Spaniards expected, the English ships sailed out and attacked the Spanish ships from behind and fought one ship at a time. The English were better fighters, and their small boats were quicker and more easily managed. They could strike a blow and get away before a Spanish ship could turn around into position to fire. So gradually they sank or destroyed the big Spanish boats one by one.

Then the English set some old boats afire and started them drifting toward the Spanish fleet. As all boats at that time were of course made of wood, the Spaniards became frightened at these burning piles drifting down upon them, and part of the fleet sailed away. The rest tried to get back to Spain by sailing the long way round, north of Scotland. But a terrible storm struck them, and almost all the boats were shipwrecked, and thousands of dead bodies were washed up on shore. So the great Spanish Armada was destroyed, and with it ended the power of Spain at sea. She was no longer the great nation she had been.

At the beginning of Elizabeth's reign, the largest and most powerful country in the world was Spain; at the end of her reign it was England that was the most powerful. Ever since then her fleet, which King Alfred started far back, has been the largest, and the saying is, "Britannia rules the waves."

People at that time thought it impossible for a woman to rule as well as a man, but under Elizabeth's rule England in turn became the leading country of Europe. Then people said Elizabeth ruled *like* a man, that she had a man's brain, a man's will. In fact they said she was more man than woman—that she was a tomboy grown up—that's why I call her "King Elizabeth."

65

The Age of Elizabeth

THIS story is about the Age of Elizabeth.

My father always told me that it was impolite to talk about a lady's age.

But I'm not going to tell you how old Elizabeth was, though she did live and reign a great many years.

I'm going to tell you some of the things that happened during her long life, for the time when she lived is what is called the Age of Elizabeth.

There was a young man named Raleigh living when Elizabeth became queen. One day when it was raining and the streets were muddy, Elizabeth was about to cross the street. Raleigh saw her and, to keep her from soiling her shoes, ran forward, took off his beautiful velvet cape, and threw it in the puddle where she was about to step, so that she might cross upon it as upon a carpet. The queen was greatly pleased with this thoughtful and gentlemanly act, and she made him a knight, so that he was then called Sir Walter Raleigh, and ever after that he was one of her special friends.

Sir Walter Raleigh was much interested in the new country of America. Cabot had claimed a great part of it for England almost a hundred years before, but England had done nothing about it. Raleigh thought something should be done about it; he thought English people should settle there, so that other countries like Spain, which had made so many settlements in America, would not get ahead of England. So Raleigh got together several companies of English people and sent them over to an island called Roanoke, which was just off the coast of the present State of North Carolina. At that time, however, almost the whole coast of the United States as far north as Canada was called Virginia. It had been named Virginia in honor of the Virgin Queen Elizabeth.

Some of these Roanoke colonists became discouraged with the hardships they had to suffer and so gave up and sailed back home again. Those who remained all disappeared. Where? No one knows. We think they must either have been killed by the Indians or have died of starvation. At any rate, not one was left to tell the tale. Among these Roanoke colonists was the first English child born in America—a girl, who had been named Virginia Dare, for the queen was very popular and a great many girls were named Virginia after her.

Some tobacco was brought back from Virginia, and Sir Walter Raleigh learned to smoke. This was such a strange and unknown thing at that time that one day while he was smoking a pipe a servant who saw smoke coming out of his mouth thought he was on fire and, running for a bucket of water, emptied it over his head.

Virginia is still famous for its tobacco. At first tobacco was supposed to be very healthful, for the Indians seemed to have very good health and they smoked a great deal. Afterward, however, in the next reign, King James so hated tobacco that he wrote a book against it and forbade it to be used.

After Queen Elizabeth had died, Raleigh was put in prison, for it was said he was plotting against the new king James, who came after Elizabeth. The prison where he was placed was the Tower of London, the old castle that William the Conqueror had built. Here Raleigh was kept for thirteen long years, and to pass the time away he wrote a "History of the World." But at last he was put to death as many other great men were also.

During the reign of Queen Elizabeth, there lived the great writer of plays, the greatest writer the world has ever known. This man was William Shakspere.

Shakspere's father could not write his name. Shakspere himself spent only six years at school. As a boy he was rather wild, and he was arrested for hunting deer in the forest of Sir Thomas Lucy at Stratford.

Shakspere reading to Elizabeth.

When still a boy Shakspere married a girl older than himself named Anne Hathaway. After he had been married a few years he left her and their three children, left the little town of Stratford, and went up to the great city of London to seek his fortune. There Shakspere got a job working around a theater, holding the horses of those who came to see the plays. Then he got a chance to act in the theater, and he became an actor, but he did not become a very good one.

In those days the theaters had no scenery. A sign was put up to tell what the scene was supposed to be. For instance, instead of forest scenery, they would put up a sign saying, "This is a forest," or instead of a room scene a sign saying "This is a room in an inn." There were no actresses. Men and boys took the parts of both men and women.

Shakspere was asked to change some of the plays that had already been written, so that they could be better acted. He did this very well; then he started in to write plays himself. Usually he took old stories and made them into plays, but he did it so wonderfully well that they are better than any plays that have ever been written before or since.

Though Shakspere left school when only thirteen years old, he seems to have had a remarkable knowledge of almost everything under the sun. He shows in his plays that he knew about history and law and medicine, and he knew and used more words than almost any writer who has ever lived. Indeed, some people say that with the little education he had, he could not possibly have written the plays himself, and so they have tried to prove that some one else must have written them. Some of the greatest of Shakspere's plays are "Hamlet," "The Merchant of Venice," "Romeo and Juliet," and "Julius Cæsar."

Shakspere made a good deal of money for those times—almost a fortune. Then he left London and went back to live in the little town of Stratford where he was born. Here at last he died and was buried in the village church. People wanted to move his body to a greater and handsomer place, to a famous church in London. But some one, perhaps Shakspere himself, had written a verse which was carved on his tombstone. The last line of this verse said, "And curst be he who moves my bones"; so they never were moved, for no one dared to move them.

66

James the Servant
or
What's In a Name?

WHAT does your name mean?

If it is
Baker or
Miller or
Taylor or
Carpenter or
Fisher or
Cook,

it means that at some time one of your ancestors was a

baker, or
miller, or
tailor, or
carpenter, or
fisher, or
cook.

If your name is Stuart or Steuart or Stewart or Steward, it means that at some time one of your ancestors was a steward for in olden days people knew very little about spelling, and they spelled the same name in different ways. A steward was a chief servant.

There was a family named Stuart in Scotland, and from chief servants or stewards they had become rulers of the Scots. Mary Stuart, whom Elizabeth had beheaded, was one of them.

As Queen Elizabeth never married, she had no children to rule after her. She was the last of the Tudor family. So the English had to look around for a new king, and they looked to Scotland.

Now, Scotland, as I have told you, was then a separate country and not a part of England as now. The son of Mary Stuart was then king of Scotland. His name was James Stuart. As he was related to the Tudors, the English invited him to come and rule over them. He accepted the invitation and was called James I. So we speak of his reign and that of his children as the reign of the Stuarts.

The Stuart family reigned for about a hundred years, that is, from 1600 to 1700, all except about eleven years when England had no king at all.

Many times the English must have been very sorry that they had ever invited James to be their king, for he and the whole Stuart family lorded it over the English people. They acted as if they were "lords of creation," and the English people had to fight for their rights.

A body of men called Parliament were supposed to make the laws for the English people. But James said that Parliament could do nothing that he didn't like, and if they weren't very careful he wouldn't let them do any governing at all. James said that whatever the king did was right, that the king could do no wrong, that God gave kings the right to do as they pleased with their subjects. This was called the Divine Right of Kings. Naturally the English people would not put up with this sort of thing. Ever since the time of King John they had insisted on their own rights. The Tudors had often done things that the people didn't like, but the Tudors were English. The Stuarts, however, were Scotch, and the people looked on them as foreigners; what they permitted in one of their own family they wouldn't stand in these strangers whom they had invited into their family. So, of course, a quarrel was bound to start. But the real fight came with the next king and not with James.

James was very fond of beefsteak, and one particular cut from the loin of beef he liked especially well. It was so delicious he thought it should be honored in some way, and so he made it a knight as if it were a brave and gallant gentleman and dubbed it "Sir Loin," which we still call it to-day—although people have forgotten all about how it got such a name, and some even say this is only a story and that he never did such a foolish thing, anyway.

During King James's reign the Bible was translated into English. This is probably the same Bible you read and that is called the King James Bible.

Nothing much happened in England during James's reign, but in some other countries a great deal did happen, although the king had little to do with it. English people made settlements in India, that far away country of the Brahmanists, which Columbus had tried to reach by going west; and these settlements there grew until India at last belonged to England. The English made settlements also in America, and these grew until at last part of America, too, belonged to England.

One of these settlements in America was made in the South, and one was made in the North. Raleigh's settlement at Roanoke had disappeared, as I told you; but in 1607 a boatload of English gentlemen sailed over to America looking for adventure and hoping to make their fortunes by finding gold. They landed in Virginia and named the place where they settled Jamestown after their king, James. But they found no gold, and as they were not used to work, they didn't want to do any. But their leader, Captain John Smith, took matters in hand and said that those that didn't work shouldn't eat. So then the colonists had to go to work.

Back in England people had learned to smoke, and so the colonists began to raise tobacco for the English people. The tobacco brought the colonists so much money that it proved to be a gold-mine—of a different kind—after all. But the colonial gentlemen wanted some one to do the rough work for them. So a few years later some negroes were brought over from Africa and sold to the colonists as slaves to do the rough work. This was the beginning of slavery in America, which grew and grew until in the South almost all the work was done by colored slaves.

A little later another company of people left England for America. These people were not looking for fortunes, however, as the Jamestown settlers had been. They were looking for a place where they might worship God as they pleased, for in England they were interfered with, and they wanted to find a place where no one would interfere with them. So this company of people left England in 1620 in a ship called the *Mayflower* sailed across the ocean and landed in a place called Plymouth, in Massachusetts, and there they settled. More than half of them died the first winter from hardship and exposure in the bitter weather that they have in the North, but, nevertheless, none of those who were left would go back to England. This settlement was the beginning of that part of the United States called New England. You will hear more about both settlements later when you study American History. But at present we must see what was going on in England, for there were great "goings on" there.

67

A King Who Lost His Head

HAVE you ever sung, "King William was King James' son"?

Well, that must have been some other King James, for King Charles was this King James' son, and he was Charles I.

Charles was "a chip of the old block." Like his father he believed in the Divine Right of Kings, that he alone had the right to say what should be done or what should not be done, and he treated the English people as King John had; that is, as if they were made simply to serve his pleasure and to do as he said.

But this time the people didn't carry him off, as they had King John, to agree to a paper. They started to fight. The king made ready to fight for what he thought his rights. So he got together an army of lords and nobles and those who agreed with him. Those who took his side even dressed differently from those who were against him. They grew their hair in long curls and wore a broad-brimmed hat with a large feather and lace collars and cuffs of lace even on their breeches.

Parliament also got together an army of the people who wanted their rights. They had their hair cut short and wore a hat with a tall crown and very simple clothes. A country gentleman named Oliver Cromwell trained a regiment of soldiers to be such good fighters that they were called Ironsides.

King Charles and Oliver Cromwell.

The king's army was made up of men who prepared for battle by drinking and feasting. The parliamentary army prayed before going into battle and sang hymns and psalms as they marched.

At last after many battles the king's army was beaten and King Charles was taken prisoner. A small part of Parliament then took things in their own hands, and though they had no right to do so they tried King Charles and condemned him to death. They found him guilty of being a traitor and a murderer and other terrible things. Then he was taken out in front of his palace in London in the year 1649 and his head was cut off. People now feel that this was a shameful thing for the parliamentary army to do to the king, and even at that time only a part of the English people were in favor of it. He might have been sent away instead of being killed, or he might have had his office of king taken away from him.

Oliver Cromwell, the commander of the parliamentary army then ruled over England for a few years. He was a coarse-looking person with very rough manners, but honest and religious, and he ruled England as a stern and strict father might rule his family. He would stand no nonsense. Once when he was having his picture painted—for there were no photographs then—the artist left out a big wart he had on his face. Cromwell angrily told him, "Paint me as I am, wart and all." Cromwell was really a king although he called himself Protector, but he did a great deal that was good for England.

When Cromwell died his son became ruler after him, just as if he were the son of a king, but the son was unable to fill his father's shoes. He meant well, but he hadn't the brains or the ability that his father had, and so in a few months he resigned. Oliver Cromwell had been so strict that the English people had forgotten about their troubles under the Stuarts. So in 1660 when the English found themselves without a ruler they invited back the son of Charles I, whom they had beheaded, and once more a Stuart became king. This was Charles II.

Charles was called the Merry Monarch because all he seemed to think about was eating and drinking, amusing himself, and having a good time. He made fun of things that were holy and sacred. To revenge himself on those who had put his father to death he had those of them who were still living killed in the most horrible way one could think of. Those that were dead already, Oliver Cromwell among them, were taken from their tombs; then their dead bodies were hung and afterward beheaded.

In his reign that old and terrible disease, the plague, broke loose again in London. Some people thought that God had caused it, that He was shocked by the behavior of the king and his people especially toward holy things, that He was punishing them. The next year, 1666, a great fire started and burned up thousands of houses, and hundreds of churches were destroyed. But the Great Fire, as it was called, cleaned up the disease and dirt and was therefore really a blessing. London had been a city of wooden houses. It was rebuilt of brick and stone.

Only one more Stuart ruler shall I tell you about—or rather a royal pair, William and Mary—because in their reign the fight between the people and their kings was once for all finally settled. In 1688 Parliament drew up an agreement called the Declaration of Right, which William and Mary signed. This agreement made Parliament ruler over the nation, and ever since, Parliament and not the king has been the real ruler of England. So I think we have heard enough of the Stuarts for a while.

68

Red Cap and Red Heels

THE last Louis I told you about was a saint—the Louis who went on the last Crusade.

The two Louis I'm going to tell you about now were not saints—not by any means.

They were Louis XIII and Louis XIV and they ruled France while the Stuarts were reigning in the seventeenth century in England.

Louis XIII was king in name only. Another man told him what to do, and he did it. Strange to say, this other man was a great ruler of the church called a cardinal, who wore a red cap and a red gown. The cardinal's name was Richelieu.

Now, you are probably sick and tired of hearing about wars, but during the reign of Louis XIII another long war started, and I must tell you something about it for it lasted thirty years. It was therefore called the Thirty Years' War. It was different from most wars. It was not a war of one country against another. It was a war between the Protestants and Catholics.

Cardinal Richelieu was of course a Catholic and the real ruler of France, which was a Catholic country. Nevertheless, he took sides with the Protestants, for they were fighting a Catholic country called Austria, and he wanted to beat Austria. Most of the countries in Europe took part in this war, but Germany was the battle-ground where most of the fighting was done. Even Sweden, a northern country of Europe which we have not heard of before, took part. The king of Sweden at this time was named Gustavus Adolphus, and he was called the Snow King because he was king of such a cold country, and also the Lion of the North, for he was such a brave fighter. I am mentioning him particularly because of all kings and rulers in Europe at this time he was the finest character. Indeed, most of the other rulers thought only of themselves, and they would lie and cheat and steal and even murder to get what they wanted, but Gustavus Adolphus was fighting for what he thought was right. Gustavus Adolphus was a Protestant, and so he came down into Germany and fought on the side of the Protestants. He was a great general, and his army won. But unfortunately he himself was at last killed in battle. The Protestants came out ahead in the Thirty Years' War, and at last a famous treaty of peace was made called the Treaty of Westphalia. By this treaty it was agreed that each country should have whatever religion its ruler had; it could be Protestant or Catholic as the ruler wished.

During the Thirty Years' War the plague, that old deadly contagious disease we have heard of before, broke out in Germany. A little town named

Oberammergau prayed that it might be spared. The townspeople vowed that if they were spared they would give a play of Christ's life once every ten years. They *were* spared, and so every ten years, ever since then, with only a few exceptions, they have been giving what is called the Passion Play. As it is the only place in the world where it is ever given, tens of thousands of Christians from all over the globe travel to this little out-of-the-way village to see these peasants act the stories of Christ's life. The play is given on Sundays during the summer of the tenth year and lasts all day long. There are about seven hundred people who take part, half of all the people in the town. It is a great honor to be chosen to play the part of a saint; it is the highest earthly honor to be selected to play the part of Christ; and it is a disgrace to be left out entirely.

The next French king to rule after Louis XIII and Richelieu was Louis XIV.

The people in England had at last succeeded in getting the power to rule themselves through their Parliament. But in France Louis would let no one rule but himself. He said, "I am the state," and he would let no one have a say in the government. This was the same as the Stuarts' Divine Right of Kings, which the English people had put an end to. Louis ruled for more than seventy years. This is the longest time that any one in history has ever ruled.

Louis XIV.

Louis XIV was called the Grand Monarch, and everything he did was to show off. He was always parading and strutting about as if he were the leading character in a play and not just an ordinary human being. He wore corsets and a huge powdered wig and shoes with very high red heels, to make himself appear taller. That, I suppose, is why some ladies to-day wear high heels called French heels. He carried a long cane, stuck out his elbows, turned out his toes, and strutted up and down, for he thought these things made him seem grand, important, imposing.

All this may sound as if Louis were a silly person with no sense, but you must not get that idea. In spite of his absurd manners he made France the chief power in Europe. He was almost constantly fighting other countries, trying to increase the size of France and to add to his kingdom, but I have already told you so much about so many fights, that I'm not going to tell you any more about his just now, for you would probably not read it if I did. So France had her turn as leader of all the other countries as Spain and England had had.

Louis built a magnificent palace at Versailles in which were marble halls, beautiful paintings, and many huge mirrors in which he could see himself as he strutted along. The palace was surrounded by a park with wonderful fountains. The water for the fountains had to be brought a long distance, and it cost thousands of dollars to have the fountains play just for a few minutes. Even to-day sight-seers visit Versailles to see the magnificent palace rooms and to watch the fountains play.

But Louis surrounded himself not only with beautiful things. He also surrounded himself with all the most interesting men and women of his time. All those who could do anything exceptionally well, all those who could paint well or write well or talk well or play well or look well, he brought together to live with him or near by him. This was called his *court*. Those in his Court were "in society." They were the chosen few who looked down on all the others who were not in society.

Louis XIV getting ready for bed.

This was all very fine for the people who were lucky enough to be "in society"—in Louis's court. But the poor people of France, those not in his court, were the ones who had to pay Louis's expenses and those of his court. They were the ones who had to pay for his parties and balls and feasts and for all sorts of presents which he gave his friends. So we shall see presently what happened. The poor people would not stand that sort of thing forever. "The worm will turn," we say.

69

A Self-Made Man

WHO was the Father of His Country?

I know what you will say:

"George Washington."

But there was another man called "The Father of His Country" before Washington was born, and he was not an American.

In the east of Europe there is a great country as large as our own, and its name is Russia. Very little had been heard of Russia before the Year 1700, for although it was the largest country in Europe, its people were only about half civilized. The Russians were a branch of the great Aryan family called Slavs, but although they were white people, they were living so close to the yellow people in China that they had become much like them in many of their ways. Then, too, the terrible Genghis Khan and his yellow Mongols had conquered Russia in the thirteenth century and ruled over the land. So although the Russians were Christians, they were in every other way more like the people of the East than like Europeans. The men had long beards and wore long coats. The women wore veils like those the Turkish women wore. The people counted with balls strung on wires as the Chinese did.

Well, just before 1700 there was born a Russian prince named Peter. When a small boy, Peter was very much afraid of the water. But he felt so ashamed that he, a prince, should fear anything that he forced himself to get used to the water. He would go to it and play in it and sail boats on it, although all the time he was almost scared to death. And so at last he not only got over this great fear but he came to like the water and boats more than any other playthings.

When Peter grew up the thing he wanted more than anything else in the world was to make his country important in Europe, for before this time it had not been. It was big but not great. And his people had to be civilized. But before he could teach his own people, who were most of them very poor and ignorant, he had to learn himself. As there was no one in Russia who could teach him what he wanted to know, he disguised himself as a common laborer and went to the little country of Holland. Here he got a job in a shipbuilding yard and worked for several months, cooking his own food and mending his own clothes. While he was doing this, however, he learned all about building ships and studied many other things besides, such as blacksmithing, cobbling shoes, and even pulling teeth.

Then he went to England, and everywhere he went he learned all he could. At last he returned to his own country with the knowledge he had gained and set to work to make Russia over. First of all, Peter wanted Russia to have a fleet of ships as other nations had. But in order to have a fleet he had to have water for his ships, and Russia had almost no land bordering on the water. So Peter planned to take a sea-shore away from the neighboring country of Sweden.

Now the king of Sweden at this time was Charles. He was the twelfth king named Charles that Sweden had had. Charles XII was hardly more than a boy, and Peter thought it would be an easy matter to beat this boy and help himself to whatever land he wanted on the water. But Charles was not an ordinary boy. He was an extra-ordinary boy, extra-ordinarily bright and gifted, and he had been unusually well educated besides. He knew several languages; he had learned to ride a horse when he was four years old and how to hunt and to fight. Besides all this, he feared neither hardship nor danger. Indeed, he was such a daredevil that people called him the Madman of the North. So at first Peter's army was beaten by Charles.

But Peter took his beating calmly, simply remarking that Charles would soon teach the Russian army how to win. Indeed, so successful was Charles at first in fighting Peter and all others who threatened him that the countries of Europe began to think of him as Alexander the Great come to life again, and they feared he might conquer them all. But at last the Russians did win against Charles, and Peter got his sea-shore. Then Peter built the fleet for which he had been working and planning for so many years.

The capital of Russia was Moscow. It was a beautiful city but near the center of that country and far from the water. This didn't suit Peter at all. Peter wanted a fine city for his capital, but he wanted it right on the water's edge, so that he could have his beloved ships close to him. So he picked out a spot not only on the water but mostly water, for it was chiefly a marsh. Then he put a third of a million people to work filling in the marsh, and on this he built a beautiful city. This city he called St. Petersburg in honor of his patron saint, the apostle Peter, after whom he himself had been named. The name of St. Petersburg was later changed to Petrograd and recently to Leningrad. Then Peter improved the laws, started schools, and built factories and hospitals and taught his people arithmetic, so that they could count without having to use balls strung on strings. He made his people dress like other Europeans. He made the men cut off their long beards, which he thought looked countrified. The men thought it indecent to have no beards so some saved them to be placed in their coffins in order that at the day of resurrection they could appear before God unashamed. He introduced all sorts of things that he found in Europe but which were unknown in his own country, and he really made Russia over into a great European nation, so that is why he is called Peter the Great, the Father of his Country.

Peter fell in love with a poor peasant girl, an orphan named Catherine, and married her. She had no education, but she was very sweet and lovely and bright and quick-witted, so the marriage turned out happily. The Russians were shocked at the idea of having a queen who was not a princess and was so low-born. But Peter had her crowned, and after he died she ruled over Russia.

70

A Prince Who Ran Away

IF you put a P in front of Russia it makes—Prussia. This is the name of a little country in Europe, which is now a part of Germany. Russia was big, and Peter made it great. Prussia was small, but another king made it also great. This king was named Frederick. He, too, lived in the eighteenth century, but a little later than Peter, and he, too, was called "the Great"—Frederick the Great.

Frederick's father, who was the second king of Prussia, had a hobby for collecting giants—as you might collect postage-stamps. Wherever he heard of a very tall man, no matter in what country and no matter what it cost to get him, he bought or hired him. This collection of giants he made into a remarkable company of soldiers which was his special pride.

He was a very cranky, cross, and bad-tempered old king. He treated his children terribly, especially his son Frederick, whom he called Fritz. Fritz had curls and liked music and poetry and fancy clothes. And his father thought he was growing up to be a girl-boy. This disgusted his father, for he wanted a son who would be a soldier and fighter. His father when angry used to throw dishes at him, lock him up for days at a time, and feed him on bread and water and whip him with a cane. Finally Fritz could stand it no longer, and he ran away. He was caught and brought back. His father was so angry with his son for disobeying and acting as he had done that he was actually going to have him killed—yes, put to death—but at the last minute was persuaded not to do it.

But here is a funny thing: When Fritz grew up to be Frederick, he turned out just what his father wanted him to be—a great soldier and fighter. He still loved poetry and even tried to write poems himself, and he was very fond of music and he played the flute very well, indeed. But Frederick wanted above everything else to make his country important in Europe; for before his time it was of little account, and no one paid much attention to it.

Now, the neighboring country to Prussia was Austria. Austria was ruled over by a woman. This woman was named Maria Theresa. Maria Theresa had become ruler of Austria at the same time that Frederick had become king of Prussia. Some people thought a woman was not a fit person to rule over a country. Frederick's father had promised to let Maria Theresa alone—he had promised not to fight a woman—but when Frederick became king he wanted to add a part of Austria to his own country, and so he simply helped himself to the piece of Maria Theresa's country that he wanted. He didn't care if she was a woman or whether it was fair or not. Of course this started a war.

Before long almost every country in Europe was fighting either with Frederick or against him. But Frederick not only succeeded in getting what he was after; he succeeded in holding on to it.

Maria Theresa, however, would not give up. She wanted to get back what had been wrongfully taken away from her. So she began quietly and secretly to get ready for another war against Frederick. Quietly and secretly she got other countries to promise to help her. But Frederick heard of what she was doing, and suddenly he attacked her again, and for seven long years this next war went on. So this was called the Seven Years' War. Frederick kept on fighting until he had beaten Austria for good and until he had gained his purpose, which was to make his little country of Prussia the most powerful country in Europe. He still held on to the part of Austria that he had at first taken away. Maria Theresa was a great queen, and she would have won against Frederick had he been an ordinary king. But she had too strong a ruler against her. Frederick was one of the world's smartest generals and too much for her.

The Seven Years' War, strange to say, was fought out not only in Europe but in far-off America, also. England had taken Frederick's side. France and other countries had taken sides against him. So the English settlers in America, who were on Frederick's side, fought the French settlers, who were against him. When, therefore, Frederick won in Europe, the English in America also won against the French in America. I am telling you all this because that is why we in America speak English instead of French to-day. If Frederick had lost, France would have won, and we here in America would probably now speak French instead of English.

Frederick, like some other kings we have heard of before, thought nothing of lying or cheating or stealing if he had to in order to get the better of other countries. Fair means or foul means made no difference to him. But his own people he treated as if they were his children and did everything he could for them. Like a lioness with her cubs, he fought for his family, even with the world against him.

There was a mill close by Frederick's palace that belonged to a poor miller. As it was not a pretty thing to be so near, the king wanted to buy it in order to tear it down and get rid of it. But the miller would not sell. Although Frederick the Great offered the miller a large sum of money, he refused. A great many kings would simply have taken the mill and perhaps put the miller in jail or put him to death, but Frederick did neither, for he thought his lowliest subject had his rights and that if he didn't want to sell he shouldn't be made to. So he left the miller undisturbed, and the mill stands to-day as it did then, close to the palace.

Though Frederick was a German, strange to say, he hated the German language. He thought it the language of the uneducated. He himself spoke French and wrote in French and only spoke German when he had to talk to his servants or those who did not understand French.

71

America Gets Rid of Her King

DID you know that we once had a king?

His name was George.

No, George Washington wasn't a king.

This was another George.

You remember the Stuarts in England—James, Charles, and the rest of the family who ruled England for a hundred years from 1600 to 1700. Well about 1700 England ran out of Stuarts—there were no more Stuart children.

As England had to have another king, they asked a distant relative of the royal family over from one of the German states to rule England. Yes, from Germany to rule England. His name was George, and the English called him George I. George couldn't even speak English. He was German and loved his own country much better than England, but he had agreed to come and rule over England, and he did so. You can imagine what sort of a king he was. His son, George II ruled after him, although he, too, was more German than English. But when the grandson, George III, came to the throne he was a born and bred Englishman. It was in this grandson's reign, in the reign of George III, that our own country, the United States, was born.

When a wheel turns over we call it a *revolution*, which is a big name for a little thing.

When a *country* turns over we also call it a revolution, which is a big name for a big thing.

Our country had started with the two little settlements, or colonies, as they were called, of Jamestown and Plymouth. But it had grown and grown until there were now a number of settlements along the coast of the Atlantic Ocean. Most of the people who had settled here were English, and the king of England ruled over them. The king asked all these people to send him money, which was called taxes. Now, the money collected from taxes was not, of course, for the king to put in his pocketbook to use as he liked. It was supposed to be spent on the people who were taxed, to be used for roads, schools, police, and such things that are for the good of all.

So these people along the coast who were paying money or taxes to the king far off across the water thought they ought to have a vote to say how this money should be spent and on what it should be spent. But they did not have a vote, and so they thought they ought not to have to pay taxes to the king away off in England.

One of the leading citizens of America at this time was a man named Benjamin Franklin. He was the son of a candlemaker, but from a poor boy who had once walked the streets of Philadelphia with a loaf of bread under each arm he had risen to a very honored position in the country. He had learned to be a printer and had started one of the first and best newspapers in the United States. He was a great thinker and had invented a stove and a lamp and had succeeded in getting electricity from the lightning in the clouds by flying a kite with a wire during a storm. He was one of the Wise Men of the West.

Franklin was sent over to England to try to get the king to change his mind about taxing the colonies or to bring about some sort of agreement with him. But King George was hardheaded, and Franklin was unable to stop the king from doing what he had made up his mind to do.

So the people in America, finding that talking did no good, started in to fight. They raised an army. Then they tried to find a good man to command the army. Such a leader must be honest and brave; he must have a good mind; he must love his country; and he must be a good fighter. So they looked around for a man who had all these qualities, and they found one. The man they picked was honest and brave, for when he was a boy, he had cut down a favorite tree of his father's just to try a new hatchet he had been given. In those days to cut down a cherry-tree was a crime for which by law a man could be put to death. When this boy was asked by his angry father if he had done it he said, "I cannot tell a lie; I did." Of course, now you know who it was—George Washington.

George Washington surveying Lord Fairfax's farm.

George learned to be a surveyor—that is, a man who measures land—and when only sixteen years old he was employed to survey the large farm of Lord Fairfax in Virginia; that showed he had a good mind. He then had been a soldier and had fought the Indians bravely and well; that showed that he loved his country and was a good fighter. So George Washington was chosen to lead the American army against the English.

The Americans did not at first think of starting a new country. They simply wanted the same rights that Englishmen in England had. But they soon found out that there was only one way to get those rights, and that was to start a new country independent of England. So a man named Thomas Jefferson wrote a paper which was called a Declaration of Independence—can you say it?—because it declared that the colonies were going to be independent of England. There were fifty-six Americans chosen by the people to sign it. Each one of the signers would have been put to death as a traitor to England if the United States had not won, and each signer knew it, yet he signed it nevertheless. But just signing this paper didn't make England give up the colonies. Oh, no! King George's armies tried to stop the colonies from getting away from the rule of England.

Washington had a very small army with which to fight the English army, and very little money with which to pay the soldiers or to supply them with food or clothes or powder and shot. One winter the soldiers nearly froze and starved to death, for they had little clothing and hardly any food but carrots, and it seemed as if the war could not go on unless they got help. Yet Washington kept up their spirits.

Benjamin Franklin was sent across the ocean, not to England this time of course, but to France to see if he couldn't get some help from that country. France hated England because she had lost part of America, Canada, in the Seven Years' War, but at first France would not help. She took little interest in the fight for Washington's army had lost a number of battles against the English, and people don't like to back a loser. But the year after the Declaration of Independence the American army beat the English badly at a place called Saratoga in New York State. Then the king of France became more interested, and then he sent help to the colonies to carry on the war. A young French nobleman named Lafayette hurried over from France and fought under General Washington and did so well that he has made a great name for himself.

England, seeing that things were going against her, now wanted to make peace with the Americans and give them the same rights that English citizens had, but it was then too late. At the beginning of the war the Americans would have agreed to this and been glad to agree, but now they would agree to nothing less than entire independence of England; and so the War went on, for England would not let the colonies go.

The English had been beaten by the Yankees, as they called them in the North, at a place called Saratoga. So then they sent their general, Lord Cornwallis, to the south of our country to see if he could beat the people there. General Greene was put in command of the Southern American soldiers. Lord Cornwallis tried to fight Greene, but Greene led Cornwallis a merry chase round the country until he was all tired out and finally went into a little place called Yorktown in Virginia. Here Cornwallis and his army were caught fast so that they could not get out. On one side was the American army, and on the water side were the French war-ships that had been sent over to help. So Cornwallis had to surrender.

King George then said, "Let us have peace"; and in 1783 the war was ended by a treaty of peace, eight years after it had started, and the colonies were independent of England. This was called the Revolutionary War, and after it was over our country was called the United States.

There were just thirteen of these original colonies that joined as partners in this Union. That is why there are just thirteen stripes in our flag. Some people think thirteen is an unlucky number; but our flag with its thirteen stripes still waves over the land, and it has brought us good luck; don't you think so?

Washington was made the first President, and so he is called the Father of His Country; the First in War, the First in Peace, and the First in the Hearts of his Countrymen.

72

Upside Down

MEASLES and Mumps are very catching.

So are Revolutions.

Just a little later than the Revolution of the thirteen colonies, the people in France had a Revolution, too. They saw how successful the Americans had been in their fight against the king of England, and so they rebelled against their own king and queen in France. This was called the French Revolution.

The reason the French people rebelled against their king was because they had very little, and the king and his royal family and nobles seemed to have everything. Both the Americans and the French rebelled against paying taxes. With the Americans, however, it was a matter of principle more than anything else. Their taxes were not very large, but they thought them unjust. The French taxes, however, not only were unjust but they took almost everything away from the people.

I have already told you how bad things were under Louis XIV, and they got worse until the people could stand it no longer.

At this time the king of France was Louis XVI, and his queen was named Marie Antoinette. Although the people were so poor they had hardly anything to eat except a very coarse and bad-tasting kind of bread called black bread; they were compelled to pay the king and the nobles money so that they could live in fine style and have "parties"; and they had to do all sorts of work for them for nothing or next to nothing. If any one complained he was put in a great prison in Paris called the Bastille and left there to die. In spite of the fact that all the people were so terribly poor, the king and the queen and their friends lived in luxury and extravagance with everything in the world they wanted, all paid for by the poor people.

Neither the king nor his wife was really wicked. They were simply young and thoughtless. They meant well, but like a great many well-meaning people they lacked common sense and did not know how others lived. They didn't seem to understand that people *could* be poor, for they had so much themselves. Marie Antoinette was told that her subjects had no bread to eat. "Then why don't they eat cake?" she is said to have asked.

To right the wrongs of the people, a body of many of the best men from all France gathered together and, calling themselves the National Assembly, tried to work out some plan to do away with all the injustice the people had been suffering. They wanted to make every one free and equal and give everybody a "say" in the government.

But the poor had become so furiously mad at the way they had been treated by the rich that they would stand things no longer and a wild and angry mob of them attacked the old prison of the Bastille. They battered down the walls and freed the prisoners and killed the guards of the Bastille simply because they were servants of the king. Then they cut off the heads of the guards and stuck them on poles and, carrying them aloft, paraded through the streets of Paris. There were only about half a dozen prisoners in the old jail, so that freeing them didn't matter much, but this attack was to show that the people would no longer allow the king to imprison them.

The Bastille was stormed on July 14, 1789. This is the beginning of what is called the French Revolution, and this day is celebrated in France in almost the same way that our Fourth of July is, for it is the French Declaration of Independence against kings.

Lafayette, who was now back in France, the same Lafayette who had helped the Americans fight their king, sent the key of the Bastille over to George Washington as a souvenir that his own country had now overthrown its king and declared its independence.

The king and queen were living in the beautiful palace at Versailles, the palace that Louis XIV had built. All the king's nobles, when they heard what was taking place in Paris, became frightened and, deserting their king and queen, took to their heels and left the country. They knew pretty well what was going to happen, and they didn't wait to see.

Meanwhile the National Assembly drew up what was called a Declaration of the Rights of Man, which was something like our Declaration of Independence. It said that all men were born free and equal, that the people should make the laws and the laws should be the same for all.

Soon after the Declaration of Rights had been made, the mad mob from Paris, ragged and wild-looking, carrying sticks and stones, and crying, "Bread, bread!" marched out the ten miles to Versailles, where Louis and Marie Antoinette were still living. Up the beautiful grand staircase of the palace they rushed. The few guards remaining round the king were unable to hold them back. They captured the king and queen and took them prisoners to Paris. There they kept Louis and Marie Antoinette prisoners for several years. Once the king and queen tried to escape in disguise but were caught before they could get out of the country and brought back.

Then it was that the National Assembly drew up a Constitution—a set of rules by which the country should be justly governed. This the king agreed to and signed.

French revolution crowd and guillotine.

But that still wasn't enough. The people wanted no king at all to rule over them. So about a year later they started a real republic like our own, and the king was sentenced to death. A Frenchman had invented a kind of machine with a big knife for chopping off heads. This was called the guillotine, and it was used instead of an ax, for it was quicker and surer. So the king was taken to the guillotine, and his head was cut off.

But the people did not settle down quiet and contented when they had got rid of their king. They were afraid that those who were in favor of kings might start another kingdom. The people chose red, white, and blue as their colors and the "Marseillaise" as their national song; and everywhere they marched they carried the tricolor, as they called the three-colored flag, and as they marched they sang the "Marseillaise."

Then began what is called the Reign of Terror, and this is a tale of blood. A man named Robespierre and two of his friends were leaders in this Reign of Terror. Any one whom the people suspected of being in favor of kings they caught and beheaded. The queen was one of the first to have her head cut off. If any one even whispered, "there's a man, or there's a woman, or there's a child who is in favor of kings," that man, woman, or child would be rushed to the guillotine. If any one simply hated another and wished to get rid of him, all he had to do was to point him out as in favor of kings, and off he would be taken to the guillotine. No one was sure of his life for a day. He never knew what moment some personal enemy might accuse him. Hundreds, then thousands, of suspected people were beheaded, and a special sewer had to be built to carry off the blood. But the guillotine, fast as it was, was too slow for the Terrorists. It could cut off but one head at a time, and so prisoners were lined up and shot down with cannons.

People seemed to have gone wild, crazy, mad! They insulted Christ and the Christian religion. They put a pretty woman called the Goddess of Reason on the altar of the beautiful Church of Notre Dame and worshiped her instead of the Lord. They pulled down statues and pictures of Christ and the Virgin Mary. In their places they put statues and pictures of their own leaders. The guillotine was put up in place of the cross. They did away with Sundays. They made a week ten days long, and every tenth day they made a holiday instead of Sunday. They stopped counting time from Christ's birth, because they didn't want anything that had to do with Christ, and they began to call the year when the republic was started in 1792 the year 1.

But Robespierre wished to rule alone, and he plotted against his two friends. One of these he had beheaded, and the other was killed in his bath-tub by a girl named Charlotte Corday, who was in a rage at what he had done. So Robespierre was left alone. At last the people, in fear of this man who was such a monstrous and inhuman tyrant, rose up against him. When he found that he too, was to be put to death, he tried to commit suicide, but, before he could do so he was caught and taken to the guillotine, where he went to the same death to which he had sent countless others, and the Reign of Terror was ended. It was a pity that he hadn't a thousand lives with which to pay for the thousands of lives he had taken away.

73

A Little Giant

At last the Revolution was stopped.

It was stopped by a young soldier only about twenty years old and sixty inches tall.

The Government was holding a meeting in the palace while a mad mob in the streets outside were trying to attack the palace. A young soldier had been given a few men and told to keep the mob away. The young soldier pointed cannons down each street that led to the palace, and no one dared to show himself. This young soldier was named Napoleon Bonaparte. He made such a fine record that people wanted to know who he was and where he came from.

Napoleon had been born on a little island called Corsica in the Mediterranean Sea. He was born just in time to be a Frenchman, for the island of Corsica had belonged to Italy and had only just been given to France a few weeks before he was born. As soon as he was old enough, he was sent off to a military school in France. There his French schoolmates looked upon him as a foreigner and didn't have much to do with him. But Napoleon made high marks in arithmetic, and he loved hard problems. Once he shut himself up in his room to work over a hard problem, and there he stayed for three days and nights until he had found the answer.

Napoleon showed by the way he put an end to the French Revolution that he was going to be a fine soldier, and so when he was only twenty-six years old he was made a general.

Now, at this time all the other countries of Europe had kings. France had caught the fever of revolution from the Americans all the way across the ocean and had got rid of her kings. The kings of these other countries were afraid their people might catch the fever of revolution, too. So all of these other countries became enemies of France because France had put an end to her kings.

Napoleon was sent off to fight Italy. He had to cross the Alps, which Hannibal in the Punic Wars had crossed long before. But Hannibal had no heavy cannons when he crossed; it seemed impossible for Napoleon's army to cross with cannons. Napoleon asked his engineers, the men who were supposed to know about such things, if it could be done. They said they thought it was impossible.

"Impossible," Napoleon angrily replied, "is a word found only in the dictionary of fools." Then he shouted:

"There shall be no Alps!" and went ahead and crossed them. His army won in Italy, and when he returned to France he was greeted by the people as a conquering hero. But the men who were then governing France were afraid of him. They feared he might try to make himself king because he was so popular with the people. Napoleon, however, asked to be sent to conquer Egypt because he had an idea he could get the better of the English there. He thought he might then cut England off from India, the new country that they had won in the reign of James I. England had lost America, but she didn't want to lose India.

The French Government was very glad to get rid of Napoleon, and so they sent him off to Egypt as he asked. He quickly conquered Egypt as Julius Cæsar had done, but there was no Cleopatra to upset his plans. While he was conquering Egypt, his fleet, which was waiting for him at the mouth of the Nile, was caught and destroyed by the English fleet under a great admiral, if not the greatest that ever lived. His name was Lord Nelson.

Napoleon had no way to take his army back to France. So he left his army in Egypt under command of another. He himself, however, managed to find a ship to take him back home. When he reached France he found that the men who were supposed to be governing were quarreling among themselves, and, seeing his chance, he had himself made one of three men chosen to rule France. He was called first consul; and there were supposed to be two assistant consuls, but the assistants were little more than clerks to do Napoleon's bidding. It was only a very short time before he was next made first consul for life. Then, not long after that, he became emperor of France and also king of Italy.

The other countries of Europe began to fear that Napoleon would conquer them, too, and make them also a part of France. So all the other countries joined together to beat him. Napoleon planned to conquer England first, and he got ready a fleet to cross over to England. But his fleet was caught off Spain near a point called Trafalgar by the same English admiral, Lord Nelson, who had beaten him in Egypt. Before this battle, Nelson said to his sailors, "England expects that every man will do his duty," and they did it. Napoleon's fleet was utterly destroyed, though Nelson himself was killed.

Napoleon then gave up the idea of conquering England, and he turned his attention in the opposite direction. He had beaten Spain and Prussia and Austria. Almost all Europe either belonged to him or had to do what he said. Then he attacked Russia. It was a great mistake he made, for Russia was far off, and it was wintertime and very cold. Still, he managed to reach Moscow way off in the center of Russia with his army. But the Russians burned the city and destroyed all the food, so that Napoleon had nothing with which to feed his army. It was terribly cold; there were deep snows; and, in retreating, his army suffered enormous losses. Napoleon himself soon made a bee-line to Paris leaving his army to get back the best way they could. Men and horses died of cold and hunger by the thousands. Napoleon reached Paris, but his fortune had turned. All of Europe was getting ready to put an end to the tyrant, and it was not long after this that he was hemmed in and beaten by his enemies.

When Napoleon saw that he was beaten, he signed a paper saying that he would give up and leave France. And so he did, sailing away to a little island called Elba, just off the coast of Italy, not far from the island where he was born.

Napoleon at St. Helena.

But Napoleon on the island of Elba got an idea that all was not lost and that he might return to France and get back his power again. So all of a sudden, to the surprise of France and the rest of the world, he landed on the coast of France. The French Government at Paris sent an army of his old soldiers against him with orders to meet him and bring him to Paris in an iron cage. But when his old soldiers met their old general they went over to his side, and so with them he marched on to Paris. The English and German armies were north of France and preparing to fight. Napoleon quickly got together an army and went forth to meet them. At a little town called Waterloo, Napoleon fought his last battle, for there he was utterly beaten by an English general named Wellington. This was the Year 1815. We still speak and probably always will speak of any great defeat as "Waterloo."

There is a peculiar sentence which reads backward the same as forward. It is what Napoleon might have said after all was over. It is:

ABLE WAS I ERE I SAW ELBA

After Napoleon was beaten at Waterloo, the English took him away and put him on a little island far off in the ocean where he could not possibly escape. It was a lonely spot named St. Helena after the mother of Constantine. Here he lived for six years before he died.

Napoleon was probably the greatest general that ever lived, but that does not mean that he was the greatest man. Some say he was the worst, for just to make himself great, he killed hundreds of thousands of people and brought destruction and ruin to the whole of Europe wherever he fought his battles.

This brings us up into the nineteenth century, for Napoleon died in 1821. How long ago is that?

74

From Pan and His Pipes to the Phonograph

Frogs croak;
Cats me-ow;
Dogs bark;
Sheep bleat;
Cows moo;
Lions roar;
Hyenas laugh;

But only birds and people *sing*. All other animals simply make noises. But people can do what birds cannot. They can also make music out of *things*.

Have you ever made a cigar-box fiddle or a pin piano or musical glasses?

In the long-ago story-book times Apollo took a pair of cow-horns and fastened between them seven strings made from the cow's skin. This was called a lyre. These strings he picked with his fingers or with a quill, making a little tinkling sound that could hardly have been very beautiful. Yet Apollo's son Orpheus is said to have learned from his father to play so beautifully on the lyre that the birds and wild beasts and even trees and rocks gathered round to hear him.

Pan, the god of the woods, who had goat's horns and ears and legs and feet, tied together several whistles of different lengths and played on these as you might on a mouth-organ. This instrument was called Pan's pipes.

The lyre and Pan's pipes were the two earliest musical instruments. The first was a stringed instrument; the second a wind instrument. The long strings and long pipes made low notes; the short strings and short pipes made high tones.

From Apollo's lyre we get the piano with its many, many strings. Did you ever look at the inside of a piano and see the many strings of different lengths? They are, however, not picked as the strings of a lyre or harp are picked, but hammered by little felt-covered blocks as you touch the keys.

From Pan's pipes we get the great church organ with its pipes like giant whistles. You don't, of course, blow the pipes with your mouth as you do a whistle. The pipes are so big you must blow them with a machine like a tire-pump, and you do this as you touch the keys.

We know what the instruments in olden times were like, but we don't know what the music that people made was really like; there were no phonographs to bottle up the sounds and, when uncorked a thousand years later, to pour forth the old notes once again. The music went off into thin air and was lost.

It was not until about the Year 1000 A.D. that music could even be written down. Before then all music was played "by ear," for there was no written music. A Benedictine monk named Guy, or, in Italian, Guido, thought of a way to write down musical notes, and he named the notes do, re, mi, fa, and so on. These were the first letters of the words of a hymn to St. John which the monks sang like the scale.

Another Italian is sometimes called the "father of modern music." His name is Palestrina, and he died about 1600. He set the church service to music, and the pope ordered all churches to follow it, but the people didn't like his music very much; that is, it was not what we call "popular."

It was not until a hundred years later—that is, about 1700—that the first great musician lived who wrote music that was really popular, that the people loved, and that we still love to-day.

He was a German named Handel. His father was a barber, a dentist, and doctor, and he wanted his boy to become a great lawyer. But the only thing the boy liked was music.

In those days there were no pianos. There was a little instrument with strings which was played by touching keys. This was called a clavichord. Sometimes it had legs like a table. Sometimes it had no legs and was just laid on a table.

Handel is found in the attic.

Handel, though only six years old, got hold of one of these instruments, and, without any one finding out about it, he had it put up in his room in the attic of his house. After every one had gone to bed at night he would practise on this clavichord until late, when he was supposed to be in bed. One night his family heard sounds up under the roof. Wondering what it could be, they took a lantern, and, quietly climbing the attic stairs, they suddenly opened the door, and there sat little Handel in his night-clothes on a chair with his feet reaching only half-way to the floor, playing on the clavichord.

After that Handel's father saw it was no use trying to make his son a lawyer. So he got teachers for him, and before long the boy amazed the world with his playing. He went to England, lived there, became an Englishman, and when he died the English people buried him in Westminster Abbey, a church in which famous Englishmen were buried.

Handel "set the Bible to music." These songs with the Bible words to be sung by a chorus of voices were called *oratorios*, and one of these oratorios named "The Messiah" is sung almost everywhere at Christmas-time.

Living at the same time with Handel was another German musician named Bach. Bach played divinely on the organ as Handel did on the clavichord and wrote some of the finest music for the organ that ever has been written. Strange that both Handel and Bach went blind in their old age, but to them it was sound, not sight, that counted most. Here is another good subject for an argument: would you rather be deaf or blind?

Almost all musical geniuses have been musical wonders when they were still babies. They have been great musicians even before learning to read and write.

One such genius was born just before Handel died. He was an Austrian named Mozart.

Mozart when only four years old played the piano wonderfully. He also wrote music—composing, it is called—for others to play.

Mozart's father and sister played very well, so the three went on a concert tour. Mozart, the boy wonder, played before the empress, and everywhere he went he was treated like a prince, petted and praised and given parties and presents.

Then he grew up and married, and ever after he had the hardest kind of a time trying to make a living. He composed all sorts of things, plays with music called operas, and symphonies, which are written for whole orchestras to play; but he made so little money that when he died he had to be buried where they put people who were too poor to have a grave for themselves alone. People afterward thought it a shame that such a great composer should have no monument over his grave, but then it was too late to find where he was buried. A monument was put up, but to this day no one knows where Mozart's body lies.

A German named Beethoven had read the stories of the boy wonder, Mozart, and he thought he, too, would like to have a boy wonder to play before kings and queens. So when his son Louis was only five years old he kept the boy practising long hours at the piano until he became so tired that the tears ran down his cheeks. But Louis Beethoven, or Ludwig, as he was called in German, finally came to be one of the greatest musicians that have ever lived. He could sit at the piano and make up the most beautiful music as he went along—improvise, as it is called—but he was never satisfied with it when written down. Time and time again he would scratch out and rewrite his music until it had been rewritten often a dozen times.

But Beethoven's hearing began to grow dull. He was worried that he might lose it entirely—a terrible thing to happen to any one, but to one whose hearing was his fortune nothing could be worse. And at last he did become deaf. This loss of his hearing made Beethoven hopelessly sad and bad-tempered, cross with everything and everybody. Nevertheless, he didn't give up; he kept on composing just the same, even after he could no longer hear what he had written.

Another great and unusual German musician named Wagner lived until 1883. Though he practised all his life, he never could play very well. But he composed the most wonderful operas that have ever been written, and he wrote not only the music but the words, too. He took old myths and fairy-tales and made them into plays to be sung to music. At first some people made fun of his music, for it seemed to them so noisy and "slam-bangy" and without tune. But people now make fun of those "some people" who don't like it!

I have told you in other places of painters and poets, of architects and wise men, of kings and heroes, of wars and troubles. I have put this story of music of all ages in one chapter which I have tucked in here between the acts, to give you a rest for a moment from wars and rumors of wars.

When I was a boy I never heard any great musicians play. Now you and I can turn on the phonograph any time and hear the music of Palestrina or Mozart, of Beethoven or Wagner, of dozens of other masters, played or sung to us whenever we wish; the greatest musicians become our slaves. No caliph in the "Arabian Nights" could command such service to his pleasure!

75

The Daily Papers of 1854-1865

IF you could go up into your grandfather's attic or the attic of somebody else's grandfather, or would dig down into some old trunk, you might find some of the newspapers that were printed during the years from 1854 to 1865. Then you might actually read in these daily papers the happenings that I am now going to tell you about. Many people still alive have taken part in some of these events themselves or know those who have. Under the heading, "Foreign News," you would probably find some of the following things told about:

ENGLISH NEWS. At this time the queen of England was named Victoria. She was much beloved by her people because she had such a kindly nature and Christian spirit. She was more like a mother to her people than like a queen. She ruled for more than half a century, and the time when she ruled is called the Victorian Age.

The English news of 1854 would tell about a war that the English were then fighting with Russia. Russia was a long way off, and so the English had to send their soldiers in boats through the Mediterranean Sea to the end, then past Constantinople in to the Black Sea. There in a little spot of land that jutted out from Russia into the Black Sea most of the fighting was done. This little spot of land was called the Crimea, and the war therefore was called the Crimean War. In this war in that far-off land thousands of English soldiers died from wounds and disease.

Now, there was living in England at the time of this war a lady named Florence Nightingale. She was very tender-hearted and always looking out for and taking care of those that were sick. Even as a little girl she had played that her dolls were sick with headache or a broken leg, and she would bandage the aching head or broken leg and pretend to take care of her sick patient. When her dog was ill she nursed him as carefully as if he were a human being.

Florence Nightingale heard that English soldiers were dying by the thousands in that distant land far away from home and that there were no nurses to take care of the wounded. So she got together a number of ladies, and they went out to the Crimea. Before she arrived almost half the soldiers who were wounded died—fifty soldiers out of a hundred; after she and her nurses came, only two in a hundred died. She went about through the camps and over the battlefields at night carrying a lamp looking for the wounded. The soldiers called her the Lady of the Lamp, and they all loved her.

When at last the war was over and she returned to England, the Government voted to give her a large sum of money for what she had done. She, however, refused the money for herself but took it to found a home for training nurses. Nowadays trained nurses are thought almost as necessary as doctors, and any one who is sick can call in a trained nurse to take care of him, but at that time there were no trained nurses and no one had ever heard of such a thing. Florence Nightingale was the first to start trained nursing, and so she is looked upon almost as a saint by trained nurses.

In one battle in the Crimea a company of soldiers mounted on horseback were given by mistake an order to attack the enemy. Though they knew it meant certain death, they never hesitated but charged, and two-thirds of them were killed or wounded in less than half an hour. Lord Tennyson, the English poet, has told this story in verse which you may know. It is called "The Charge of the Light Brigade."

JAPANESE NEWS. Japan is a group of islands near China. Although I have not told you about it before, it was an old country, settled in its ways even before Rome was founded. In Europe there have been constant changes of kings and rulers and people and countries. But in Japan they have had the same line of kings since before Christ.

Japan wanted no white people in her country, and, with a very few exceptions, she had always kept them out. But in 1854, the same year that England began the Crimean War, an American naval officer named Commodore Perry went to Japan and made an agreement, or treaty, as it is called, by which Japan allowed white people to come in and do business with her people. The Japanese seemed hungry for knowledge, to learn how to do things in the white man's way. When Perry first went to Japan the Japanese lived the same way they had a thousand years before. They knew nothing of the white man's inventions or ways of living. But in fifty years' time they have jumped a thousand years in civilization!

These are some of the things you might read about in those old newspapers. Such news would probably have taken up little space; perhaps they would have been found down at the bottom of a column if the newspaper were American. But if the paper was printed between 1861 and 1864, the greater part of it would be about a war that was going on in our own country at that time. This was a war between our own people, a family quarrel, which we call the Civil War.

Two parts of our country, the North and the South, did not agree on several matters, chief of which was the question whether the South could own slaves. So they went to war with each other. Each side fought for what it believed was right, and thousands upon thousands gave their lives for what they believed. The war lasted for four years, from 1861 to 1865, before it was decided that no one could ever again own slaves in the United States.

Some of you who read these pages had grandfathers or great-grandfathers who fought in this war. Some of these fought for the South; some fought for the North. Some of them may have died for the South; some of them may have died for the North.

The President of the United States at this time was a man named Abraham Lincoln. Lincoln was a very poor boy who had been born in a log cabin. He had taught himself to read by the light of a blazing knot of wood at night after his day's work was done. As he was very poor, he had only a few books, and these he read over and over again. One of these books was the same "Æsop's Fables" that you read. When Lincoln was a young man, he became a storekeeper. One day he found that he had given a poor woman a smaller package of tea than she had paid for, and so he closed the store and walked many miles to her house in order to return the change. People began to call him Honest Abe after that, for he was always very honest and kind-hearted.

Lincoln visiting camp and shaking hands with the soldiers.

He studied hard and became a lawyer and at last was elected President of the United States. One day while he was in a theater watching a play he was shot and killed by one of the actors who thought Lincoln had not done right in freeing the slaves.

Lincoln was one of our greatest Presidents. Washington started our country; Lincoln prevented its splitting into two parts, and kept it together as one big united land to grow into the great country it now is.

76

Three New Postage-Stamps

WE are getting pretty close to the present time, to "Now."

Let us look backward a minute to see what had been going on in Europe since the time of Napoleon.

After Napoleon had been sent to Elba, the French had to have another ruler. They wanted their old kings back again. The family name of their old kings was Bourbon. So the French thought they ought to have a Bourbon ruler over them. Accordingly they tried out three Bourbons one after the other, all relatives of their last king, whom they had beheaded.

But all of them proved no good, the French people had given the Bourbon family a good tryout, and so at last they stopped worrying with kings and started another republic.

Now, a republic has a president instead of a king, so that the people had to choose a president; and whom do you suppose they picked out? Why, the nephew of Napoleon. The nephew of Napoleon was named Louis Napoleon. He had planned and plotted again and again to make himself king of France, but again and again he had failed. And now he was elected president! But Louis Napoleon didn't want to be *only* president. He wanted to be like his uncle the great Napoleon. He dreamed of being emperor and conquering Europe, and so it was not long after this before he had himself made emperor, and he called himself Napoleon III.[5]

[5] Napoleon I had a young son who might have been Napoleon II if he had lived. The story is, that when Napoleon III was made emperor his name was printed simply with three exclamation marks after it—"Napoleon!!!" and this was by mistake read Napoleon III.

Napoleon III was jealous of the neighboring country of Prussia. She was getting to be too strong, he thought. Prussia had a king at this time named William who was very able himself, and he had an able assistant or prime minister named Bismarck, who was looking for an excuse to fight France. So presently a war was started between the two countries in 1870. Napoleon soon found he had made a bad mistake in picking the war with Prussia. Prussia was not *getting* too strong; she was already too strong.

Napoleon III was completely beaten by Prussia, and he with a large army had to surrender. Then in disgrace he went to live in England.

The Prussians marched into Paris and made the French agree to pay them a billion dollars. When some of the French towns said they couldn't pay, Bismarck lined up the leading citizens of the place and told them they would be shot if they didn't raise the money that was demanded. So France paid, and to the wonder and amazement of everybody she paid this immense sum in two years' time. But the French and the French children have never forgotten the way they were made to pay and the way they were treated by the Prussians, and so ever since then there has been deadly enmity between these two countries. This war was called the Franco-Prussian War, as it was between France and Prussia.

There were a number of little countries near Prussia. They were called German states. But though their people were related, the countries or states were separate. As a result of this war, Prussia was able to join all these German states together and to make for the first time one big, strong, powerful nation called Germany, feared by other countries on account of her great army of fighting men. William was made emperor of all Germany and called kaiser. He was crowned in the French palace at Versailles that Louis XIV had built.

The French thought the Germans had been able to win this war because they had public schools in which all their children were trained, and because of the way their soldiers were drilled. So France set to work and started public schools everywhere in France and imitated the German way of drilling their army so that they would be ready for them in the next war.

Ever since then France has been a republic with a president and an Assembly chosen by the people.

At that time Italy was not a single country as now but like Germany a collection of small states. Some of these were independent, some were owned by France, some were owned by Austria. The king of one of these Italian states was Victor Emmanuel. He wanted all the Italian states to unite and become one single country like our United States. He was helped by his prime minister, a very able man named Cavour, and by a rough but romantic popular hero named Garibaldi, who was called the hero of the Red Shirt.

Garibaldi, who had been a candle-maker in New York City, was always poor and seemed not to care for money. He was so popular that whenever he called for soldiers to fight with him for his beloved Italy, they at once flocked around him ready to fight to the death.

And so at last these three, Victor Emmanuel, Cavour, and Garibaldi, succeeded in making their country one big nation. The Italians erected monuments to them and named streets after them. To Victor Emmanuel they built a magnificent building on a hill in Rome overlooking the city, a building that was intended to be more beautiful than anything built in Athens during the time of Pericles or in Italy during the Renaissance.

If you collect postage-stamps it would be interesting for you to get, if you can, stamps of these countries at that time, the New French Republic, United Germany, and United Italy.

77

The Age of Miracles

YOU may think the Age of Miracles was when Christ lived.

But if a man who lived at that time should come back to earth now he would think *this* the Age of Miracles.

If he heard you talk over a wire to a person a thousand miles away, he would think you a magician.

If you showed him people moving and acting on a movie screen, he would think you a witch.

If he heard you start a band playing by turning on a phonograph, he would think you a devil.

If he saw you fly through the air in an airplane, he would think you a god.

We are so used to the telephone, telegraph, and phonograph; to steamboats, steam railroads, and trolley-cars; to electric lights, motor-cars, moving pictures, radio, and airplanes, that it is hard to imagine a world in which there were none of these things—absolutely none of these things. Yet in the Year 1800 not a single one of these inventions was known.

Neither George Washington nor Napoleon ever saw a steam-engine, a steam-car, nor a steamboat. They had never used a telephone nor a telegraph nor a bicycle. My own grandfather never saw a trolley-car nor an electric light. Even my father never saw a phonograph, a moving picture, an automobile, nor a flying-machine.

More wonders have been made in the last hundred years than in all the previous centuries of the world put together.

A Scotchman named James Watt was one of the first of these magicians whom we call inventors. Watt had watched a boiling kettle on the stove and noticed that the steam lifted the lid. This gave him an idea that steam might lift other things as well as the lid of a tea-kettle. So he made a machine in which steam lifted a lid called a piston in such a way as to turn a wheel. This was the first steam-engine.

Watt's steam-engine moved wheels and other things, but it didn't move itself. An Englishman named Stephenson put Watt's engine on wheels and made the engine move its own wheels. This was the first locomotive. Soon funny-looking carriages drawn by funny-looking engines were made to run on tracks in America. At first these trains ran only a few miles out from such cities as Baltimore and Philadelphia.

Then a young fellow named Robert Fulton thought he could make a boat go by putting Watt's engine on board and making it turn paddle-wheels. People laughed at him and called the boat he was building "Fulton's Folly," which means "foolishness." But the boat worked, and Fulton had the laugh on those who had laughed at him. He called his boat the *Clermont*, and it made regular trips up and down the river.

No one had ever before been able to talk to another far off until the telegraph was invented. The telegraph makes a clicking sound. Electricity flows through a wire from one place to another place which may be a long distance off. If you press a button at one end of the wire you stop the electricity flowing through the wire, and the instrument at the other end makes a click. A short click is called a dot, and a long click is called a dash. These dots and dashes stand for letters of the alphabet, so you can spell out a message by dots and dashes.

A is · —   dot-dash

B is — ···   dash-dot-dot-dot

E is ·   dot

H is ····   dot-dot-dot-dot

T is —   dash

An American painter named Morse invented this wonderful little instrument. He built the first telegraph line in America between Baltimore and Washington, and this was the first message he clicked across it: "What hath God wrought!"

A school-teacher named Bell was trying to find some way of making deaf children hear, and in doing so he invented the telephone. The telephone carries words as the telegraph carries clicks. You do not have to know a special alphabet or spell out words by dots and dashes as you do on the telegraph. With the telephone any one can talk from one side of America to the other.

Many inventions now in every-day use have been partly invented by several people, so that it is hard to say just which one thought of the invention first. Several people thought of a way to run a machine by feeding it electricity. This was the electric motor. Then others thought of a way to run a machine by exploding gas. This was the motor used in automobiles.

Electric lights, such as we use indoors, were invented by Thomas Alva Edison. Edison is called a wizard, because in the Middle Ages wizards were supposed to be able to do and to make all sorts of wonderful and impossible things, to turn lead into gold, to make people invisible, and that sort of thing.

But Edison has done things that no wizard of a fairy-tale had ever even thought of. Edison was a poor boy who sold newspapers and magazines on a train. He was interested in all sorts of experiments and fitted up a place in the baggage-car where he could make experiments. But he made so much of a mess in the car that at last the baggage-man kicked Edison's whole outfit off the train. Edison invented many things connected with the phonograph and the movies, and he has probably made more useful and important inventions than any other man who has ever lived, so that he is much greater than those mere kings who have done nothing but quarrel and destroy—without whom the world would have been much better off if they had never lived!

Thousands of people who have lived in the past ages have tried to fly and failed. Millions of people have said it was impossible to fly and foolish to try. Some have even said it was wicked to try, that God meant that only birds and angels should fly. At last, after long years of work and thousands of trials, two American brothers named Wright did the impossible. They invented the airplane and flew.

An Italian named Marconi invented the radio, and others every day are still making wonderful inventions, but you will have to read about these yourself, for we are near the end of our history.

Here is a good subject for an argument or debate: Are we any happier *with* all these inventions than people were a thousand years ago *without* them?

Life is faster and more exciting; but it is more difficult and more dangerous. Instead of enjoying a book curled up in the corner of a sofa by a crackling fire, we leave a steam radiator and go out to the movies. Instead of singing or playing the violin, we turn on the graphophone or the player-piano and miss the chief joy in music, the joy of making it ourselves. Instead of the jogging drive in an old buggy behind a horse that goes along through the country-side almost by himself, we speed on in dangerous autos, to which we must pay constant, undivided attention or be wrecked.

78

GERMANY FIGHTS THE WORLD

The last chapter was one of the few without a fight in it. But now, to make up for that, I must tell you about the greatest and the worst fight in history.

There is a little country in Europe called Serbia. It is next door to Austria. A young man who lived in Serbia shot an Austrian prince. Little Serbia apologized to Austria for what one of her people had done. But Austria insisted that the Serbian nation was to blame for what had been done; she refused to accept the apology and started in to punish Serbia.

I once saw a little dog snap at a big boy. The owner of the little dog apologized to the big boy for what his dog had done. But the big boy did not accept the apology, and he started in to thrash the little boy for what his dog had done. Presently a crowd gathered round, the friends of each boy took sides, and there was a general free-for-all "scrap."

So it was in this case. One of Austria's big friends, Germany, took sides against Serbia, and Russia took the side of Serbia. Ever since the time of the Franco-Prussian War and Bismarck and William, Germany had been in training for a fight, and so had her neighbors. Nearly all the countries of Europe had for years been getting together into two groups, made up of the friends and the enemies of Germany; and the two were ready to jump at each other as soon as Austria, or Germany, or anybody else, struck at any one.

But Germany didn't strike at Serbia; Austria didn't really need her help against Serbia. Germany was sure that France, who was her enemy and Russia's friend, would take sides against her; and so she rushed at France to destroy her before Russia could hit hard from the other side. Now, to get at France Germany had to get through the little country of Belgium. She and France had agreed that neither would march armies through Belgium, but when the war began her armies marched in anyway and pushed aside the Belgians, who tried to stop them. And so her armies rushed on toward the capital of France, Paris. She got as far as a little stream called the Marne, only twenty miles from Paris. But here the French under General Foch stopped her army. This battle of the Marne is probably the most famous of all the battles you have heard about in history, for though the war was not ended for four years after this battle, if the Germans had won at the Marne, the war would have been over, with Germany victor, and the rest of the world would have had to do what Germany said.

Germany was the first to use poison gas, trying to smother her enemy; she fought with submarines from under the sea; she attacked passenger ships that could not fight back. The English navy was the strongest, and it was only with submarines that Germany could fight at sea. This war was the first one in history in which battles were fought not only on land but up in the air and down under the water.

England took sides with France and Russia—and these were called Allies—to fight against Germany and Austria, and at first the war was between these countries only. Before the war ended, however, almost all the countries of the world had taken sides against Germany, for they knew that if she won she would be able to tell the rest of the world what to do. Then all of a sudden Russia had a revolution. The Russian people killed their ruler, the czar, and his family, and refused to fight any longer. Things began to look pretty bad for the Allies.

The United States did not start into the war until 1917, almost three years after it had begun; then she did so because German submarines were sinking American passenger ships and killing Americans.

Surrender of Germans.

America was so far off—three thousand miles away—and across an ocean that it seemed impossible that she could do much in the war. But in a very short time she had sent two million soldiers across in ships. Under General

Pershing they fought great battles. At last Germany was utterly beaten, and on Armistice day, November 11, 1918, Germany signed a paper agreeing to do everything the Allies asked; and so the greatest war in history ended. The kaiser went to live in Holland, and Germany became a republic.

79

Yesterday, To-day, and To-morrow

THERE is a candy shop near where I live. On its sign it says, "Made Fresh Every Hour." History is being made every day. It is being made fresh almost every hour. The newsboy even now is calling outside of my window, "Extra! Extra!" Is it a new war? Is it a new discovery? If you had clipped head-lines from the papers since the World War, here are some of the things you might have pasted in your scrapbook.

TREATY OF PEACE
SIGNED AT VERSAILLES

Nations Agree on Terms of Peace

The Mohammedan Turks in the East Are
Again Threatening the Christian
Nations of the West

THE IRISH FREE
STATE ESTABLISHED

After Centuries of Struggle to Become
Independent of England, Ireland at
Last, with England's Permission, Has
Set Up a Government of Her Own

COLUMBUS OF THE AIR

Read, an American, Crosses Atlantic
Ocean for First Time in an Airplane;
Lands at the Azores and Then in
Portugal; Several Others Soon Follow,
and the Ocean Is Crossed a Number of
Times

WOMEN CAN VOTE AT LAST

All Through the Ages Women Have Had
Little or No "Say" in the Government;
Now, for the First Time, They Can
Vote in Our Country and in Most
Other Civilized Countries

STRONG DRINK PROHIBITED

The Use of Wine and Strong Drink,
Which Has Caused So Much Crime,

Disease, Death and Unhappiness, Has
Been Forbidden in the United States
and Limited in Many Other Countries;
in the Generations to Come, Men Will
Probably Marvel That There Was Once
a Time When People Drank Poison for
Pleasure

From now on you will have to read your history in the daily papers.

Up to this time, history has been marked by the story of one war after another, some big, some small, some short, some long. Almost always a fight has been going on somewhere. It has been War, War, War; Fight, Fight, Fight. Children scratch, kick, and bite. But the older we get, the less do we use our fists and feet to settle quarrels. So fighting seems to be a sign of childhood—that we are "kids"—and our fights, that we call wars, a sign of how young the world really is and we really are; a sign that the world is still but a minute or two old.

Now, we admire and praise as heroes Horatius, Leonidas, Joan of Arc, and General Foch and those others who have defended their countries against the attacks of the enemy, as we would admire a man who shoots a burglar or a murderer that attacks his family in the night. But those, whether kings, generals, or princes, who do the attacking and take life with no other excuse than to add to their power or wealth or glory, are no better than burglars who go forth with a gun and a blackjack to waylay, rob, and murder for the same purpose. War kills, war destroys, war costs millions of lives and billions of dollars—money that could be used to make us happy, instead of causing bitterness, suffering, misery, and unhappiness; blind men and cripples, widows and orphans. No one is better off, not even the winner. It is a terrible game, in which even the winner loses. And yet in the long run who knows? It may be the only way the world can grow!

But this is certain: if wars do not end, they will be fought with something more deadly, more terrible than shot and shell. Sooner or later, some man of science will invent a disease more catching than the terrible plague, more deadly than the Black Death with which to attack the enemy. But if such a disease is let loose, once started it will spread from one being to the next till every one has caught it and died and no one will escape. Or he will invent a poison to poison the air we breathe that will spread like the wind or like wildfire in dry grass, and there will be no stopping it. The air that wraps the globe will be a sea of poison gas. Every thing that breathes will take only one breath, and every man, woman, and child, every beast of the field, every bird and flying thing will drop dead. Or he will invent something a million times more powerful than gunpowder or dynamite—something so explosive that when discovered by some Mr. Swartz it will blow him, his house, his town, his country, and the whole world to kingdom come—and that will be the end of this little spark off the sun.

Perhaps you have looked through a microscope at what seem to be wars between germs. As germs might look up at the eye of the microscope through which we watch their life-and-death struggles, and wonder what is up above on the other side looking down at them, so we may look up at the blue eye of heaven above us and wonder what all-seeing, all-knowing, all-powerful being up there is watching our own life-and-death struggles here below.

Our little world, which seems so immense to us, is really only a tiny speck, only one of countless other specks floating in space; it is like one of the tiny motes which you may see any time in a sunbeam that shines in at the window. Who has an eye so keen that he can count the moving motes in such a beam of light? Who would miss one such grain of dust if it should disappear? So this grain of dust we call the World and all of us who live upon it could vanish without ever being noticed!

This story ends here, but only for the present, for history is a continued story and will never end.

If you were living in the Year 10,000 A.D., as some boy will be, your history would only be just begun when you had reached where we are now. Even the World War would then seem as long ago as the fights of the Stone Age men seem to us. You might think of us and all the inventions we consider so wonderful as we think of the discovery of copper and bronze.

Will the history that is written in the Year 10,000 have any wars to tell about? If the wars on Earth cease, will there be wars with other worlds?

And if there are no more wars, what will history tell about? Will it be new inventions? What kinds? Will it be new discoveries? We know every corner of the world now. Will it be the inside of this world or other new worlds or a spiritual world?

Perhaps then people will no longer use trains, steamboats, automobiles, or even flying-machines, but go from place to place as on some magic carpet, simply by wishing. Perhaps then they will no longer use letters, telephones, or telegraphs, or even radio, but read each other's thoughts at any distance.

And so on—World without end—AMEN!

www.ingramcontent.com/pod-product-compliance
Ingram Content Group UK Ltd.
Pitfield, Milton Keynes, MK11 3LW, UK
UKHW031346260325
456749UK00003B/619